CW01665051

1066

Fulford

The battle and its consequences

Describing the coordinated invasions of Anglo-Saxon England

Charles Jones

WPS 2025

©Charles Jones 2025

All rights and intellectual property are reserved. No part may be reproduced or utilised by any processing, printing or storage system without the consent of the copyright owner.

ISBN 9781780185170
Kindle edition 9781780185163

This book is dedicated to those whose faith and hard work made it possible including Peter Addyman, Richard Hall and Keith Challis who mentored the early project.

Thank you all.

Declaration

This work, the research and the images are all the work of the author.

First published 2025 by WPS

Other works on this topic by Charles Jones include:

Finding Fulford 9781780180502 – Documents the archaeological projects to find the site. 2011

The Forgotten battle of 1066, Fulford 9780752443263 – A historical perspective that predates the archaeological analysis. 2005

Special thanks to Sue, Michelle and Ali for editorial advice and assistance.

Table of Contents

Cover images

The background is the author's photograph of the English muster at Battle Abbey in 2016. No armies of reenactors have yet had the opportunity to muster at Fulford.

Two sections of the Battle of Fulford Tapestry, completed in 2006, feature the outflanking move by King Harald (on the back cover) followed by his victorious entry into York with Earl Tostig.

The 6m long tapestry was designed by the author as part of the generous UK National Lottery Funded project whose rules required some lasting memorial to be created. There was little certainty, at the time, that the battle site could be confidently located. Therefore, the tapestry employed the Norse literature in the design, so it is a visual expression of the verses in the Sagas and Jan Messant was generous with her advice.

Archaeology subsequently demonstrated the accuracy of the ancient stories and provided the location, confirmed by excavations.

The assistance of the teams at the Bayeux Museum and the V&A was invaluable, as was the help of the late Jill Goodwin with the threads and the dye colours. She correctly identified the plants employed which science only confirmed in 2023. The aim was to match the iconic Bayeux Tapestry in every aspect of its creation including the natural dyes, threads and linen cloth used.

Foreword

This book tells the story of the first of the three battles in England during a fateful four weeks in the autumn of 1066. It has three aims.

- The first is to describe the battle in remarkable detail, made possible by over two decades of archaeological research.
- The second is to profile the people that promoted this campaign who have been largely overlooked.
- The final purpose is to explain the importance of the Fulford encounter to any proper understanding of the events of 1066.

The battle of Fulford was the opening, and arguably largest[1], of the three 1066 battles. As it is the first battle of these invasions, the context for the people and the politics that precipitated the end of the era of Anglo-Saxon monarchs is included. The stories of some of the marginalised players, sheds light on the whole campaign where a clear plan for two coordinated invasions emerges.

This narrative starts with the wider political context followed by the stories of the key people who planned, or precipitated, these events. This is followed by a detailed account of the battle itself. The last section deals with the consequences of the battle and draws together the evidence that the two invasions were designed to be simultaneous, and examines what went wrong.

The battle described here is a wonderfully clever, if tactically complicated. Some important information has been annexed rather than being incorporated into the main text as it would risk slowing the fast-paced battle-narrative.

The decades of archaeological investigation at Fulford allowed the descriptions provided by contemporary scribes to be tested against the landscape of 1066. Later, excavations provided evidence that served to reinforce the credibility of the early sources that described the battle. This permits this confident and detailed description of the build-up to the battle and the action itself.

Another challenge when reporting history is to identify what is evidence-based and what is speculation; I have tried to indicate this in the way matters are expressed. This volume does not explore every interpretation but presents my considered conclusions. There are occasional sorties into some detailed evidence, and how it was assessed, to enable an informed decision

[1] See page 207 comparing the three battle 'sizes'.

among the alternatives. This happens especially when assessing the thinking of the combatants which went undocumented.

The clear evidence for the coordinated invasions illuminates subsequent events. As the supplicant, Earl Tostig, the exiled Earl of Northumbria who was also King Harold II's brother, necessarily shared some details with the invading commanders. Attacking from the north, the semi-retired King of Norway, Harald, and from the south his kinsman through marriage, Duke William of Normandy. Providence provided what might in military terms be seen as an unlikely resolution and one which Tostig had definitely not planned.

Quite why Fulford and its leading combatants have been so neglected is a mystery. The historian F M Stenton, who wrote his classic work on Anglo-Saxon England soon after a reliable catalogue of Norse literature became available to scholars, questions this neglect; ' ....the battle of Stamford has always impressed historians. It ended more than two centuries of Anglo-Scandinavian conflict in a manner which brought great honour to the last old English King. In comparison, the battle of Fulford has aroused little interest. Nevertheless, it deserves to be remembered in any attempt to get beneath the surface of events which followed it.'[2]

Once the campaign leading to Fulford is included in the 1066 narrative the picture that emerges adds unexplored dimensions to the stories currently told about those events. This volume therefore addresses the challenge posed by Stenton by discussing Fulford's impact on subsequent events. This leads to a significantly different view of the people involved as well as of the subsequent two battles in that fateful year.

Chas Jones

July 2025

Oxford

---

[2] F M Stenton *Anglo-Saxon England* The Clarendon Press, 1970, P 528. Professor Stenton was completing this great work in the early years of WWII. His preface is dated 27 August 1943.

Introduction

The core of this volume is an evidence-based, detailed description of the first of the three battles in the autumn of 1066 that ended the Anglo-Saxon era in England. The sections either side of the battle provide, first, the perspective, and later, the consequences of the Fulford battle.

The project to find the battle of Fulford, which has already lasted over 20 years,[3] allowed the descriptions provided by ancient scribes to be tested against the landscape which itself had to be archaeologically 'reconstructed' to understand how it looked almost a millennium ago. The unique location suggested by these early writings, coupled with the landscape studies, then allowed some excavation to be planned thirteen years into the project.

These digs provided finds-evidence and served to reinforce the credibility of the early sources describing the battle. Without such physical confirmation, any story based on the written record alone becomes, at best, a work of informed fiction.

History's complexity allows for different interpretations. To help navigate this maze, genealogies, maps and timeline have been included for reference.

Absence of evidence is neither a license to fabricate nor an excuse ignore a story. The political and personal narratives are designed to help fill gaps left in the written record. However, the reporting must not omit evidence if the jury of readers is to reach their own informed verdict.

But the devilish details of this lengthy investigation would produce a volume that is both overlong and boring.[4] The risk of providing the edited highlights to achieve brevity is that it calls for an element of trust. The formal investigative methodology that was followed at Fulford might justify such trust as it required all alternative views about the battle's conduct or location to be entertained and tested.[5]

Some degree of humility must also be expressed about the interpretations put forward. This may not be correct in every detail, even though the

---

[3] Engineering work planned for 2027 will give access to previously inaccessible layers at the heart of the action. Archaeology is never 'finished'.

[4] Ironically it has taken just as long to write this short book as the 700+ page unpublishable volume which has all of those details.

[5] A chapter in the report *Finding Fulford* is devoted to assessing all of the published alternative sites noting that the area defined for the investigation was based on these pre-existing views.

archaeological project sought to address every anomaly that arose. On occasions, the sought evidence was simply lacking.[6] However, this essay sets out the successful synthesis that has tied up all of the loose ends relating to the conduct of the battle.

An ambition of this book is to convey the subtlety of the actors that is revealed through their actions. What these leaders were thinking or had planned has left no trace in surviving records and physical evidence is silent or ambiguous. However, their actions in the years before the battle helps provide some insight into their personalities and a reasonable guide to their decisions during the battle. This is one motivation for the first section which introduces the key characters and their political context.

This story pits some good guys against three egocentric narcissists, which was seemingly a qualification for dominance in that era of change. This narrative assesses the actions of the losers favourably which might be seen as bias and I apologise to readers who take a different view. The battle at Fulford actions are a credit to all of those who fought there.

The historical canvas in this volume includes several meanders away from what might initially be viewed as relevant to a narrative restricted to the battle. These are necessary to provide some overlooked perspectives but is limited to people and events just one stage removed. For example, I note how war with King Macbeth helped open the way for a member of the southern Godwinson family to become Earl of Northumbria and how the millennial revival of the Church of Rome impacted the threat that could be mounted by the Normans in 1066. Lady Godiva even plays her part in the background. Because the invasions discussed here come from two widely separated European territories the focus cannot be parochial.

After a short preface to introduce the written sources, this book has three equal sections and some annexes. The first provides the political context for this battle. The evidence set out here is that this first battle of the autumn of 1066 was one part of the plan to remove King Harold from the throne.

The main plotter was Harold's brother, Tostig. This view differs from the received version of events given to us by the Norman victors at Hastings. Evidence is presented to explain the role of Tostig, his wife Judith, and

[6] The investigative approach has been published and sets out why simply letting the facts speak for themselves does not work when hunting battlefield: Instead, questions were posed and interpretations investigated with all the tools available to reach a conclusion that was beyond any sensible doubt.

Matilda, the wife of Duke William, as the brains and coordinators of the events that brought the Anglo-Saxon era to an end.

The second section is the core of the book, describing the battle. It sets out the exquisite game of bluff and deception leading up to, and during, the battle. The lengthy prelude to the fighting is important as it provides evidence of the sophistication of the leaders, which is relevant to understanding the wider 1066 campaign.

The extensive literature plus the archaeology permits the battle itself to be described in detail which is remarkable for such an ephemeral event from long ago. The clever way it is fought is an inspiring story, provided one accepts warfare as a legitimate way to settle disputes, because all of the leaders and, as far as can be discerned, all of the soldiers, fought their best battle possible.

This is not a battle of two lines of warriors slogging it out but one of manoeuvre and counter attacks. History is so much more intricate and nuanced than the usual portrayal in films and stories. The battle landscape at Fulford also played an unusually dynamic role. When the armies deployed, an extensive water-filled ditch separated them. It is the way both commanders tried to turn this flood to their advantage which determined the outcome.

The final section is more than a postscript addressing the consequential events, including the fate of the main characters of this story, and explores the impact of northern events on the timing of the Norman invasion.

After the narrative itself, the annexes are designed to provide more context. The first expands what we know about the armies, their organization, arms and tactics and touches on their motivation. The role played by archaeology, which allowed this story to be composed, is explored and explains how it added credibility to the written sources. The archaeology annex also examines the challenge of interpreting what was found rather than the technical details of the find assemblages, which are reported elsewhere.

The discussion here is also confined to the fate of England since the rulers of the surrounding nations of Wales, Ireland and Scotland were only marginally impacted by the events of 1066, with their governance and territory initially unaffected. However, all of England's continental neighbours played a significant role in the events that culminated at Fulford.

It is unclear why Fulford continues to be ignored by most historians when there is so much written evidence to work with even though confining a study of our history to the words alone foreshortens one's perspective.

Perhaps the Fulford project will encourage others to dig a little deeper into what is written to enable a more accurate and realistic picture to be reported.

The archaeological approach to ancient literature, for example, identifies the perspective of observers thereby providing additional context to their particular record. It reveals that some key observations can only be understood in the context of their location within the complex battle landscape. Such analysis was vital to allow a consistent narrative to be synthesised using every available account of this battle.

Another annex presents Fulford's remarkable geological setting, expanding the role that the flood-scape played in this battle.

An essay discussing why historians have invented and continue to employ a non-existent place for this battle is annexed to help rescue this heritage asset from obscurity. To conclude there is a short excursion into what should be considered credible tracing Harald's banner that fell at Stamford Bridge.

Friends of the project were anxious that I should include a narrative of the planning battle fought, and lost, to save the site from the builders but in the oft-repeated words of my mother, 'if you have nothing good to say about someone, say nothing'.

The police, whose work is based on evidence, the Fulford Parish Council, who know their community, the lawyers who provided their skills *pro bono*, plus the army of volunteers and funders, are the only heroes of this project. There were many more villains.[7]

---

[7] Our work to investigate the site was begun long before any planning permission was granted. When asked to register the site English Heritage (Now Historic England) responded '5.4 Given the planning history of this site, EH is currently considering responding to the request to Register with advice which recognises that Germany Beck is likely to be the location of the Battle, but that, given the planning situation, refrains from adding the site to the Register.' (*Ref BP2012/3/E 2 Feb 2012)* Registration would have required the builder to investigate and offer the site some bargaining power. No houses have been constructed on the battlesite but the access road was driven into the heart of the battle.

Some conventions in the text

The Day and Date of the battle

A consensus among the sources say that the battle took place on a Wednesday. A little confusion arises when Norse sources specify the date with respect to St Matthew's Day. Some sources leave out the words 'on the eve of'. The saint's day was Thursday in 1066 but two sources actually name Wednesday as the day, and this day is consistent with subsequent events, giving 20 September 1066 as the battle's date.

Adjusting dates

In this text, the Julian dates are used because they are the ones recorded in the relevant written sources describing the battle. The shift from Julian to Gregorian calendars took several centuries in Europe, causing some historic dates to be changed.

In 1582, 10 days were skipped in Britain. The adjustment was made recognising that the Julian and Gregorian calendars were coincident in 325 AD. The calendar adjustment required varies for subsequent years according to the formula of inserting 'leap centuries'. In 1066 the difference between the Julian and Gregorian dates was 6 days. 20 September 1066 in the Julian calendar became 26 September 1066 in our modern Gregorian calendar.

All the calculations for tides and sunrise timings have to be adjusted to back-calculate the days lost. It is these derivative dates that are used here with the necessary adjustment. So sunrise or tide times quoted are those that were experienced by the warriors in 1066.

The place name

We find Fuleforde (currently indexed by the National Archive as Foleforde/Fuleford/Fuleforde) and Fuletorp mentioned in the Domesday survey of 1086. In common with most place names, the name attached to Fulford has changed, or perhaps evolved, over time. The English Placename Society catalogues these usages:

- Fuletrop, Fuleford, Fuelforde & Foleforde from 1086 Domesday Survey
- Water Fuelforde 1156
- Fulford 1230
- Overfolforth 1366
- Gayt & Gatefulfurthe 1519, Foulfurthe 1542, Fowforth 1587
- Overfulford 1615
- Fulfords Ambo (Both Fulfords)

Consistent spelling is a recent obsession. The early literature provides two 12th century writers who refer to the place of the battle as Fulford, or more precisely Fuelford or Fuelforde, and in the 19th century the same area was referred to by a cocktail of names when the parish church was relocated.

Domesday also mentions Fultorp: If 'torp' represents the suffix 'thorp', (Norse derivation – hamlet) then the existence of a settlement, as well as a nearby fording place might be a reasonable conclusion. If one follows this conjecture, the settlement of Fultorp has a Scandinavian origin. Were there perhaps two locations, one was the place of the ford and the other a settlement? No Norse era settlements have been confidently located but might be the settlement that was later known as Gate Fulford.[8]

An article explores why this battle is wrongly referred to by historians as either Gatefulford or Fulford Gate, a name that is untraceable in the records. (see Annex D *What's in a name?*)

Genealogy charts

The charts illustrate the relationship between the people in this story so siblings that are not relevant to this narrative are often omitted, except where their inclusion is necessary for continuity. Many females are omitted because their existence was frequently ignored by ancient record keepers.

Name and titles convention

This text standardises the place and personal names employed but those in old sources are sometimes not changed. On a very few occasions it is necessary to expand on why people identified in texts might be wrong. In one case, Waltheof, the correct name is substituted based on the discussion within the text.

Women suffer the fate of sometimes having their given-name changed upon marriage. There are several Ediths and Emmas[9] so for clarity they are called by one consistent name within the cast for this drama where their important roles in the Fulford narrative are explored.

There are three Sweyns in this story but they are distinguished by using the Saxon form Swegen, Sweyn for king *forkbeard* and Swein, Tostig's cousin, to

[8] Place name 'evidence' for battles is popular with those whose study is limited to the literature. Oliver Rackham, the doyen of landscape archaeology, notes 'Place-name scholars have a tradition of clutching at straws and reading into place-names more than they say'.

[9] The 'twice-Queen' Emma is always referred to as Ælfgifu in royal documents.

assist with keeping them separate. Nothing can be done to avoid confusion between two key combatants, Harold II, King of England, and Harald Sigurdson, King of Norway, also known as Harald *Hardrada*. Happily King Harold of England does not arrive until just after Fulford so Harald, King of Norway, is our focus at Fulford. We are normally on first name terms with kings, counts and earls because it is tedious to provide their title each time we encounter them.

The suffix,-son, and occasionally-dottir for females, refers to a family: So The Godwinsons is a collective reference to the children of Earl Godwin.

Maps & landscape drawings

The Ordnance Survey kindly granted the project a licence and some of their data has been employed in composing the diagrams, such as contour lines or spot heights and obviously the OS grid-north.

Most maps are compositions which reflect the land surface from nearly a millennium ago. These freehand sketches were based on early air photographs, typically from the 1940s, and the extensive survey and augering investigation of the subsurface undertaken during the project. The aim is to convey an impression of the understood landscape during the battle while providing some reference points to modern features to allow them to be related to the ground by visitors.

Archaeological images

Where rust or concretion obscures the shape, the items have been drawn. Technical details of the finds have been or will be published elsewhere and wherever possible on accessible academic websites.

Distances and speed

Metres and kilometres are used. For those unfamiliar with the metric system, a metre is roughly a yard and a kilometre is about 5/8 of an English mile (1,760 yards). Twenty five millimetres are needed for a single inch.

Flanks

The term flank suggests the vulnerable end of any line of warriors. In a shieldwall, one side's left flank faces their opponent's right flank. Commanders choose a pitch for their battle that will not allow the opponent to outflank, and get behind, their army. Fulford was a complex battle and flanks play an extremely important role in the outcome, illustrated below.

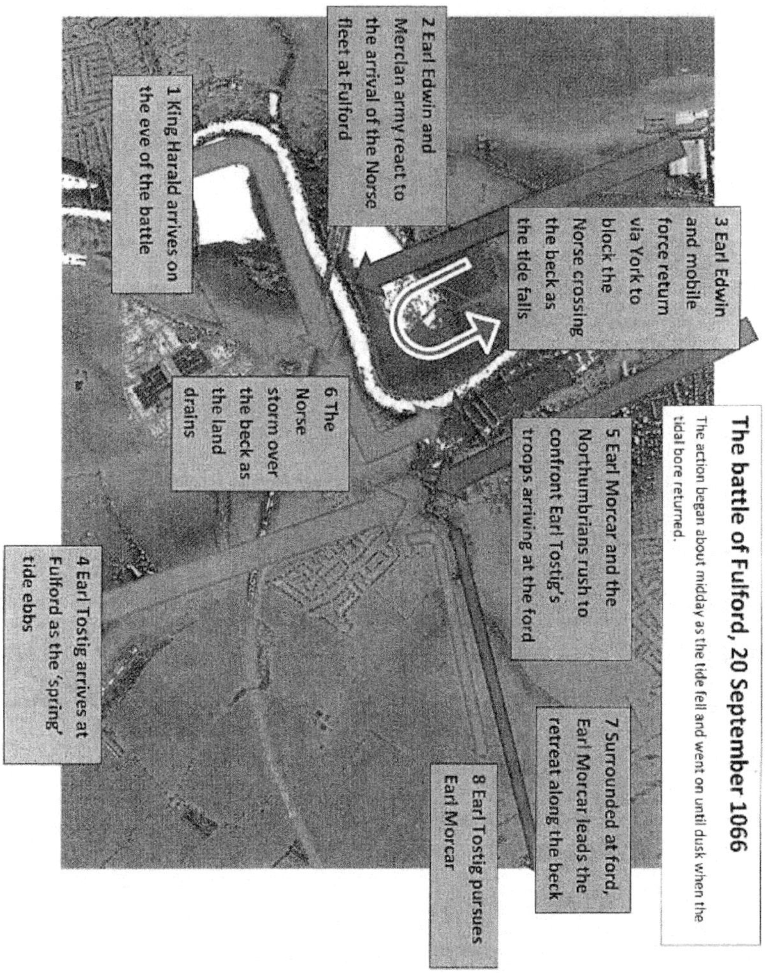

The actions over the 24 hours of this battle are noted on this topographic LIDAR map. The large white areas were covered in water when this data was gathered (water does not reflect the measuring microwaves), illustrating how the area is still prone to flooding. Tidal flooding plays a crucial part in the following battle narrative. Since this image was taken, an access road and junction has been built in the centre of this map for the new housing estate.

The ancient written sources discussed

The starting point for the archaeological investigative project was a study of all the surviving ancient written sources that mention the battle. It is important to understand how, when and by whom they were written to help assess their credibility.

The sources are fortunately extensive but, like any records, may incorporate bias and errors. Bias is occasionally overt but can also be innocent and simply reflect the perspective of the writer because they report only what they can observe. This 'first person' perspective is evident in several accounts of the Fulford battle and suggests these are authentic reports rather than a narrative that was later agreed or aggregated to present a victor's version. The surviving accounts were checked by seeking physical corroboration at Fulford, as well as being checked against each other. Their accuracy and consistency is impressive.

Anglo-Saxon Chronicle (The abbreviation ASC is employed)

By the eleventh century, what had begun as the Wessex version of events was being maintained in various monasteries around England. This provides regional versions, identified by a letter A-F, giving national coverage although still with some southern bias. The twenty words devoted to the battle by ASC version D recorded,[10] are hardly a spoiler since they do no more than identify the participants and the victor. 'And Morcar the earl, and Edwin the earl, fought against them; and the king of the Norwegians had the victory.' This tells us nothing about the battle itself or its location, although another version tells us a little more.

In what might have been intended as the 'official' chronicle of events around England, whose upkeep was possibly formalised at the time of King Alfred, there is another version which records; 'Then he [King Harold of England] went northward, day and night, as quickly as he could gather his forces. Then, before that King Harold could come there, Edwin the Earl and Morcar the Earl gathered from their earldoms as great a force as they could get together; and they fought against the army, and made great slaughter: And there was much of the English people slain, and drowned, and driven away in flight; and the Northmen had possession of the place of carnage. And this fight was on the vigil of St Matthew the apostle, and it was Wednesday [20 September].'

[10] https://www.academia.edu/43540851/The_Literary_Sources_for_the_1066_Battle_of_Fulford P 7

We have these different ASC versions because several monastic centres were responsible for the upkeep of the Chronicle. It is a truism that the victors get to write history and the Stamford Bridge battle receives more coverage in the ASC, including limited details of the battle action[11]. However, it provides little to help us identify the location although careful reading does suggest that the second battle of 1066 was eventually fought over an extensive landscape. We are given similarly scant information about the battle action we know as Hastings a few weeks later recorded in the contemporary English chronicles.

Perhaps details of the battle were deemed irrelevant to the purpose of the Chronicle where the result, rather than the method, was all that was relevant. A belief that outcomes were divinely ordained possibly made reporting the actions irrelevant, even irreligious. The focus of the chroniclers was always on the transfer of power and authority. They are not works of military history.

The Anglo-Saxon Chronicles were not composed by reporters who had been on the spot. The monasteries had clerks, or clerics, who annually recorded events deemed significant to those in charge. So raids on coastal monasteries get well reported. The later outbreak of English written histories draws on these various monastic records to amplify such events. These have value since not all of their sources survive. But we can see that these early scholars were slaves to what had previously been recorded, even copying errors, while promoting the political and religious orthodoxy.

The Norse sources

If one had to rely on such a sparse record, any description of the battle would necessarily be either a work of fiction or imagination. Happily, a much fuller story is provided by the victors of Fulford and remarkably these same sources record details of their subsequent destruction at Stamford Bridge suggesting perhaps that the Norse sources come from more even-handed, secular reporters rather than monastic scribes.

The best descriptions we have of the battle of Fulford come from what are collectively referred to as 'the sagas'. In English the term 'saga' is almost pejorative since it implies much is made-up, so it is worth discussing how they came to be written down, especially given the time that elapsed between the events and their use by historians. The compilation of Norse histories

[11] The incident of the lone Norse on the bridge was added as a gloss subsequently to one version describing the action during the retreat of the Norse after their defeat at Stamford Bridge.

several centuries after the event by several separate authors is conventionally taken to undermine the credibility of these 'saga records'.

In the 11th century few people were able to read, limiting access to what was recorded. Instead, within the Nordic countries there was an active oral tradition and great man even kept a poet close to record their deeds in poetry.[12] Such poems, known as skaldic verses, were presumably recited regularly, but around the 13th century the situation changed.

Some early Norse historians include the original poems, and an international feat of scholarship has traced, catalogued and translated surviving early verses because many individual verses had indeed been written down by the time they were used to compile the Kings' histories. Some of the key events relating to the battle of Fulford can be traced from these contemporary poems to the written histories, implying that what was written is a record of people who actually witnessed the event. It is these Kings' sagas which are employed in this investigation.

One of those compiling a history using these verses laments the fact that people were no longer memorising the poems nor even taught to understand the poetic references. Perhaps the spread of Christianity discouraged reference to the ancient beliefs reflected in the traditional stories. The spread of literacy might account for a simultaneous outbreak of history writing in England, recognising that there was an audience beyond the bounds of churches and monasteries.

There are certainly many Norse works of fiction. These mythological and creative stories were termed 'edda'. There is also a distinct sub-group of family sagas, known as the Kings' Sagas, which set down the information contained within the oral tradition.

The relevant Kings' Sagas are known as *Agrip, Morkinskinna, Fagrskinna, Heimskringla, Orkneyinga saga* and *Flateyarbok.* We owe a debt to the scholars who have assembled what was sometimes a jigsaw of fragments to provide the translated texts we can employ to tell this story about Fulford.

Because we will be relying on these texts, it is worth introducing the different kings' sagas to understand the context in which they were written to see how much we can rely on them.

---

[12] An oral tradition probably thrived in England and France but little survives with the Battle of Maldon poem and the Carmen of Hastings provide examples, with the latter noting that the format is designed to be memorable for ordinary folk.

Agrip

The *Agrip*, composed before 1200, makes reference to a Latin history in Niardos,[13] providing a paper trail of sources dating back to the time of battle of Fulford. This source gives us no information about the battle's conduct or location beyond implying that it took place in Northumbria. It tells us more about Stamford Bridge, the demise of Harald *Hardrada* with a focus on his son, Olaf.

Of interest to the English historic narrative is its record of Ælfgifu, who was Cnut's partner before Queen Emma displaced her. Ælfgifu and one young son were packed off to govern Norway, with mother acting as regent until the death of Cnut when they retreated to Denmark aware of *'their own unpopularity'*.[14] She seems to have made the mistake, repeated by Tostig, of alienating the nobles by attempting to impose a more central administration than they were willing to tolerate.

Fagrskinna

Fagrskinna literally translates as 'Fair vellum' but the inscribed title of the work is *A Catalogue of the Kings of Norway.* This work or its antecedents are believed to have been completed before 1210. Scholars suggest the *Fagrskinna* was authored by 'a conservative arranger of earlier written sources' which favourably interpreted the actions of strong rulers.[15] It provides us with some well-observed biographical notes.[16]

This source provides a detailed description of the discussion of Tostig's travels and discussions with the Kings of Denmark and Norway as he sought support to return to England by force.

---

[13] Niardos is the Latin name for the place that is now part of Trondheim. Olaf Tryggvason made it his base; It was also the base of the lords of Lade, the powerful family of the west coast. Trondheim was an important Christian base in Scandinavia during the mediaeval period. Local opposition to Christianity however led to Olaf Haraldsson's exile then his defeat and death although Olaf was recognised as a martyr and canonized.

[14] Chapter 35. This Anglo-Saxon interregnum left some antipathy towards the English which is noted in other narratives

[15] Alison Finlay Introduction to 2004 edition *Fagrskinna* 9004131728 Brill

[16] The 2003 translation of *Fagrskinna* became available after the likely location of the Fulford battle was identified. As such it provided new data to test the understanding of the events at Fulford. It provided several pieces of information which fitted the proposed location well and not previously available in older translations.

Morkinskinna

Morkinskinna can be translated as 'Rotten' or 'Mouldy Parchment' which scholars assess was written about 1220 and relied more on oral traditions. Two possible editor/compliers have been suggested. Over half the content relates to Harald Sigurdson (Harald *Hardrada*, the victor at Fulford) and Magnus Olafsson, his half-brother, making this a valuable source. Earl Tostig's successful attempt to persuade Harald to launch his invasion of England is reported.

The translators assess that many of the stories about King Harald came from oral sources because they 'had a better chance of surviving if they engaged the listener's sense of 'wisdom and ingenuity'[17].

Heimskringla

This was the last and is the most quoted version of the Kings' Sagas. We also know the name of the compiler. Snorri Sturluson was an Icelander who engaged in politics rather than warfare and served as the law speaker so was effectively an elected judge. He possibly earned that role because he had recorded past legal judgments, making precedents easier for him to cite. His version of Fulford matches other sagas and provides supplementary information suggesting that he accessed some other sources to describe the battle. King Harald is the focus of all of his reporting so this limits the perspective Sturluson provides of this battle.

More than 70 skalds are quoted within *Heimskringla*.[18] Although the last of the early compliers, it is not obvious that Snorri Sturluson made use of the earlier histories. It is possible that his own methodology precluded using material he himself had not sourced; in fact he explains why some stories were adopted and others rejected:

'In this book I have had old stories written down, as I have heard them told by intelligent people, concerning chiefs who have held dominion in the northern countries, and who spoke the Danish tongue; and also concerning some of their family branches, according to what has been told me. Some of this is found in ancient family registers... and part is written down after old songs and ballads which our forefathers had for their amusement. Now, although

[17] Intro by Andersson and Gade, *Morkinskinna* Cornell Uni Press 2000 080143694X pp63

[18] Stephanie Wirth writing in *Learning and Understanding in the old Norse World* Ed Quinn, Heslop, Wills 978250352808 Brepols 2007

we cannot just say what truth there may be in these, yet we have the certainty that old and wise men held them to be true.' This helps the reader to assess the credibility where Snorri, like a modern scholar, recognised that it was important to explain his evidential criteria.

Snorri adds this when writing about King Harald Sigurdson: 'Yet many of his deeds have not been set down, both because of our lack of information and because we do not wish to put down in writing stories not sufficiently witnessed.'[19] In these words Snorri encapsulates the dilemma of every historian when he recognises the need to exercise his judgment about the sources of information. Happily he felt some were well-attested and could be included to give us our portrait of a remarkable warrior.

Snorri's account of the battle concludes with the skaldic verse known as *Haraldsstikki* describing how 'the Norsemen could go dry-foot over the fen.' This ghoulish observation provides a credible image of the landscape of the ford, which was excavated to discover the ancient road and the pool around the crossing.

Heming

The Orkney sagas contain the story of Heming. It describes how in a series of increasingly outrageous challenges the young Heming gets the better of the ageing King Harald until Heming is challenged, on pain of death, to undertake a suicidal ski run to the edge of a cliff. The saga has him miraculously saved by St. Olaf, Harald's elder half-brother, which caused Heming to retreat to exile in England.

While some parts of this saga are not credible, the description of the turning point of the battle is described in detail and not found in other sources. The observations are consistent with what the other histories report. The key point to note is that Heming had been exiled by Harald. He was now fighting on the English side, enabling him to observe his nemesis, Harald, outflank the English. This is discussed later in the context of the battle action.

These overlapping saga versions provide different perspectives; one challenge of the project was to reconcile all of them. Heming's account illustrates the need to understand where on the battle each reporter was located because none of them were in a position to observe all the action. This was an important 'discovery'. No single saga tells the whole story. They only reported what they observed.

---

[19]From ch36 *Heimskringla*

Critics

Nevertheless, these Kings' Sagas have some severe critics. '..- it is sad that we cannot trust for a moment the noble narrative of the *Heimskringla*, the grandest battle tale among all the Sagas. So many of its statements are utterly incorrect that we cannot accept the rest'.[20] This is unfair, not least because Snorri actually records how he omits any unverifiable claims. In the modern era, social media demonstrates how outrageous claims gain traction which subsequent refutations cannot dislodge. Sadly this academic view, dating from 1910, is still widely held even though the provenance of the saga stories has been studied and understood.[21]

One must however concede that when it comes to names, many errors occur. Norse sources get English names wrong while the reverse is also true. But this observation is valuable since it suggests that in some cases the different English, Norse and French versions did not draw on a common source or copy each other as they make different mistakes with names.[22] Conversely, the repetition of a mistake by multiple chroniclers, noted in later English chroniclers who faithfully copied each other does not make the original error go away. Repetition of an error does not provide it with credibility. All of the sources employed had to be checked and challenged against evidence uncovered on the ground.

Mistakes with names can be identified but are fortunately not relevant to the descriptions of landscape and actions that are provided by the sources. During the archaeological project to locate the Fulford battlefield our sources were systematically investigated and remarkably, none could be falsified.

The credibility of these sources is arguably enhanced by the way that they do not seem to sanitise or modify the skaldic verses that provided the source material for the subsequent Norse historians. Modern historians might be tempted to inject some sense of foreboding into their narratives, mindful of the eventual outcome. However, such previews of the outcome are entirely absent, suggesting these historians were slaves to their source material.

---

[20] Charles Oman *England before the Norman Conquest*, Methuen 1910

[21] One of the earliest versions of Snorri's work *The Sagas of Olaf Tryggvason and of Harald the Tyrant* came from a double-translation, Old-Norse to Norwegian then Norwegian to English. It employs somewhat dramatic language and some errors can be identified in this early translation.

[22] Later English chronicles relied on previous scribes so once a mistake is made it is then faithfully copied.

Perhaps with the exception of Snorri Sturluson, their reports are apolitical and not subject to religious censorships.

Chroniclers based in England

Symeon of Durham

Symeon was writing his *Historia* about 50 years after the battle and is one of only two among the ancient chroniclers to actually name the battlesite as Fulford. For those unfamiliar with the geography of the region, Durham is the nearest Episcopal See north of York. Symeon could be said to be a 'local', certainly when compared to the other scribes, which might explain why he was able to add some detail not found in the brief ASC accounts about the battle.

Geoffery Gaimar

Gaimar also names *Fuleford* as the place of the battle. The name matches the one used in the Domesday survey although spelling consistency was not an issue. Gaimar refers to the English as Engeleis, Engelis and Engeles in his Norman-French history and indeed records his own name as Geffrei and Geoffroy

"Earl Tosti with his fleet ....and with a quick voyage they entered the mouth of the river Humber and so sailing up the Ouse they landed at a place called Richale, and took York after a hard struggle. The Brother earls Edwin and Morcar with a large army, joined battle with the Norwegians at Fulford, near York, on the northern bank of the River Ouse ...'[23]

He had the job of translating the English chronicles into Norman 'French' and wrote a poetic version of England's story, in a style that had some similarities to the Norse 'skaldic' or Norman 'carmen' tradition. We would recognise him as a professional writer and he gives us details of the journey along the Rivers Humber and Ouse by King Harald's contingent, whose journey was different from the main army which landed at Riccall (Richale).

[23] Translation from Ian Short *Gaimar History of the English* OUP 2009 9780199569427

Orderic Vitalis

Orderic was born in 1075 of Anglo-Norman parents and was sent at the age of 10 to the monastery of St. Evroul. "So, weeping, he gave me, a weeping child, into the care of the monk Reginald, and sent me away into exile for love of thee and never saw me again." Various monastic visits provided the opportunity to study other early histories and we can estimate that he was writing about the events of 1066 within 50 years. He died in 1142.

Orderic was a shrewd commentator on the events of his own time which covered the rise to supremacy of the Normans in his native land which he does not always review with favour. He only records the Norse invasion in one of his late works but makes no specific mention of Fulford, in common with others writing in France, there is no indication that he was aware of the battle. He might be self-censoring because he almost relishes in the 'great heaps' of the bones that marked the site of the Stamford Bridge battle where those he termed 'Danes' were slaughtered at the next northern battle.

Orderic gives us the name Senlac (Sandlacu - Sand stream) as the place of the subsequent battle and reports Edwin and Morcar submitting to William and their later rebellions. He would almost certainly have known about Fulford, and because he was a good recorder, we must regret this omission from his writing.

Norman Sources

Norman sources are silent about Fulford but this provides a context to visit the motivations for not simply writing but also examining the spin applied to what was recorded. The archaeological investigations at Fulford allowed the location of some reporters to be identified which obviously impacted what they recorded.

David Bates in his essay "*Lives, Identities and the Historians of the Normans*" writes 'All the historians are working within contemporary moral forms of discourse that sought to make sense of, and even to improve, the disturbed and often violent world of their times.' Noting that many early writers express this motivation suggests that to term their contributions as 'propaganda' is of 'dubious value'.

Citing Elizabeth van Houts, Bates notes that they 'wrote to please God' and concludes that 'having major public profiles' historians 'were aware of the responsibilities that went with this'. The same can arguably be said of early historians who were reporting English events while the immediacy of Norse skalds required them to please their patron and a critical audience.

A gentler word than propaganda is arguably necessary to recognise their condemnation of King Harold as well as other editorial judgements. Eadmer, the first English historian since the epic work of Bede, recorded his motives which were first, to assist those making decisions in the future and then to report with 'a good purpose'. These motivations help explain the story of 1066 that is currently accepted.

Translation

In seeking to describe past events one is dependent not only on what the ancient scribes recorded but then upon the wonderful work of translators. There are at least three linguistic layers of interpretation to be applied when studying ancient texts before the words can be employed as archaeological data.

1. First is the translation of the words and matching it to an equivalent in the target language. It was necessary to explore the full sense of several of the original landscape words employed when investigating the site and on a number of occasions academic specialists in philology had to be consulted to see if terms such as 'fen', 'down-along' or 'beside' adequately matched what had been identified on the ground.
2. Archaeology requires the full meaning of key words therefore the concept that is embodied in some words must be explored. Translating the Latin *apud* to mean 'at' while the context suggests it is expressing proximity or 'nearness' rather than providing a physical designation of being adjacent, as some translations suggest.
3. Finally one should also be aware of the sense that the author might be trying to convey with the word or expression. The words flank, arm, horn or wing might have specific meanings for a soldier but are employed interchangeably by translators. One short sentence telling us that 'They retreated to a place where there was no armed opposition' is loaded with military meaning and is a location that can be uniquely identified in the Fulford landscape.

There are six references to movement in translations of the battle action, and it is extremely important to understand the direction each army is heading. The retreat of the Mercian contingent under Earl Edwin back towards York is also confirmed as he moved 'up along' and some 'got away' from the battle. A researcher must perhaps re-interpret some words in the context of the landscape to understand the battle action.

'Errors'

Determining what are errors and how to reconcile these, was an issue for the methodology being followed during the project to discover the site of the battle of Fulford. The rule followed was that what was written should be accepted as accurate. One cannot pick and choose among whatever words survived. The need to reconcile different descriptions drove many of the research projects.

One later English chronicler mentions the 'northern bank of the river Ouse' which provided one such challenge. There is no northern bank of the Ouse and other sources are consistent with a battle taking place on the east bank. The Ouse runs roughly north-south, giving east and west banks below York until it is briefly deflected by the sub-surface glacial terrain at Fulford Hall towards the west. The river then follows the geology until it reaches Bishopthorpe where it returns to the north-south route. It is therefore difficult to place the action of the battle south of York while at the same time placing it on the north bank of the Ouse except by positing it in the wetland at Middlethorpe and there are many reasons to initially dismiss this as the location for the main action.[24]

The matter was resolved when it was appreciated that the Mercian army deployed to this short section in the action which is explained later. This justifies mentioning the northern bank and one might even conjecture that this scribe was visiting Bishopthorpe, now the site of the Archbishop of York's palace, where he could justifiably perceive the battle being fought from the north bank.

The axis of the battle is a stream known as Germany Beck, which has a north and south bank so could equally justify citing the northern bank. Any skald attached to Harald would see the north bank as the location of their outflanking battle while a reporter with Tostig would record that the south bank was the heart of the battle. But both these locations are on the east bank with respect to the River Ouse suggesting that any cardinal points had to be closely qualified to be meaningful.

---

[24] Assessing alternative locations forms the topic of another report which notes that each proposal contains at least one element of this complex tactical battle.

There is a risk of labouring this point but critical pedants like to question an entire evidential base by fixating on a single word. Science certainly requires an explanation for every anomalous measurement. However, the words bequeathed to us by ancient scribes cannot be measured in the same way. The Norse scribes upon who we rely for landscape descriptions were also reporting what they could see so they describe what were in effect different battlescapes.

The Fulford investigative methodology followed the maxim that the exception probes the rule, and much effort was expended on every anomaly encountered. Perhaps a better expression of the rule that was followed is that nothing recorded by the ancient scribes can be ignored but it must be reconciled with the evidence. If that proves impossible, then more research was required illustrated by the story of Heming which did not 'fit' until it was discovered that this Norwegian was fighting for the 'wrong' side.

One can forgive scribes who were economical with their word-count when parchment and the writing required so much resource. Modern investigators might have appreciated a verbose prose style but happily the surviving, economic prose allowed the area of the battle to be identified, confirming the accuracy of what the ancient scribes recorded.

Part One: Politics and people

Europe takes shape

This section gives expression to one theme of this volume. History is an interconnected tapestry of people and places which is more complicated but also more interesting than the stories that are normally told. Invasions do not happen in isolation.

These historic sketches are designed to provide the perspective that is relevant to our focus on these invasions. They are abbreviated but summarise how rulers emerged in Normandy, Norway and England.

In the eleventh century Europe there were two superpowers, the Holy Roman Empire and France. The purpose here is to paint this picture as we approach the year of destiny for England because it impacts the motivations of all those who sought to be king in England.

The superpowers were composed of many states which were individually similar in size and status to England. Unlike almost all of the Continental lands, kings on the British Isles did not inherit obligations to an overlord with a superior title such as emperor. As in the Nordic lands, England's borders were contested but around 1066 a phase of formalising national boundaries and kingdoms in Europe might be seen as ending.

The island of Britain was a thriving Christian outpost when the centralised Roman government ended at the start of the fifth century. This northern culture had developed its own Christian art and calendar. The Book of Kells and the Lindisfarne Gospels illustrate its vibrancy.

At the end of the sixth century Pope Gregory nevertheless sent the monk Augustine to bring the Roman version of Christianity to these islands after two centuries of 'Celtic Christianity'. Almost simultaneously, the 'People of the book' began to expand another Abrahamic religion from its birthplace in Arabia. These two great religions brought some standard legal principles, religious practices and a clerical system to western Europe.

The perceived order and good government associated with a Europe ruled from Rome had lasted over three centuries. Roman military dominance had collapsed in part through internal political discord, exacerbated by migrations of national populations into 'Roman Europe'. The Franks, Goths, Avars, Bulgars, and Magyars are among the better-known groups that repopulated Europe and North Africa, pushing the Britons and other Celtic peoples to the west. Lazily referenced by the term 'The Dark Ages', it is better thought of as a 'Migration era' whose mobile populations have left limited documentary and archaeological evidence.[25]

By the nineth century the waves of migrations from the east to the west seems to have stabilised with new tribal territories carved from the forested tracts, possibly incorporating or destroying diverse ethnic settlers as they did so. From these settlements one new super-power emerged within a century.

This new era in Europe is conveniently marked by the reign of Charlemagne, or Charles *the Great*, but it was his father, Pepin, who imposed a hierarchy over much of what we would recognise as Western Europe. He called on the Pope to recognise his family as the effective rulers of Europe and therefore the natural successor to the Roman Empire. Pepin's structure of one super-king and many clients would persist for centuries.

This picture was formalised following the selection, or nomination, of Pepin's son, Charlemagne, as the 'Holy' Roman Emperor by Pope Leo in the year 800. Leo had himself only been restored the previous year as Pepin's 'European order' asserted itself. The Roman Church had notionally recruited a new line of 'Roman' Emperors as protectors. The spiritual and the secular rulers of western Europe were now aligned, at least in theory.

The Roman territories controlled by Charlemagne roughly coincided with the Western half of the old Roman Empire but not the Eastern Roman empire, which was still ruled from Constantinople. The Pope, perhaps emboldened by his secular protector, chose this time to challenge the Eastern Church for supremacy of the whole Christian church. It would be 1054 before the churches mutually excommunicated each other marking the split of 'Orthodox' East from the 'Roman' west.

The origin of the word king suggests that rulers had to be qualified by birth, being 'of the kin' from an elite family. Charlemagne, working with the invigorated Church of Rome, effectively changed the rules that underpinned anointed rulers. The complex and often contradictory

---

[25] The unravelling of ancient DNA might in time shed more light on these migrations.

practices of the clerical and secular that emerged would be tested in 1066 with an attempt to assert secular martial rights by a northern invader with a Papal 'crusade', led by William, in the south. 1066 was a victory for Rome.

Charlemagne institutionalised the idea of an overlord who exercised some form of unifying administration while imposing military obligations on its components. Backed by their overlord, rulers inherited their titles. Charlemagne's will divided the new 'Roman' Empire into three zones, ruled by his three sons: We would now recognise these divisions as Germany, France and Italy although it would be another thousand years before these nations' boundaries would be stabilised.[26] Charlemagne likely appreciated the limitations imposed by slow communications necessitating significant local independence.

Fraternal wars and fluid alliances dominated the following century but it provided the context where a young Willam, Duke of Normandy, had to seek the aid of his overlord the King of France in order to survive, defeating other Normans claimants at the battle of Val ès Dunes in 1047. In 1066 William would seek a crown which was not subject to any overlord.

England and the Norse lands were not a part of this Post-Charlemagne system although the latter managed, through coastal raids and the establishment of trading settlements, to carve out some territory for the Northmen from the French 'over-king' during the early part of the 10th century. [27] Around the same time a ruling lineage descended from Alfred *the Great* claimed to be supreme King in England although it would be his grandson who, by defeating allcomers in battle, was first styled King of all England. Alfred's England was focused on Wessex.

A century and a half later these institutions could not be described as stable. The insularity of England brought some prosperity allowing Norse invaders and raiders to be bought off with coin. The local superpowers across the Channel had been joined by the Byzantine and Islamic Empires

---

[26] The Prussian dominated Germany was born in 1890 and Italy's 'unification' in 1861 while the late 18th and early 19th century revolutions in France removed the head of the regional, ducal aristocracy to establish a truly national entity.
[27] The French rivers and coasts were seemingly more attractive to early Norse raiders.

leaving England and the Norse lands as outposts whose occupation would not disturb any of the major western powers.

The influence of the Roman Church

While weapons and armies still provided the hard power, through the anointing of Charlemagne the Roman Church had assumed an agency for legitimising western European kings. This soft power gave Popes a role in the many disputes over succession where boundaries were challenged. Duke William's successful appeal for Papal support was one of the factors that allowed him to rally support for his invasions of England in 1066. Since the Pope at that time relied on Normans to stay in power, papal support was arguably more secular than spiritual.

The previous half century had seen King Macbeth from Scotland followed by King Cnut, who was at that time ruler of Denmark, Norway and England and Earl Tostig Godwinson, one of the key players in our Fulford story, each make their way to Rome because spiritual blessing evidently brought some temporal benefits. The church was able to extract tax from faithful countries and many rulers recognised that it was wise to have ecclesiastical backing.

It was seemingly safe for royal pilgrims to cross Europe and visit Rome. In 1050, Macbeth became the only Scottish king to make a pilgrimage to Rome. He gave money to the poor of Rome 'as if it were seed.' The Pope at that time, Leo IX, was a reformer campaigning against the sale of ecclesiastical offices and married priests. During his tenure, there were also attempts to align the hierarchy of bishops, and the Sees over which they exercised control, with the current national boundaries.

King Macbeth might have been making a bid for ecclesiastical independence to match his own claim of sovereignty but it would not be until 1472, when competing popes traded favours to gain support, that an independent bishop for Scotland was recognised. Innocent VIII made Glasgow an archdiocese, removing it from the See of York. Ironically within a century the Church of Scotland broke with the Church in Rome.

At a practical level, the church provided the clerks, to keep records which were vital for any government which used the universal language, Latin. Ambitious knights in western Europe would, for many centuries, engage in the volatile political events of southern Europe. In the decade just before 1066 Norman warriors were siphoned off for crusades and as mercenaries to fight for and against the Eastern and Western Church even carving out new kingdoms of their own. These distractions probably helped Duke William hold his fractious territory at the northern edge of France together.

In 1059 Bishop Hilderbrand arrived in Rome to wage war against Benedict X, who was termed an anti-Pope. As Pope Nicholas II, Hilderbrand's indebtedness to his Norman supporters encouraged Duke William to seek, and gain, papal support against King Harold, claiming the latter had ignored the late King Edward's will, plus Harold had broken the sacred oaths illustrated on the Bayeux Tapestry.

This was not William's first negotiation with the power of the Papacy. Norman bishops at the Council of Rheims initially condemned William's marriage to Matilda in 1050. But the Prior of Le Bec, Lanfranc, who would later be appointed Archbishop of Canterbury, visited Rome and a penance was agreed to legitimise their marriage[28] providing a rehearsal for the support sought to give the 1066 invasion the status of a crusade.

The picture painted here is one where national leadership was contestable and with a spiritual component. We should interpret the events of 1066 as another scene in the unfolding drama to determine national domination.

Normandy emerges

Before looking at the succession issue, the links between the two 'nations' that will launch invasions in 1066 and England need to be examined but only picking out the threads which will lead us towards the battle at Fulford from the complicated European political picture. The Vikings, which the English Chroniclers always refer to as Danes, took advantage of the post Roman instability setting up trading posts at the fringe of Charlemagne's empire. However the northern coast of France offered long sandy beaches and secluded harbours suitable for their ships to raid and trade. Many migrated south in the 10th century after some costly clashes with the Germanic tribes who made their trading centres in the Lowlands untenable.

In 911 the King of the West Franks offered Rolf title to part of the northern coast to defend on behalf of his overlord following invasions. Rolf and his people would convert to Christianity and he was granted the title of Duke, ruler over the land of the Northmen where Vikings groups from Ireland and elsewhere had already settled. The new duchy was a frontier land for the Franks who were carving territory out of the neighbouring Bretons,

---

[28] The twin minsters in Caen were built as a lasting memorial of this agreement.

who still maintained cultural links with the Britons of Cornwall and Wales (Kernow and Kymry).

While the sovereignty of Normandy was subject to the King of the Franks, in Norway the jarls (earls) were even more reluctant to relinquish their independence to any overlord.

Norway

The emergence of the westerly Norse land as a kingdom exemplifies the interconnectedness of European lands. The loosely defined Viking era saw migrants and raiders sail from the northern lands in their resilient longships to the south and west. The defeat of the northern invasion from Norway in 1066 is often taken as the end of the Viking Age which from England's perspective had lasted about 250 years.[29]

Harald *Fairhair* who dominated Norway until 930, is credited as the first king of a unified Norway although this was fragile and a rather loose model of overlordship. One of his sons Haakon *The Good*, who had grown up in England, attempted to introduce Christianity perhaps under pressure from the Holy Roman Emperor Otto II but after Haakon's death in 960 some powerful jarls rebelled.

Olaf Tryggvason, is thought to be a great-grandson of Harald *Fairhair*, although his eventful life is not reliably documented. His story includes the three year-old escaping from the anarchy in Norway with his mother only to be enslaved in Estonia before being bought and brought to Novgorod where he enjoyed royal protection, having revealed his heritage. Meeting and murdering his captor precipitated his departure where a fortuitous shipwreck led to a love-match with Queen Geria of the Wends. Here he honed his skill as a warrior, restoring control over rebellious Wendish territories and being obliged by his father-in-law to join the Holy Roman Emperor, Otto II, on a crusade to speed the adoption of Christianity, defeating the fractious pagans of his homeland.

Heartbroken at the early death of his first queenly wife, he sailed west. He began raiding the south-east English coast when, after four years as an archetypical Viking, landed in the Scilly Isles to seek out a famous seer

[29] The first recorded attack on Lindisfarne was in 793. Viking settlement in Ireland by comparison caused the petty kings to unite and they had driven the invaders out to 'Normandy' and into Mercia in about a century.

who either converted, or confirmed, Olaf in the Christian faith.[30][31] But in 988 he attended a 'thing', or assembly, that had been called by Queen Gyda, widowed sister of the King of Dublin, who sought a new husband and where the scruffy seafarer was chosen above other suitors. The raiding continued.

In 991 his raiders were camped on the island of Northay in the mouth of the river Blackwater in Essex and demanded money to stop his raiding when confronted by Earl Byrthnoth who allegedly offered to pay him with spears. Determined to rid England of these raiders, the aging earl consented to let Olaf bring his army to land where the long and bloody battle is described in the epic poem of Maldon.[32] Another levy of ship-tax paid off Olaf who probably then felt he had both the money and reputation to allow him to accept the invitation to return home in 995 where the sitting king was quickly deposed.

Olaf and his wife subsequently travelled around England illustrating perhaps that Viking raiding had become a somewhat formulaic, fund-raising activity. Resistance to Christianity was still strong in Norway and the processes of unification and conversion were forcefully extended during his short reign in Norway which reached its dramatic conclusion when he jumped from his longship, the Long Serpent, to avoid capture by pagan rebels who had the support from all the neighbouring countries.[33]

Olaf Haraldson, the half-brother of the man who would later lead the northern invasion of England in 1066, emerged as 'top king' in 1016. He institutionalised many aspects of the Church in Norway establishing a priesthood at the time his southern rivals, the Danes were distracted, invading England. But eventually the powerful Norwegian jarls united with Cnut, King not only of the Danes but now of England, to drive Olaf into exile. This allowed Cnut to add Norway to his portfolio after the battle of Stiklestad in 1030 where Olav was killed and his injured half-brother

---

[30] An English account has Olaf being baptised in 994 at Andover

[31] His band of followers did not take kindly to his rejection of pagan ways and almost killed him, an eventuality for which he had been forewarned by the seer.

[32] A 325-line fragment survives as do images of the wall hanging made to commemorate the gallant Byrthnoth.

[33] The fatal expedition was provoked by his third marriage to a 'queen', the sister of king Sweyn I of Denmark whose invasion in 1015 began the succession crisis that would be resolved in 1066.

Harald began his epic wanderings that would end in 1066 at Stamford Bridge.

Cnut appointed his first wife and their younger son, as regents conveniently removing them from England as he cultivated his relationship with Normandy, leading to a second marriage for Emma, wife of the late King Ethelred. The fates of Normandy, Norway and England were intertwined long before 1066.

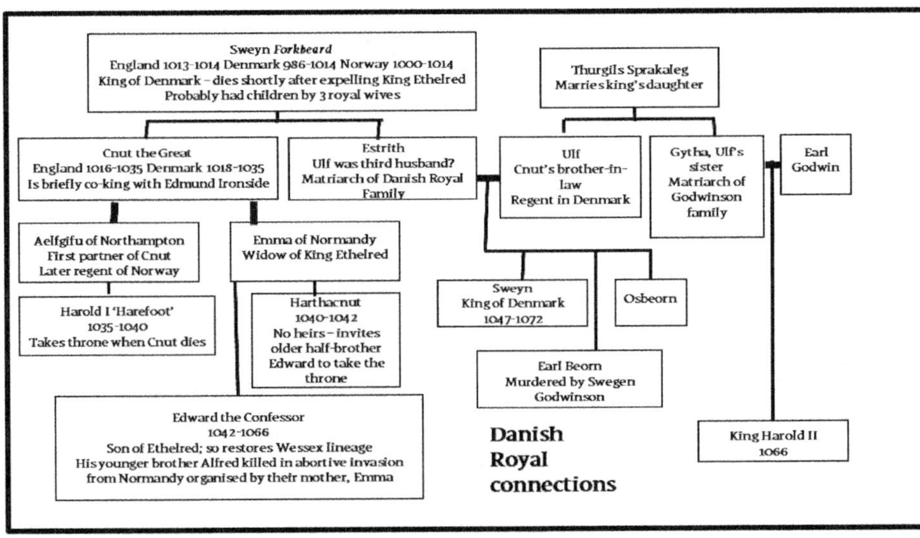

Danish Royal connections

Succession issues

As with so much historical telling, there can be no simple and no 'right answer' to the question of who should occupy the throne of England after Edward by right of birth. The interconnectedness of the Danish, Flemish, Norman and English ruling families makes that impossible. Power and opportunity were the practical governors of who would take the throne. As the Prussian General Clausewitz wrote in the early 19th century 'War is a mere continuation of politics by other means'.[34] Battles do not take place in isolation. They emerge from the preceding events when matched powers are not prepared to compromise. With power concentrated in the person of a king or emperor, the prize was seen to justify the cost and risk.

---

[34] "Der Krieg ist eine bloße Fortsetzung der Politik mit anderen Mitteln". Clausewitz; *Vom Krieg: Princeton University Press. 9780691018546 #87*

The concept of primogeniture was not yet fully established although both the revitalised Church of Rome and the dynastic ambitions of those already occupying thrones certainly favoured this seemingly simple solution.[35] England often followed a system where kings were chosen from among those previously designated as atheling, or throne-worthy, by their right of birth. However, neither the procedure nor the 'electors', often thought of as the Witangemot, were formalised. Strong kings commonly nominated their successor followed by a spiritual coronation, leaving little scope for secular debate. It would be many centuries before there was an undisputed succession-code. The five kings of England prior to 1066 had each followed a different path to the throne.

Edward *the Confessor* had lived in Normandy for nearly 30 years until invited back by his half-brother whom he succeeded as king in 1042. Young Duke William was 14 at that time but was doubtless well-acquainted with Edward's ties to Normandy through Emma, who was William's aunt. The childless Edward was second cousin to William providing him with a claim through bloodlines and family relationships which could be recognised as legitimate qualifications when claiming a throne.

This Norman entanglement began with an attempt to deny a base for the raiding Vikings by King Ethelred who set aside his first wife and married Emma, sister of Duke Robert of Normandy who was later to father William. This marriage made Normandy a natural maternal refuge for the English royal family when the Danes invaded in 1014 and subsequently the long term home of the future Edward *the Confessor* when his own claim was set aside after his mother married King Cnut. The royal alliance through Emma ironically had little impact on the Viking raids in England as noted with Olaf Tryggvason whose ship-money, or 'Danegeld', continued to enrich the Norsemen and finance this claimant to the Norwegian throne.

In 1051 there is some evidence that William visited Edward to confirm the plans for succession. One version of the ASC reports 'Count William came

[35] This often meant the eldest male although within a century of the successor to the Norman invasion, Henry I made the nobles and bishops accept his daughter Matilda as their sovereign. Pregnant at the time of her father Henry's death, her rights were usurped by her cousin Stephen, leading to England first post-conquest civil war euphemistically recorded as 'The Anarchy' lasting 15 years.

from overseas' although this event is not reported by the Canterbury and Abingdon scribes maintaining the ASC who might have been expected to record this local event, hinting at the possibility that it was clandestine. The omission is more likely due to the unravelling of Edward's plan within the year, possibly before the official entry for that year was composed, so a failed plan was not deemed noteworthy therefore went unreported.

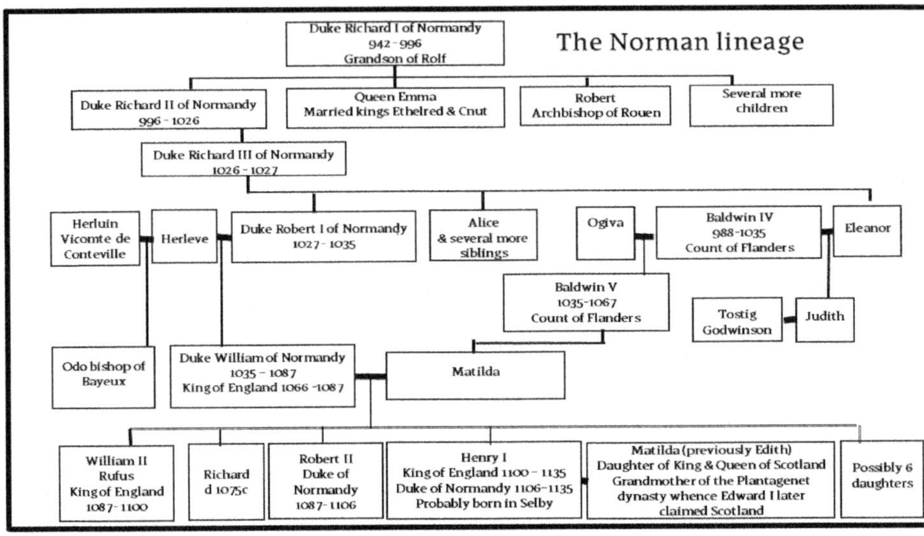

The French chronicler, William of Poitiers, joins his namesake William from Jumièges in reporting that Abbot Robert of Jumièges delivered Edward's message nominating William as his successor possibly shortly after contriving the exile of the Godwinson family in 1051. Edward was indebted to the Normans not only for providing a refuge, but William of Jumièges reports that the Norman Duke regarded the exiles as brothers and had demanded Cnut restore them to their rightful place in the succession[36]. When this was refused by the ailing Cnut, Robert assembled a fleet at Fécamp although the fate of this plan is ambiguous.[37]

The removal of Earl Godwin's youngest son, Gurth, and Swegen's son, Hakon,[38] as hostages to Normandy, plus the arrival of a contingent of

---

[36] Overlooking the many sons that Ethelred has fathered with his first wife.

[37] Relationships between Cnut and the Normans were complicated as there are Danish reports that his half-sister, Estrid was betrothed and according to Danish sources married to Duke Richard II's son, Robert.

[38] This implies that Swegen was already seen as an heir presumptive although he was to die very shortly returning from his pilgrimage of penance to Jerusalem.

Norman knights to provide some hearthtroops for Edward, lend credence to a visit by William presumably to formalise his appointment as Edward's successor. The saintly aura that was subsequently attached to Edward by the Norman Church is belied by such conspiratorial actions.

January 1035 saw William formally designated as Robert's heir, with the Norman magnates swearing fealty to him and this succession was endorsed by their overlord, the French King Henri I. Robert then died at Nicaea, returning from pilgrimage to the Holy Land. William became duke when he was eight. The young William had to call on his overlord, Henri I, to assert his rights to the title and lands of Normandy, defeating his rivals in battle.

There is another pointer suggesting that the plan for William to inherit England was well known. It might be coincidence, but in 1052 King Henri of France formed alliances to address William's growing power. William's English involvements perhaps alarmed his northern French contemporaries who wanted to counter this growing Norman power. History would justify their fear.

The restoration of the Godwinson family in 1053, is discussed later but Edward was unable to win the support of his other earls, effectively thwarting his plan to link the Norman and English domains. Ironically by exiling the Wessex earls Edward might have precipitated an awareness among the English elite of the consequences of rule from Normandy.

This nationalist unity would be demonstrated again in 1066 when the English earls choose Harold Godwinson as the new king. They seemingly recognised that solidarity was vital if they were not only to keep the island secure from invasion but also to ensure they were not subject to a foreign over-king. Their island was at the time a prosperous kingdom with reasonably secure borders that was less prone to the volatile alliances and flexible boundaries that were common on the mainland of Europe.

Edward was seemingly diminished by this failure. "Godwin's sons held England in their power, for Edward was content with life alone and the empty title of king".[39] The wealth of the Godwinson family probably exceeded that of the King most of whose life had been spent as an exile.

When Edward's first plan to nominate and introduce his Norman successor failed, he devised another plan. In 1054 the childless King

---

[39] *Adam of Bremen History of the Archbishops of Hamburg-Bremen* tr Tschan Colombia Uni Press 2002

Edward sent Bishop Ealdred of Worcester to visit Emperor Heinrich III in search of the only surviving member of the Wessex bloodline who could be considered Edward's heir. Edmund *Ironside* had rallied the country against Cnut until they agreed to divide the country to avoid further bloodshed. Edward the Exile was the son of Edmund *Ironside*, co- king of England in 1016 with Cnut before his untimely and suspicious death. Edmund was one of many sons from the first marriage of Ethelred although their primacy was usurped after Ethelred married Emma of Normandy.

During the turmoil at the end of King Ethelred's reign, in 1015, a surviving son, Edmund, had married Ældgyth, widowed in the succession struggle, following the Danish invasion that saw the king seek exile in Normandy. This marriage produced two young sons who were sent into exile by Cnut allegedly telling their chaperone that their deaths would be welcome. The escort took sympathy and found a safer but remote sanctuary for the infants.

Edmund *Ironside's* son, known as Edward *the Exile*, had married Agatha, of the Hungarian royal line. They had three children, Margaret, Christina, and Edgar who would all play significant parts in England's story. Bishop Ealdred, who in 1058 became the first English bishop to make a pilgrimage to Rome, was close to King Edward and acted for him to bring his great nephew, Edward *the Exile* back from Hungary. The hope was to promote this descendant of King Alfred's lineage as his successor.

In 1057 Edward's new plan was also thwarted with Edward *the Exile* dying soon after arrival in circumstances that cast suspicion on Harold at the time. His surviving children we believe were brought up at the royal court as a surrogate family. The son, Edgar, and especially his daughter Margaret, who became Queen of Scotland and later their first patron saint, would maintain the lineage of Alfred. Margaret's daughter would marry William *the Conqueror's* youngest son, Henry, connecting the Norman bloodline to the Anglo-Saxon lineage, giving birth to another redoubtable Matilda, matriarch of the Angevin dynasty.

Edgar, the only boy, who was the grand-nephew of King Edward, therefore had a good claim to the throne of England. Why in the subsequent debate Edgar's blood-line claim to the throne was overlooked until after the defeat at Hastings is confusing.

A tortuous, legalistic claim can be advanced for King Harald of Norway based on a peace treaty between Denmark and Norway. With so much intermarriage and numerous treaties in the preceding century, many claims to European titles and thrones can be advanced. From what little we know of the customs and nature of the early German settlers in this country, what the historian Tacitus wrote about the first century Germans, seemingly still applied.

He writes: 'They choose their kings for their noble birth, their leaders for their valour. The power even of the kings is not absolute or arbitrary. As for the leaders, it is their example rather than their authority that wins them special admiration - for their energy, their distinction, or their presence in the van of fight.....'.

Much time can be wasted in debating the various claims from these different traditions. The outcome was effectively decided by circumstances, although William went to some lengths to let it be seen that he had the Roman Church on his side. Ultimately a successful claim depended on timing, opportunity and military power plus an element of good fortune.

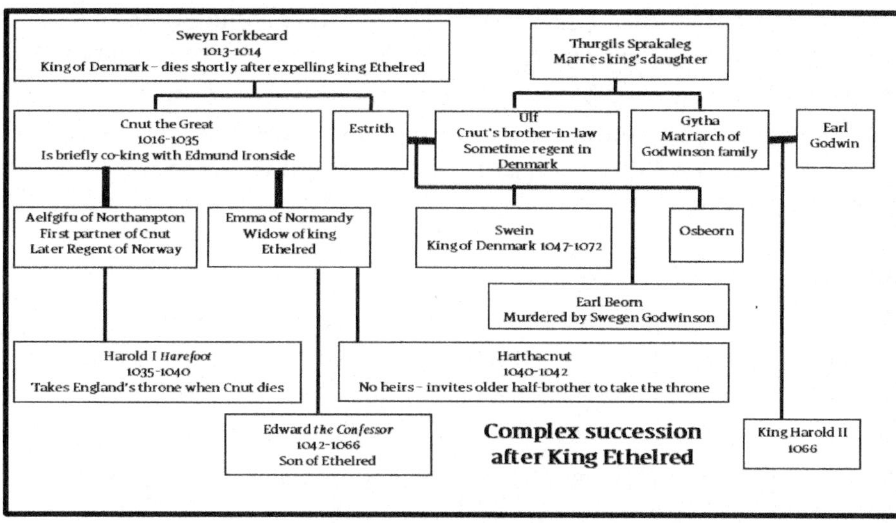

Introducing some people important to our story

Having set the political landscape and forces acting on 'national' boundaries, it is time for a brief sketch of the personalities who will tell the story of this battle at Fulford. These are not biographies but simply sketches the events that impact our story. There are four leaders, plus one who is misidentified as a leader in the sources describing the battle, who have to be introduced.

Behind these combatants lies an important supporting cast that will impact the battle even though they are not present at Fulford. Some of these, such as the Lady Godiva and King Macbeth have almost fictional status in the popular telling of history but as historic characters they are woven into the lives of those who would lead their armies to Fulford.

Earl Tostig

Earl Tostig Godwinson is the key player in our story about Fulford although his role in the events of 1066 in England has yet to be fully recognised. He is the mastermind behind the twin invasions, one in the north and one in the south of England, that displaced the Anglo-Saxon rule and brought William from Normandy to be crowned King on Christmas Day in 1066.

Revolt

Just one year before events had moved quickly and unexpectedly for Tostig. At the end of 1065 Tostig found himself an exile after a revolt against his 13-year rule as Earl of Northumbria. He was away hunting with the old King Edward whose authority and health was in decline.

A well-organised revolt caught and killed his men in York. It is possibly indicative of the lack of trust between the locals and their lord that Tostig recruited his household troops from Denmark.[40] The rebels quickly appointed the younger son of the late Earl Ælfgar of Mercia, Morcar, as their new earl. With this appointment the northern earldoms rebalanced the spread of a Wessex influence in England.

Such an appointment should however only be made by the King, and his hunting companion was clearly a close confidant to the ailing King

[40] Noted in Frank Barlow's book *The Godwins*

Edward, who was later known as *'the Confessor'*[41] after he was canonised in 1161. Edward shared and perhaps encouraged Tostig's piety. The King instructed Earl Harold, Tostig's elder brother, to confront the rebels and restore Tostig.

The King needed his protégé, who had like himself, powerful continental connections following his marriage to a countess from Flanders, as his ally in the ongoing power struggle with all the English earls, including Tostig's brother Harold.

King Edward responded with unusual decisiveness when news of the way the powerbase of his companion had unravelled so spectacularly. Perhaps he viewed this as another chance to weaken the grip of the native nobles by restoring his close ally, Tostig. The royal command however, posed many problems for the astute Harold, who as Earl of Wessex was what we might recognise as the Prime Minister but also commander of England's biggest army.

Edward summoned a meeting at Britford near the place he and Tostig had been hunting. The King heard the complaints about Tostig's rule claiming that the latter's desire for wealth had made him unduly severe, leading the rebels to declare Tostig an outlaw for what they deemed were unlawful actions. This was a legal nicety since the law allowed those termed outlaws to be pursued until they left the land.

The situation for Harold, Tostig and the King was perilous as the Northumbrian rebels had already marched south to press their case and were exacting revenge on Tostig's southern estates for his 'crimes'. They were joined at Northampton by Earl Edwin and his Mercian army, suggesting some preparation and planning had unsurprisingly preceded the rebellion. Coordination between the invading earls is made more likely as they were also brothers.

Earl Harold acting for the King met with his brother Tostig, the rebel brother-earls Edwin and Morcar plus the other earls in England to negotiate, but Harold did not bring his army to Northampton. Harold who manifested the astute sense of a politician, evidently appreciated the gravity of the situation and quickly returned to Oxford. At the Royal

---

[41] In earlier times the term *confessor* was described a person who suffered for their faith and in ecclesiastical terms might be seen ranked just below that of a martyr.

Council[42] meeting on 28 October, Harold persuaded the King to accept the demands of the rebels. Tostig openly accused his brother of fomenting the rebellion to get rid of someone upon whom the ailing King relied. The reaction of these brothers speaks volumes about their personalities; Tostig paranoid and Harold political.

Although there is nothing to suggest Harold was complicit in the rebellion it certainly did present him with multiple advantages. Harold might rid himself of a troublesome and ambitious brother, one who had the ear of the King and quite possibly with ambitions to take the throne for himself, something that was not uncommon among royal siblings. Possibly the King still planned to pass the throne to William with Tostig's aid.

Harold's motivation was unity. He recognised the threat that would soon come from William of Normandy who openly declared his intention to take the English throne. For Harold, peace and unity were more important than immediately restoring his evidently unpopular brother. But the sense of irreconcilable betrayal felt by Tostig is manifest in all his subsequent actions. Harold might have hoped that this rift could be resolved after the King died, something he belatedly tried to do when they next met on the battlefield of Stamford Bridge. Fulford is the story of how Tostig was resolute in his ambition to depose his brother.

Harold doubtless appreciated the real threat posed to the kingdom with two hostile armies in the field and just a few days march from London. Young Morcar, Tostig's replacement, was supported by his older brother, the Earl of Mercia, Edwin. Both had armies, whose combined strength matched or outnumbered the force Harold would be able to muster given time. Harold might have called upon his other brothers whose minor earldoms supported smaller armies that would be tested the following year at Hastings. But in a display of the tactical awareness that was evident the following year, the northern brothers had made their way south so quickly that they had isolated the army of East Anglia from Wessex again suggesting that this coup had been well planned.

On their way south the armies attacked some estates of the Godwinson family. Through marriage but also as an act of policy, kings since the time of Cnut had begun to mix up the land ownership perhaps hoping to

[42] We do not know of a formal constitution for such a council but it is likely to have been similar to a Witangemot which was composed of men of power and leading clerics. It had a semi formal role as the highest court as the only place where the actions of nobles could receive judgment.

weaken 'tribal' allegiances. The post-Conquest Domesday survey shows how every earl held[43] lands in territories other than inside their own titular territory. Although these raids might have been targeted at Tostig, the impact on the wealth and power of the Godwinson family if the rebels continued south, would have been clear to all.

Harold's instructions from the King were clear but he decided instead to negotiate. It was not just that the northern armies outnumbered those Harold could hope to field even if he could fully mobilise in time. King Edward was old and ill so now was a very bad time for a civil war. They were all aware that there would be a succession crisis because Edward's long marriage to Harold's sister had not borne any children.

A civil war would make the country vulnerable to the claims of William, and it was known that the ailing Edward, who had spent half his life as an exile in Normandy, favoured the duke. In addition to weakening any resistance England might offer to an invasion, civil strife presented opportunities to foreign contenders for the throne to find native allies. A defeat for Harold now could even open the way for young Earl Edwin to make a bid to be king. The Wessex domination of England would be eclipsed.

One can understand why Tostig suspected his brother of being complicit in the northern coup because the invasion of the south served him so well. Harold's subsequent actions suggest that he recognised this rebellion was his opportunity to negotiate the support he would later need from these young earls to put him on the throne of England. He probably seized the opportunity. Marriage to the rebel's sister was probably proposed as part of the peace pact. Harold demonstrated a ruthless side that accepted targeted violence but preferred peace. One might recognise a preference for political solutions from this younger son who did not display the common arrogance of heredity authority.

The rebellion presented Harold with other significant advantages. Exiling Tostig was not a harsh punishment since his wife Judith was from Flanders. Tostig even held title and lands in Flanders and Harold might have hoped that his brother could be placated with a promise to review the exile after Edward. The choice of a new monarch by the Witangemot

---

[43] The term 'held' means that it was granted by charter and was not, automatically, hereditary but was in the gift of the monarch as a way to reward or punish. There was some 'bookland' giving rights in perpetuity and was common for religious gifts.

would also be much easier without the presence of Tostig. The only downside from Harold's perspective was facing the displeasure of the king, and of course Tostig.

Harold negotiated peace and faced the king's wrath. Tostig went into exile and all of his subsequent actions suggest that he felt betrayed and that his brother had done a deal with the rebels. The Godwinson brothers would meet once more on the battlefield of Stamford Bridge where Harold's offer to restore his brother was rejected.

The old king died about 12 weeks later as 1066 dawned. He was not well enough to attend the inauguration of his great project to build a New Minster church in London, west of the old Roman city of London, which has been known ever since as Westminster. Edward was distancing the government from the Wessex capital in Winchester, to the border with Mercia, another of the three great earldoms. Westminster has remained the seat of government.

So at the end of 1065 Tostig and his wife Judith, Countess of Flanders, took their two children and returned to her home for what they might have hoped was a temporary exile. Baldwin V, Count of Flanders, installed him as castellan of St. Omer granting the exiled Tostig both status and land. The coronation of his brother Harold took place on the last day of the royal court's winter gathering at Westminster. It was perhaps rushed but this was one of only two occasions in the year when all the senior nobles and clerics were traditionally assembled. But after Harold's coronation, Tostig did not receive the call to return home.

Judith

In this context Tostig's wife, Judith, requires a proper introduction as she will play a crucial, if so far unacknowledged part in the unfolding events of 1066. Tostig married Judith in 1051 possibly just before the Godwinson family were exiled[44] and one might speculate that Edward promoted this union to benefit the one male of the Godwinsons with whom he had good relations knowing that he was plotting the downfall of the rest of Tostig's family.[45]

---

[44] The *Vita Edwardii* records that the skirmish at Dover which precipitated the exile occurred "during the very marriage celebration of Earl Tostig when he took Judith as wife" from *The Life of King Edward* Tr Barlow F

[45] Since he had not attained the rank of earl, the marriage contracted to Judith was a considerable coup for the Godwin clan. The author of the life of King

In 1051, when Judith was at least 16 she married, or as some historians term it 'was married to', Tostig. 'Judith's first marriage should be understood as something of a low-risk investment for [her half-brother]] Baldwin'.[46] But Tostig was the third son, so their 'ranks' were similar. It is perhaps relevant that both Judith and Tostig seem to have been devout[47] and intellectually matched. Baldwin was also negotiating the marriage of Judith's lifelong companion, Matilda, to Duke William.

For Baldwin creating the English alliance balanced the alliance Edward had formed with his rival, Emperor Henry who had married Edward's half-sister Gunnhild, who was the daughter of Cnut and Emma. The role of women as peace-weavers between dynastic houses is often remarked although political marriages could seemingly reinforce aggressive alliances.

Judith was the daughter of the late Count Baldwin IV of Flanders, and the consensus[48] is that her mother was Eleanor, daughter of Richard II Duke of Normandy, securing an alliance with the Normans. Baldwin IV's first wife was Otigiva of Luxembourg who died in 1030. She was the mother of the future Baldwin V, Judith's older half-brother, 20 years her senior. Judith's year of birth was therefore between 1030 and 1036 as her father died in 1035.

Judith's niece, Matilda was likely a similar age and were raised together in Bruges under the guardianship of Adele, Matilda's, mother. Both girls were evidently literate and well educated as illustrated by their patronage of written texts in their later lives. They would be schooled in power politics with the costal geography of Flanders making it an important hub for all parts of central and northern Europe.

They were likely fluent in several regional French argots, Flemish, English and Latin and possibly familiar with some Norse and Germanic languages. One can think of this as an attribute in 'the marriage market' but in assessing their future lives it might be seen as a good preparation for a life

---

Edward refers to him as earl although most records suggest he did not attain this status until after his wedding.

[46] Fleming R *Kings and Lords in Conquest England* Cambridge Uni Press 1991

[47] During her marriage to Tostig she commissioned at least four gospel books that survive. Donations to monastic institutions whose connections ensured the gifts would be recognised in perpetuity.

[48] Mary Dockray-Miller *Judith – The books and life of Judith of Flanders* Ashgate 2015 9781409468356

spent in European politics. The role of translator is seldom mentioned so one must suppose leaders were either multilingual or reliant upon their foreign brides. Positioned between the Holy Roman Empire, England, the French state, and the Norse lands, Flanders was vulnerable. The component parts of the surrounding lands turbulent with their boundaries and their spheres of influence variable.

It is an unexplained coincidence that in the same year as Judith's marriage to Tostig, King Edward sprung his trap and the Godwinson family were banished from England only to returned in 1052 after it became clear that the King lacked support among the other earls for his Norman succession plan.

Three years after the Godwin clan was restored, after their short exile, the Godwinson family was in the ascendancy and Tostig was appointed Earl of Northumbria upon the death of Earl Siward. His wife Judith who is generally accorded the tile 'Countess' not least because the English of the time had no word to honour the wife of an earl.

Judith and Matilda are both important to our narrative. With two separate invasions being planned in 1066, coordination was necessary. The timetable, which is discussed later, leaves little doubt that William was aware of the timing of the northern invasion. It is also reasonable to suggest that Judith was privy to Tostig's plan and she would have benefitted from progress-reports once he began his campaign in the early summer. Comments attributed to Tostig by one Norse source after his victory at Fulford also suggest that he was aware of the timing of William's invasion, but those will be expanded in the battle post-script.

Duke Richard II of Normandy's sister, Emma ,had been Queen of England twice: First when married to Ethelred whose childless eldest son, King Edward, sparked the events of 1066: Her second marriage was to King Cnut whose son Harthacnut would also briefly occupy the English throne before passing it onto his elder half-brother Edward. Judith's blood line was therefore close to the English royal line and Matilda shared both grandfathers with Judith, so the English, Flanders and Norman leaders were all part of a royal family to which Tostig had been admitted. Perhaps the ailing King entertained the hope that this might provide Tostig with the traction he needed to succeed him, rather than Harold, after his Norman plan failed in1052.

Both Flanders and Normandy sought to maintain good relations with their more powerful neighbour across the channel. The ASC of 1037 mentions

English nobles taking refuge in Bruges and later Emma, the widow of two English kings used it as her base to further her plans for her sons including Harthacnut and Edward, even Swegen the eldest Godwin son used it as his refuge between 1046 -1049. It was the place to which the exiled Godwinson family retreated in 1052 so one might see Flanders as at least sympathetic to those whose political position in England was perilous.

King Ethelred had actually invaded Normandy, determined to capture and abduct Richard II for his perceived failure to control the Norse raiders attacking England, but this raid failed. It was at this stage that Richard's sister, Emma, was sent as a peace-weaver to placate Ethelred.

The death of King Henri I of France in 1060 enhanced Tostig's prestige and strategic position when his brother-in-law[49] was appointed guardian to Henry's infant son, Philip I. Judith's brother was in effect ruler of France for as long as the French king was under-age. This meant that the exiled Tostig potentially had a full-time job running Flanders for his brother-in-law, probably based in St. Omer plus close marriage ties to Duke William. His subsequent choices provide an insight to his determination for revenge.

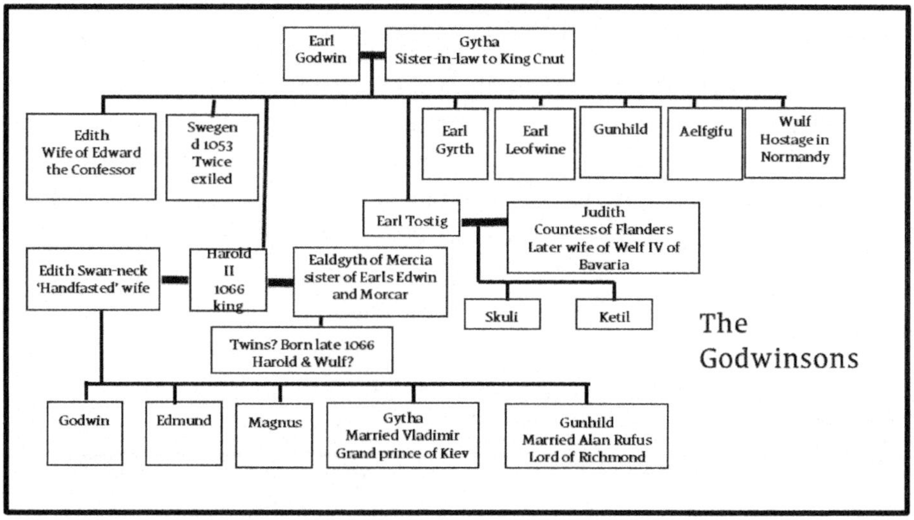

The Godwinson Exile in 1051

The Godwin family might have made preparations against the eventuality of exile with three of Godwin's sons, Swegen, Harold and Leofwine taking

[49] Realistically, the relationship was likely equivalent to father-in-law due to the two-decade age difference.

their ships, not to Flanders, but to Ireland, from where they could pose a threat and influence events. Edward had perhaps overplayed his hand in engineering a crisis and then ignoring urgings from neighbouring monarchs to allow Earl Godwin to return and prove his innocence, suggesting the old earl had good political connections and the neighbours wanted a stable England. The unrest was quickly exploited by the Welsh to launch damaging raids and Edward's fleet at Sandwich failed to intercept Earl Godwin's fleet when he made a number of landings in his native Wessex where he seemingly had a good reception before returning to comfortable exile with his in-laws in Flanders.

During this period Harold had become the senior Godwin son after the departure of Swegen for his penitential pilgrimage. Harold made several successful and damaging raids along the west coast further exposing the limits of the King's power and control. The Godwinson family then united their fleets in Flanders and launched a new strategy with landings in England to demand provisions and hostages. King Edward planned a showdown in London where he had mustered 50 ships and summoned his earl's armies. But the chroniclers suggested that Earls Leofric and Siward were slow to respond, in effect depriving the King of an army. With the support of the Londoners, Harold and Godwin surrounded the King's fleet.

Arriving to meet King Edward at his new West Minster hall, the Godwinsons were armed and arrayed ready for battle. But instead of fighting, Earl Godwin laid down his arms and demanded that he be allowed to purge himself of the treasons with which he had been charged. The King now reluctantly agreed to a 'trial' since the assembled chief men of England evidently supported this demand for 'justice'. The Witan believed Godwin and approved his restoration and then 'outlawed those Frenchmen who had promoted injustice'. The following year Godwin collapsed when dining with the King and died on 15 April 1053 aged about 60, seemingly of natural causes.

One footnote to this restoration was the departure of the group of Norman warriors who had recently arrived to provide the King with some close protection as his 'hearthtroops'. Such a 'bodyguard' was quite normal but Edward might have lacked the means and seemingly the necessary future prospects to attract men to his service during his long period in exile.

When Edward was invited to return he seemingly came without any companions and it might indeed have been impolitic to return home with a private army. Since his promotion to the throne Edward had been forced to rely on the Godwinson's to defend him. With the Godwinson's back in power these Norman warriors were unwelcome but did not return home. Instead they offered their swords to the King of Scotland, Macbeth, where in due course they would share his fate in August 1057.

More about Matilda

There are two versions of Matilda's marriage to William. A romantic one that has William having his initial amorous suit rejected, leading to an aggressive outburst and physical attack on Matilda followed by a risky second visit that was successful. The other version is that Baldwin V proposed the match of his daughter Matilda to William in 1048 although in the following year Pope Leo IX objected to the marriage on the grounds of consanguinity. Nevertheless by 1053 William and Matilda were married and six years later the marriage was recognized by Pope Nicholas II, who we noted had earlier deposed the sitting Pope with Norman help. By way of penance William and Matilda built two adjacent monasteries in Caen for breaching the Church's rules.

But Matilda's path toward true love had encountered one major detour we know of. In 1050, Brittric, a noble from Gloucester, was sent by King Edward as an ambassador to Baldwin, Count of Flanders. It was here that he met Matilda who was about 20 at the time. She fell for Brittric but he did not reciprocate. The hurt meant that as Queen of England, the previously spurned lover, persuaded William to dispossess Brittric from the manor of Avening and he is reported to have died as a prisoner in Worcester.

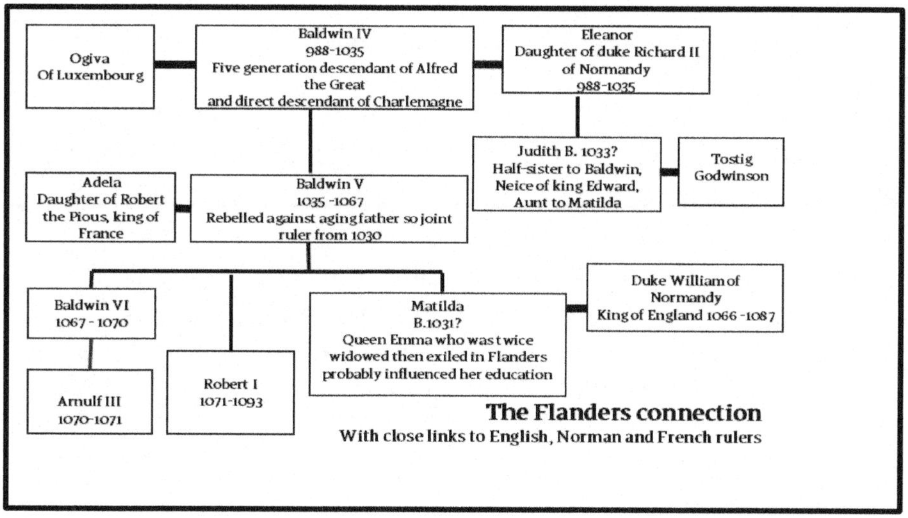

The Flanders connection
With close links to English, Norman and French rulers

Pilgrimage

At the height of his power, in 1061 Earl Tostig accompanied by Judith, led an embassy to Rome on behalf of the king. The party included Ealdred, archbishop-elect of York, who was journeying there to receive his pallium, the official insignia which had to be bestowed by the Pope in person. On the outward and return journeys Tostig is reported as demonstrating his piety by worshipping at each shrine they passed, although such formulaic expressions were the norm. As a couple, they were deemed generous for the way they devoted their tax revenues to the Church, earning praise in religious texts. The taxes extracted to support such generosity was one grievance cited by the rebels in 1065.

Pope Nicholas II, the newly elected pope, received Tostig and his companions honourably and invited the Earl to attend a synod, presumably at Easter 1061 where it is believed Tostig sat next to the Pontiff. This synod had been summoned to deal with the problem of simony in the church where the selling of permissions, positions, and pardons had become a recognised and accepted way of enriching clerical officeholders.

There was a dispute over Bishop Ealdred's election as archbishop of York and it seems that the Earl threatened to withhold the 'Peter's Pence', the annual payment from England's church to the Pope. Acting as the ambassador for King Edward, this was an important meeting recognising the rising political power of the Papacy and Earl Tostig.

Tostig's embassy became embroiled in the local struggle between the Tuscan nobility and the Papacy when members of his party were attacked on the via Cassia shortly after leaving for home. The Earl had sent Judith and most of his retinue ahead so they were unaware of what had happened to their fellows still in Rome. The attackers were led by Gerard, Count of Galeria, who was later excommunicated by Pope Nicholas II for this act of aggression.

During the attack a nobleman, named as Gospatric, enabled Tostig to escape by pretending that he was the earl. The name Gospatric was common in the north in this period and cannot be identified with certainty, but it is possible that he was either the post-conquest Earl of Northumbria but he might have been the Gospatric, son of Uhtred and his second wife, Sige, or the thegn who was slain when under the protection of Queen Edith in 1064, providing another spark for the revolt against her brother the following year.

On their return to Rome, Tostig and his companions were treated with compassion by the Pope, who gave them gifts and they departed with a benediction plus archbishop Ealdred's pallium. This is notable as it was rare for a pope to change their mind, suggesting that Tostig was both forceful and persuasive. Judith and Tostig's separate parties reached England safely in the autumn of 1061. There are reports that Judith, and possibly Tostig, visited Matilda in Normandy on their way home. Both women had families by this time. This might have provided an opportunity to meet William and create a relationship that would impact England's history five years later.[50]

During the period of Tostig's rule in Northumbria, the couple forged close links with the monastic community of St Cuthbert at Durham. Symeon of Durham describes their gifts to Durham's patron saint, St Cuthbert. Symeon is also the source for the story of Judith's desire to worship at Cuthbert's shrine in person.

Women were not permitted to enter the precincts of the church which was within this Benedictine monastery but the curious and determined Judith sent one of her maids who fell ill and died soon afterwards. This is matched by a tale of one of Tostig's officers who was miraculously struck down for violating sanctuary within the church as they sought a fugitive. The gifts from the couple are therefore portrayed as atonement but they fit into lifelong pattern of gifting practical treasures including gospel books.

Sadly no letters survive to demonstrate what Tostig planned, and he would not survive to be able to tell his version of the 1066 story. His widow would quickly re-marry and devote her energies to the struggle between rival claimants to the papacy. Matilda understood how to keep plans confidential.

Tostig's travels and meetings are well documented by Norse historians promoting the northern invasion. Perhaps mindful of security southern sources provide only circumstantial evidence to suggest that he was at the centre of a coordinated plan to conquer England in 1066 using his close continental connections.

[50] It was not until 1064, three years later, that Harold made his eventful visit to Normandy.

Macbeth

The north was, at this era, disputed territory between Northumbria and the kingdom of Alba where King Macbeth took control in 1040. Peace along the border had evidently reigned because in 1050 Macbeth went on pilgrimage to Rome, a full decade before Tostig's embassy. A canny politician, Macbeth agreed that his northern adversary, Earl Thorfinn of Orkney, also journeyed to Rome so that neither would take advantage of the other's absence. The Pope had also declared a jubilee perhaps encouraging Macbeth to leave his kingdom with secure land and sea borders. He possibly returned with holy oil that was subsequently used to anoint monarchs in Scotland.

His neighbour south of the lawless borderlands was Earl Siward of Northumbria who is best remembered for his expedition against the Scots a few years later in 1054. Siward was instructed to assist Duncan's son, Malcolm, who had been orphaned when Macbeth took the throne. Young Malcolm found refuge at his uncle's court in York after 1040 but claimed his father's throne in Scotland.

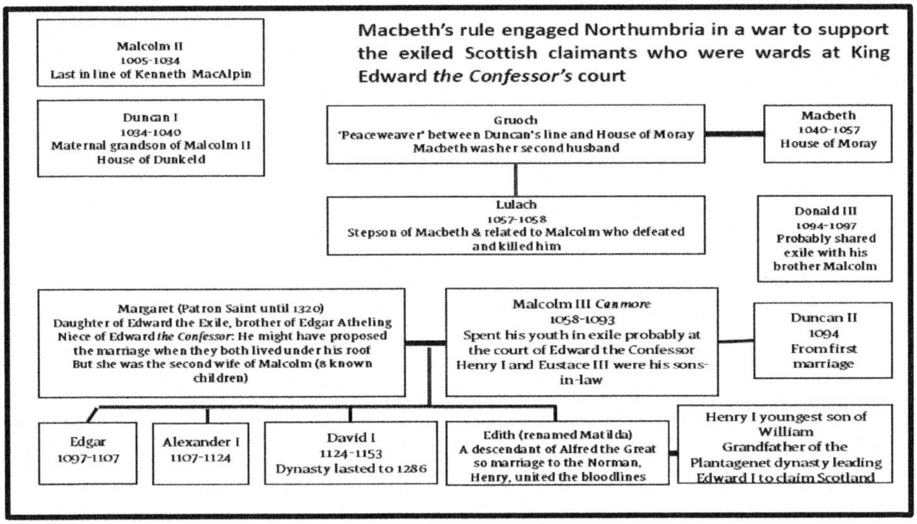

At the bloody battle of Dunsinane in 1054 the Earl was victorious at the cost of his son and other potential candidates to succeed to the earldom of Northumbria. This tragedy ultimately opened the way for Tostig and later for Morcar to assume the role of earl even though they were both 'outsiders'. Macbeth never recovered his prestige following the defeat at Dunsinane and probably died of wounds received at the battle of Lumphanan in 1057.

Harald, King of Norway

There are two Harolds in the story about Fulford. The new King Harold II, brother of Tostig, arrived too late to take part in the battle at Fulford but just five days later he would confront the other Harald, at Stamford Bridge, where both he and his brother Tostig, would both be killed by Harold's army.

King Harald of Norway is the second important character in this story of Fulford. He had been persuaded to mobilise his army when Tostig went north to Oslo in the spring, seeking support to restore him to his title and lands in England, even suggesting that he had an equal claim to the throne as his elder brother. The various Norse Sagas report the exchanges between Tostig and his royal Danish cousin where he challenged King Swein to emulate his great grandfather, Cnut, who had ruled England, Denmark, and much of Norway although the latter was governed by his first wife, Ælfgifu of Northampton.

Ælfgifu had been displaced by the dowager queen Emma when Cnut married Æthelred's widow in a political marriage. The sons of these rival wives would both be kings of England. Ironically it was King Edward *the Confessor*, the offspring of Emma's first marriage who outlasted all the sons of Cnut, restoring the Wessex lineage of Alfred. Edward's first act as king was to seize his mother's treasure and exile her perhaps as revenge for promoting his younger brothers and leaving him in exile. But this royal story is straightforward compared with Harald's route to the throne.

As a teenager, Harald had fought alongside his half-brother, Olaf, who was killed at the Battle of Stiklestad in 1030. The adventures of Harald's escape and his rise to become a leader of a Viking army should be the stuff of a Hollywood series. He went to Constantinople where he rose to be the captain of the Varangian Guards, who provided close protection for the Byzantine Imperial family.

There are credible reports that this led to various intimate relationships including with the exiled and then restored Empress Zoe. He had attained this supreme position by battling with pirates, restoring Byzantine control over Sicily and southern Italy, before escorting the Empress on a pilgrimage to Jerusalem when the warring faiths were temporarily reconciled. Such a summary cannot do justice to the exploits and intrigues into which Harald was drawn. Harald's narrative justifies the way the word 'Byzantine' is employed as a synonym for unduly complicated, untrustworthy administrative intrigue.

While Harald's biographers laud him for making this pilgrimage route safe for Christians. Credit is also claimed by a group of Normans who set out for Jerusalem with a similar objective. However, these Normans were initially diverted from their spiritual objective by 'liberating' southern Italy from Byzantine control. In the succeeding decades many Normans left home and worked as mercenaries for the Pope, the Lombard, and even the Byzantine and Muslim rulers, providing profitable employment for knights.[51] It was in 1035 that Duke Robert of Normandy, the father of William, died in Nicaea returning from pilgrimage, succumbing to disease which was probably the fate of the majority of soldiers in ancient times, leaving his infant son William to inherit the Duchy of Normandy.

The Byzantine Emperor Michael V equipped an expedition for the reconquest of Sicily and regain lost territory. The expedition was led by George Maniaces, and under his auspices Harald led the Varangian Guard. It was after this successful expedition that Michael V alleged that Harald had misappropriated funds and had not given the proper amount of tithe to the government. Harald's experiences in Constantinople honed not only his military but his political skills and made him extremely rich.

This chapter of Harald's adventures ended when he was imprisoned in a tower from which it was impossible to escape, that is until one of his imperial conquests used her rank to get him out. Two ships were quickly loaded. It was fortuitous that Constantinople was under attack by a Rus army and the navy had deployed for battle, leaving the harbour empty and lightly guarded. Two heavily laden ships set off, but only Harald's made it over the great chain that sealed the harbour. He accomplished this by getting all the people and baggage at the stern of his longship and at just the right moment ordered them to rush forward as soon as the bow rode up when it encountered the chain. The other ship was perhaps less sturdy and broke in half and sank.

The next adventure began with his marriage to Princess Elsvetta, daughter of the Russian Czar in Kyiv. Now loaded with the riches that he had won during his time in Constantinople, he began to make his way home with the ambitions to take on the mantle of his half-brother, Olaf and become King of Norway.

---

[51] No study of any beneficial impact that this exodus of warriors had on the stability of the Normandy region could be identified.

But nothing is ever simple in the telling of Harald's story. First he had to ally himself with an exiled claimant to the throne of Denmark which was at the time ruled by King Magnus, of Norway, Harald's nephew. Making and breaking alliances, he made his way home where he offered to share his fortune with the nephew against whom he had just fought in exchange for a share in the kingdom of Norway. A co-kingship deal was agreed but when Magnus, *the Good*, died Harald became king and commenced 13 years of wars with his erstwhile Danish ally, Swein, who had also reclaimed the throne of Denmark. Although Harald won many of their battles, he never managed to win this war and restore Norwegian rule over Denmark. This era of warfare under Harald ensured that he had the ships and warriors available in 1066.

The ageing warrior did not rest after concluding an unsatisfactory peace treaty with his Danish southern neighbour. This 50 year old veteran of so many battles theoretically handed over control of Norway to his eldest son who was the product of a political marriage to the family of his most powerful rival, and not his wife the Rus princess, Elsvetta with whom he had two daughters.

After 1062 King Harald devoted himself to seeking vengeance on those in his own kingdom and earned the name '*Hardrada*', literally Hard Ruler, but which is better understood as 'tyrant'. His vengeful behaviour drove some powerful families to transfer their allegiance to the Swedish king and it is also reported that brave men had to come between Harald and the son to whom he had notionally transferred the crown. He was not taking well to semi-retirement and the risk of assassination or civil war was looming.

This was the Norwegian domestic political context when Tostig arrived seeking help to return him to power in England. Freed from royal duties, profoundly unpopular and distrusted by the nobles, with an army of veterans that were perhaps getting impatient, an expedition might have been tempting. Possibly his queen Elsvetta recognised that a foreign adventure would not only save Harald from assassination but protect her position and those of their two daughters. The women might be more secure abroad than in Norway, so they set off late in 1066 for England.

It is unlikely that the reputation of King Harald, where Norwegians were yet to use his nickname *Hardrada* in any contemporary writing, was well known in England. In the days before the battle at Fulford, once his arrival had been observed, some of the many stories attached to his ventures were probably retold. He knew this was his last adventure and one that he hoped would secure his legacy as the greatest Viking.

Edwin and Morcar

On 3rd October 1065 the Northumbrian thegns met in York and chose Morcar to become their new leader. His elder brother, Edwin had himself only become Earl of Mercia a few years earlier after the death of their father. Morcar's promotion followed the coup discussed earlier when Tostig's followers were killed and his land and property seized.

One prelude to this rebellion took place in 1064 when two important thegns, Gamel and Ulf, came south under safe conduct, supposedly at the invitation of Queen Edith, Tostig's sister, and were murdered. The precise nature of this embassy from the Northumbrian earls is not clear but probably centred around the process of tax collection.

Tostig's pilgrimage and church building needed to extract more taxes. The 'clerical' way tax gathering, established in the south, largely bypassed the thegns. The traditional method afforded an opportunity for the thegns to extract a share for themselves as they collected the king's taxes.

Even Tostig's sister noted that he was sometimes unduly severe in his administration of justice and one complaint noted in the Anglo-Saxon Chronicle charged Tostig with 'robbing churches, depriving men of their lands and lives'. One rebel demand was to restore the laws of Cnut, suggesting Tostig during more than a decade as their earl had employed rules that had evolved down south into what was still recognisably Danelaw.

Morcar may not have been as passive in the rebellion as the silence of the sources suggest. His father had been the Northumbrian earl for a short time but was exiled in contentious circumstances opening the opportunity for Tostig to be appointed by the king as the Earl of Northumbria.

Their father Ælfgar is believed to have married Ælgifu, and they had at least four children. The eldest son, Burghead, died returning from Rome in 1061 providing an apparently coincidental parallel with the Godwinson family where Harold's elder brother, Swegen, perished returning from a pilgrimage to the Holy Land although we know the latter was atoning for several heinous crimes.[52]

There is circumstantial evidence to suggest that the surviving two boys and their sister were brought up by their grandmother. The celibate clerics who provided the sources for subsequent historians largely exclude reporting women from their chronicles but Godgifu, known to us as Godiva, survives in charters as well as legend. She was the wife of Leofric, and they had a single son Ælfgar. She was born about 990 and married before 1010, Leofric became Earl of Mercia under Cnut's rather brutal reorganisation of the English earls. Nothing more is known of Godiva's origins although the incident for which she is remembered suggests the lands, including Coventry, were here familial home and the historian John of Worcester tells us that Coventry Abbey was founded by Godiva and her husband.

The boys were well practiced in the forceful power politics of the time. Their father, Ælfgar became Earl of East Anglia displacing Harold when he was exiled along with the family in 1051. Harold was restored to his earldom but at Easter 1053 Godwin died, promoting Harold to the more extensive Earldom of Wessex, which opened the way for Ælfgar to return to East Anglia.

These seemingly peaceful transitions however disguise the building tensions within England. When Ælfgar inherited the Mercian title after the death of his father, the Godwinson family quickly appointed one of their own to become Earl of East Anglia.

The political tension came to the fore again in 1055 when Ælfgar was exiled for crimes which some chronicles felt were fabricated. But he raised a small fleet in Ireland and landed in Wales where Gruffydd King of Wales agreed to join forces with him. Subsequently Gruffydd would marry Ældgyth, Ælfgar's daughter. Gruffydd and Ælfgar defeated the local English lord, 'brutally sacking' Hereford.

King Edward sent Earl Harold with his Wessex army forcing the invaders back into south Wales. The issue was then resolved and Earl Ælfgar was reinstated to his earldom. Gruffydd was less fortunate. An alliance between the Mercians and the Welsh was a threat to the domination of

[52] Swegen Godwinson had first been exiled for the murder of his cousin, a possible heir to the Danish throne, and again for abducting the abbess of Leominster and 'keeping her for his pleasure and then sending her back'.

England by the Wessex earls. A price was put on his head which was in due course delivered to King Edward.

One consequence of this episode was that Edwin and Morcar's sister was a widow by 1065 and it is possible that in the critical negotiations after the Northumbrian rebellion against Tostig that Harold proposed a marriage to Ældgyth. Such a match offered the prospect of uniting the two dominant dynasties and putting an end to their rivalry. If Edwin and Morcar had contemplated staking a claim to the English throne after Edward, the prospect that nephews yet to be born would inherit the crown might have featured in the negotiations at Northampton in October 1065 before the northern earls agreed to lead their armies home.

Subsequent chroniclers would note that the brothers acted as one with Edwin putting his life on the line to support his brother at Fulford, contrasting with the fraternal conflict between Harold and Tostig Godwinson that would destroy them all.

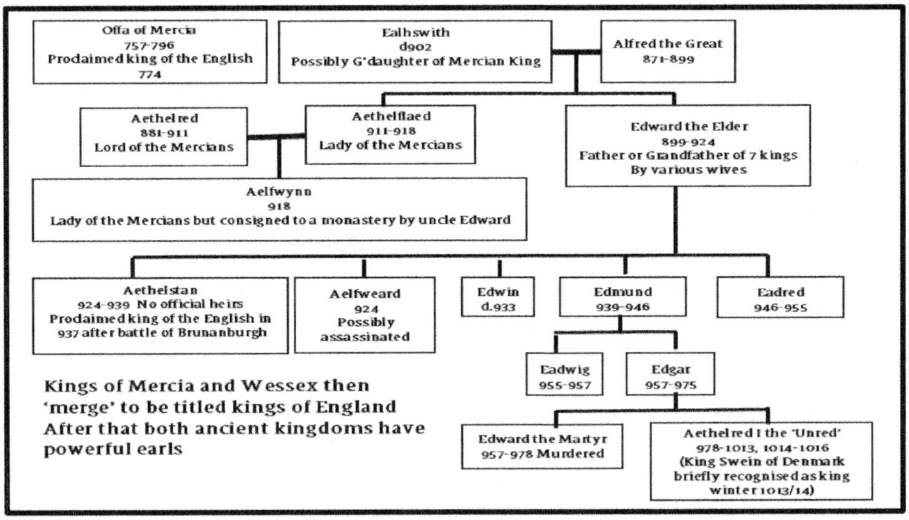

Waltheof

One last character needs an introduction. His role in the battle is tricky to unpick because the 'Earl Valtheof' reported in Norse written sources is often interpreted as a case of mistaken identity. English records state that the defenders at Fulford were led by the Earls Edwin and Morcar and this is consistent with all historical analysis.

However rather than accepting this as a case of mistaken identification there is evidence that Waltheof was indeed a prominent leader during the battle. This suggests that the sources were not wrong to identify him as a prominent leader in the battle.[53] There are good reasons to place Earl Waltheof at Fulford as the leader of the force he had contributed to the Mercian army from his southern landholding in Huntingdon.

He was a native northerner of noble stock who would in time himself be styled Earl of Northumbria by King William. Had he stayed down south he would have been engaged at Hastings and therefore not enjoyed the favour subsequently shown him by William which is another reason to place Earl Waltheof at Fulford. Those who fought the Norse invaders did not suffer the confiscations imposed on any who took part in the battle on Senlac Hill.

It is possible that Norse historians misunderstood, or misinterpreted, some of the skaldic conventions. *Wæltheow's* warriors are mentioned in *Haraldsstikki* and scholars, using this as a source for their writings, might have interpreted him as a leading earl and assumed that he was Morcar's brother.[54] We learn that Edwin brought some of his Mercian army to defend the river bank but Waltheof might have been actually giving the orders while Edwin liaised with his brother. The extraordinary setting and sequence of the subsequent battle would provide ample opportunity to discover who was opposing them.

During the project to locate the battlefield it was important to provide details whenever any early written source was challenged. The guiding principle was that one could not pick and choose from the evidence available. This quotation from Forrest Scott details the explanation for accepting this name substitution.

---

[53] There are several misidentifications in the saga source. One records that the Norse army. "... slew Morcar, Godwin's son, but Earl Gurth his brother fled out of the battle." Morcar was not Godwin's son, and the only contemporary 'Earl Gurth' was Harold's brother.

[54] Forrest Scott *An English Earl in Icelandic Sources Saga-Book Vol XIV* 1953-57 UCL, Viking Society. Scott, then an academic at Sheffield, must be credited as the first person to publish Germany Beck as the location of the battle. However Scott also repeats the mantra of students of medieval literature; "from its tone" it is "a clearly unhistoric account of Waltheof's part in the battle" rendering impossible any historic reconstruction based on the literature alone. This assessment can now be challenged because of the accuracy revealed when archaeology was used to check the landscape and battle-actions.

'E.A.Freernan [Freeman Norman Conquest, III 352,n.2.] tentatively explains Waltheof's name by suggesting that it really represents Edwin, Morcar's brother and Earl of Mercia, who is not mentioned in the Norse accounts but who did take part in the battle according to English sources, [ASC C D E] a more familiar name replacing a less familiar one. This is possible, but if so the substitution goes as far back as *Haraldsstikki* where the name Valtheof occurs and is used to alliterate; just how far back this is depends on when this very simple and conventional stanza was composed. If the poem was composed more than, say, ten years after the battle, when Waltheof had become generally famous, then the substitution may have taken place in oral tradition between the date of the battle and the composition of the poem. [Vigfusson and Powell(Corpus,II,222)] But if the poem was composed within a few years of the battle, as is quite possible, by someone who had been in Harald's army or who relied directly on tradition supplied by members of that army then it must really have been the belief of the survivors of the expedition that they had fought against Waltheof. And if so they were probably right, for Waltheof's name would not be famous enough in 1066 to have replaced Morcar's. The possibility that the Icelandic sources are right in making Waltheof take part in and escape from the battle of Fulford does thus remain, and if they are right in this it is the one original fact which they contribute to our knowledge of the life of Earl Waltheof.'

Suggesting that the expression *Valpjofslioar* is a kenning[55] for 'Northumbrians' might have led the later Norse compilers of the histories to misinterpret the meaning. If so, the poem must predate the histories discussed earlier since they all have the same 'error'. The problem is that Waltheof's tenure of the Northumbrian earldom did not occur until 1072, and it is not clear how skalds in Iceland would have learned of his promotion.

Edwin is unknown to the Norse writers whereas Waltheof's later treasons and reconciliations against the conquerors are well recorded in Norse sagas that ultimately tells us of the 'martyrdom' of Waltheof at Winchester and his subsequent burial in the Abbey of Crowland which became a place of miracles and pilgrimage. Because subsequent actions of 'Waltheof' are reported in Norse sources it further explain why Edwin's titular leadership role in the battle might have been usurped in the sagas

[55] A kenning is a two-words phrase that can replace a noun in Anglo-Saxon and Norse poems.

by Waltheof,[56] especially given the evidence for the latter's tactical leadership on the battlefield.

Having accepted the role ascribed to Waltheof there is more evidence beyond the Norse sources to support his leadership role at Fulford. Waltheof, was grandson of the famed Earl Uhtred, a member of the house of Bamburgh which had ruled Northumbria until King Cnut's fatal intervention. In 1054 a much older brother, Osbeorn, was killed in a battle with King Macbeth of Scotland. This made Waltheof a natural heir, but he was perhaps deemed too young at about 5 years of age to succeed as earl when Siward died in 1055 opening the way for appointment of Tostig. This appointment of a member of the southern Godwinson family was doubtless resented by the rival northerner factions.

In 1065 Waltheof had a second chance to assume his father's title as he was possibly 15 therefore the natural candidate to succeed Tostig after the coup. Fears about ancient animosities between the rival families of Northumbria is suggested as the reason he was again overlooked. This decision was seemingly justified by events just a few years later when, in the northern anarchy post-Conquest, his rival Oswulf seized the territory and temporarily held it.[57]

Both these local candidates were granted substantial sub-earldoms after the 1065 northern coup against Tostig, Oswulf in his ancestral area of Northumbria but Waltheof was granted extensive southern lands around Northampton. Huntingdon and Northampton had been added to Siward's territory in the 1040's, possibly through marriage, suggesting there were some fine political judgements required to establish a new political balance of power in the post-coup appointments.

Similar political judgements and compromise probably promoted the outsider Morcar who was able to keep the fractious components of the frontier land united knowing that the support of his brother, the Earl of Mercia, would protect the rebels from retribution by the Wessex faction.

---

[56] Earl Waltheof was also not Morcar's brother as is stated in some Norse sources. Evidently Norse genealogy of the noble English families was not well known and there is no evidence that any non-Norse sources were available for the writers of the histories to reference. While utterly respectful of the records provided by the saga compilers, we must accept that on some maters they are misinformed.

[57] The Bloodfeud between the Northern leaders is documented in Richard Fletcher's book of that name.

King Edwards allocation of titles would keep the contentious northern earls well separated geographically in the grants of lands in 1065.

Bloodfeud: Uhtred's murder

A final digression is necessary to explain the origins of this fatal feud within the northern clans. The old Earl Waltheof followed the Norse tradition of family feuding and wreaked his vengeance on the family responsible for the murder of his great grandfather Uthred in 1016 as a part of their ongoing bloodfeud. In a time before the 'king's justice' enforced the law, families operated under systems of compensation, there was a tariff of 'blood-money' known as wergild, or vengeance.

After Swein Forkbeard's invasion in 1013 to oust King Ethelred, Uhtred and the northern nobles submitted to the Danish king. But soon after, Uhtred switched allegiance possibly because of his marriage to Ælfgifu a daughter of Ethelred. Uhtred also accompanied Edmund *Ironside* on campaign effectively against Cnut.

When Cnut completed his subjugation of the unruly north of England, he commanded Uhtred of Northumbria to meet him at a place called Wighill (Wiheal) near Tadcaster. Despite the promise of safe conduct, Uhtred was murdered by Thurbrand *Hold* along with the forty housecarls who were slaughtered inside a gloomy hall after the warriors had, according to the custom of the time, surrendered their weapons outside the meeting hall. A bloodfeud that was initiated would last for almost 60 years.[58] This is the context that has Waltheof fighting at Fulford but not with the Northumbrian army, as one might expect, but with the Mercians. This confirms that the bloodfeud tensions were still very real.

[58] Cnut certainly had a ruthless side since he had maimed the hostages delivered to him when after the sudden death of King Swein and the English once again supported Ethelred, forcing Cnut to depart for Denmark and raise a new army.

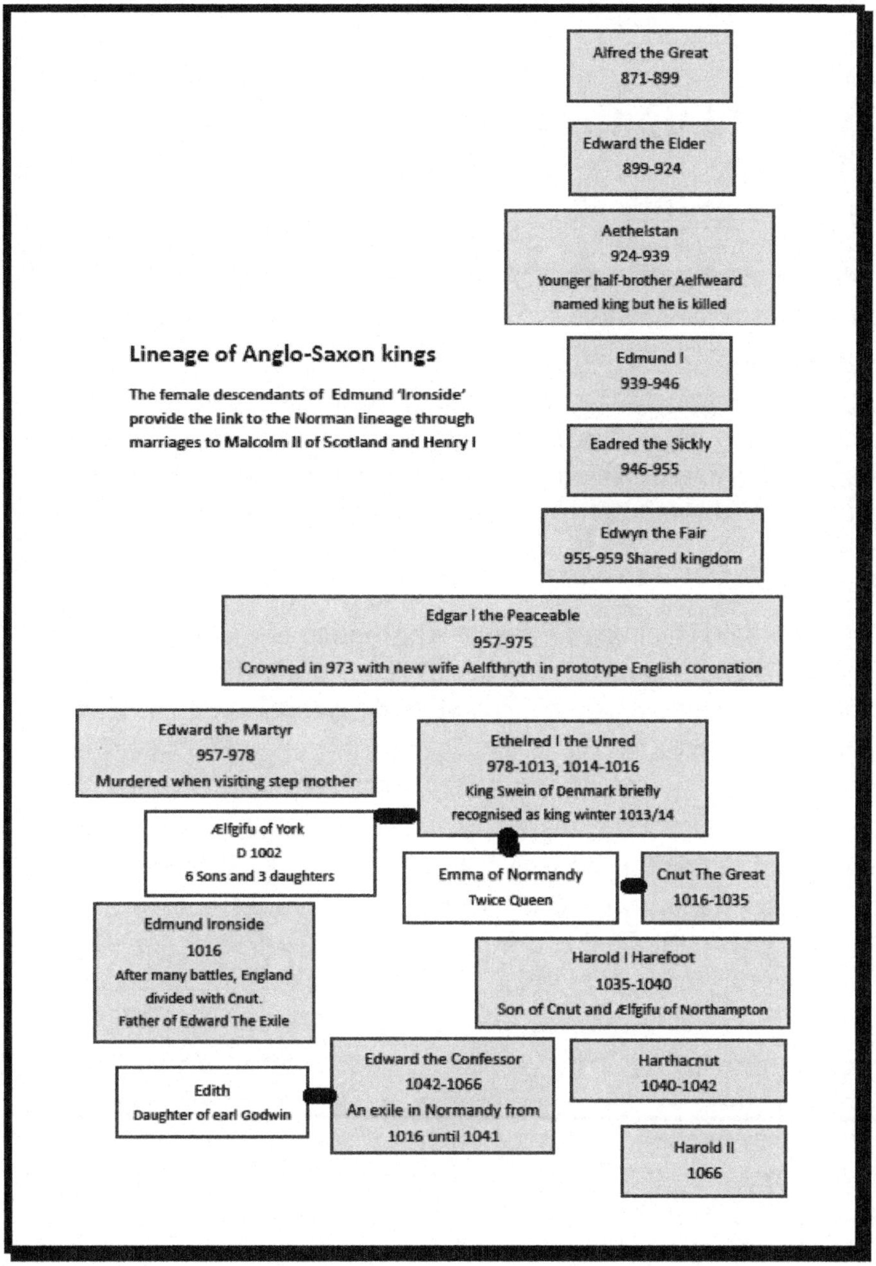
Lineage of Anglo-Saxon kings
The female descendants of Edmund 'Ironside' provide the link to the Norman lineage through marriages to Malcolm II of Scotland and Henry I
Alfred the Great 871-899
Edward the Elder 899-924
Aethelstan 924-939 Younger half-brother Aelfweard named king but he is killed
Edmund I 939-946
Eadred the Sickly 946-955
Edwyn the Fair 955-959 Shared kingdom
Edgar I the Peaceable 957-975 Crowned in 973 with new wife Aelfthryth in prototype English coronation
Edward the Martyr 957-978 Murdered when visiting step mother
Ethelred I the Unred 978-1013, 1014-1016 King Swein of Denmark briefly recognised as king winter 1013/14
Ælfgifu of York D 1002 6 Sons and 3 daughters
Emma of Normandy Twice Queen
Cnut The Great 1016-1035
Edmund Ironside 1016 After many battles, England divided with Cnut. Father of Edward The Exile
Harold I Harefoot 1035-1040 Son of Cnut and Ælfgifu of Northampton
Edith Daughter of earl Godwin
Edward the Confessor 1042-1066 An exile in Normandy from 1016 until 1041
Harthacnut 1040-1042
Harold II 1066

Part Two: The battle actions

The build-up to battle

England prepares

The selection of the new English king in the opening days of 1066 prompted actions, at home and abroad. The months preceding the autumn battles were politically busy.

King Harold II cemented domestic relationship that would see the two most powerful families in England united in marriage. His bride, Ældgyth, was widowed in 1063. This followed an expedition into Wales by Harold and Tostig Godwinson, probably in 1057, to disrupt the emerging alliance between the Welsh and the Mercians that threatened Wessex's domination.

This expeditions seemingly provoked the murder of Ældgyth's husband, Gruffydd, the dominant king in Wales.[59] Her first marriage not only made an ally for her grandfather, Earl Leofric of Mercia, but rewarded Gruffydd for his support in restoring her father, Earl Ælfgar, who had been exiled seemingly in a power struggle with the Godwinsons.

The motivation for Harold's proposal to marry Ældgyth, sister of the brother earls, Edwin and Morcar, was political. The alternative is to suggest the marriage was an impulsive gesture which is unlikely for these were sophisticated political operators. The term 'peaceweaver' is noted in ancient writing for these marriages and is certainly appropriate in this context.

It secured the support of the Mercian house and destroyed their earlier alliance with Wales. The proposed union might even have been part of the deal struck in 1065 when Harold supported the selection of Morcar as Earl of Northumbria, acting against his own brother Tostig. Perhaps in exchange the northern earls agreed to support Harold's election as king after Edward.

---

[59] The couple had at least one child, a daughter, Nest, who married the Herefordshire border lord, Osbern fitz Richard who was a pre-conquest, Norman arrival. Their son might have been the William fitz Osbern credited by some French chronicles of persuading William that an invasion was feasible.

Harold who was now King of England, felt it expedient to travel north to York and possibly to Chester in order to impress the powerful leaders in Northumbria and Mercia of his commitment to national unity after the rebellion against his brother a few month before. This was a brave and confident move.

Bishop Wulfstan of Worcester accompanied Harold on this mission north. Wulfstan was the namesake and relative of a fiery preacher who suggested in his homilies what would befall England if they did not mend their ways. Wulfstan perhaps inherited some of the esteem of his uncle and was himself promoted from the Bishop of Worcester to the Archbishopric of York and a close advisor to King Harold.

Wulfstan was evidently well respected since he was the only senior cleric to keep his post after 1066 until his death in 1095. Harold marriage to Ældgyth, made her Queen of England and probably took place during this trip although the date and location are not recorded. The presence of this bishop added authority to the match and a royal wedding in the north was a gesture of respect which his new allies would recognise.

The existence of Harold's first family provided another motive for solemnising the marriage in the north. Edith *Swanneck's* much earlier marriage to Harold is always noted as being a 'handfasted' union, which gave it formal status but avoided the need for expensive ecclesiastical intervention to dissolve it.[60]

Harold's southern family would not need to attend the marriage nor would it be advisable to travel uninvited into the territory of those who had weeks before invaded the south. As Tostig had led the English cavalry on a punitive raid to hunt Ældgyth first husband. His attendance would certainly have been awkward.

The children born from a church-marriage would have a powerful claim to the English throne. This union offered the prospect of a new dynasty from two families elevated by King Cnut.[61] There were good grounds to assume the marriage would be fertile since Harold already had 6 children with, Edith *Swanneck*, while Ældgyth had a daughter, whose name is recorded as

---

[60] It would be another two centuries before the Church of Rome monopolised the institution of marriage in England.

[61] Edith *Swanneck* was of Anglo-Danish stock with regal connections like Harold. Edith held the family lands in East Anglia after her brothers were exiled by King Edward to weaken the Danish ties established by King Cnut. Her father led the Jomsvikings so she was steeped in ancient Norse traditions.

Nest. Edith was not 'set aside' and remained part of the family undertaking the task of identifying and recovering Harold's body after the Battle of Hastings. An interesting arrangement suggestive of political sophistication.

By the time of the marriage[62], the exiled Tostig's plans to restore his fortunes were well advanced. It probably took a month for him to fully appreciate that his brother was not going to recall and restore him in England. News of Harold's betrothal doubtless travelled to Flanders where Tostig understood the implications. If Harold hoped that time would heal his brother's hurt, he was wrong. Tostig's sense of grievance evidently quickly give way to a decision to take control of his future.

Only one description of Tostig's personality has survived. 'And Earl Tostig himself was endowed with very great and prudent restraint - although occasionally he was a little over-zealous in attacking evil - and with bold and inflexible constancy of mind. *He would first ponder much and by himself the plans in his mind,* and when he had ascertained by an appreciation of the matter the final issue, he would set them in order; and *these he would not readily share with anyone.* Also, sometimes he was so cautiously active that his action seemed to come before his planning; and this often enough was advantageous to him in the theatre of the world.'

These are the inciteful and mature words of a sister who we understand gave them to the monastic scribe composing record of her late husband, Edward's life, although it is the source of much of what we know about the Godwinsons composed after 1066.

Both brothers who guided the events of 1066 had their characters described by their sister, the dowager Queen Edith.

'Both persevered with what they had begun; but Tostig vigorously, Harold prudently; the one in action aimed at success [ambition], the other also at happiness. *Both [brothers] at times so cleverly disguised their intentions that one who did not know them was in doubt what to think.* And to sum up their characters for our readers, no age and no province has reared two mortals of such worth at the same time. The King [Edward] appreciated this, and with them thus stationed in his kingdom, he lived all his life free from care on

[62] Some sources use the term handfasting instead of marriage perhaps suggesting an 'engagement' prior to church solemnisation.

either flank, for the one drove back the foe from the south and the other scared them off from the north.'[63]

Tostig's plan emerges

From the timetable we can deduce that Tostig had no doubt about his course of action. He had a comfortable position in Flanders, enjoyed the prestige of successfully debating with the Pope, as well as the opportunity to join with his 'brother-in-law' William whose plan to invade England was openly discussed. The latter would offer him an opportunity to take revenge on the northern rebels as well as his brother, now King Harold.

It seems he was not content to rely on others and sought to promote himself such that whatever the eventual outcome of 1066, his influence would be enhanced. There were too many unknowns to allow him to form a plan but he seems to have identified a number of ways to ensure his fate could be in his hands and not dependent upon other.

Tostig's travels took him first to his cousin in Denmark and then onto Denmark's enemy, King Harald in Norway. With his connections in Flanders, there would be no shortage of guides for a journey overland to Denmark. His wife Judith, a countess in her own right, could provide an escort and her brother as the Regent of France during the King's minority, provided the prestige necessary to facilitate a journey through the lands previously unified by Charlemagne.

Such powerful connections would ensure safe conduct. Tostig had recently travelled to Rome, with only one recorded mishap, and merchant routes were well established from his Flemish starting point documented in their contemporary cloth-trade records.

Travel by boat was feasible but was subject to the wind and weather. The Continental coastal route featured sandbanks where the Rhine flowed through the lowlands and into the sea. A boat would have allowed his entourage to carry their arms and armour but such an impressive embassy would not be required or necessarily advisable on his mission to persuade them to help restore his lands and title.

Navigating a maze of mudflats in winter makes it unlikely that Tostig chose sea transportation for his journey to see his kingly cousin in Denmark not least because there was no knowing exactly where they would have to travel to find the northern kings in their winter quarters. These would not necessarily have a handy harbour, so horseback provided

[63] *The Life of King Edward (Vita Edwardii Regis)* Tr Frank Balow, 0198202032 1992

flexibility. His first destination was Roskilde, on a journey that in the short days of winter might take up to 30 days but was probably accomplished in half that time.

We are not given dates for these trips, but the subsequent calendar allows only February, March and early April for Tostig's to complete all his northern negotiations and travels. This provides sufficient time for extended meetings with the kings of Denmark and Norway and ample travel time for a round trip. We can calculate when his northern travels ended because we can compute the time he embarked on the next part of his plan, coastal raiding. The appearance of a comet on 24 April 1066 is recorded[64] and it is just after this that they record Tostig's first raid in England.

Tostig meetings

While precise dates and locations for Tostig's itinerary are uncertain, happily several Norse chroniclers record the meetings and provide a good summary of what was said. Norse sources report Tostig's promotion of his personal cause and we are provided with some comments into the contrasting characters of Tostig and his kingly cousin, Swein. The latter was a realist and had concluded a peace treaty with his powerful Norwegian neighbour, King Harald, which been in force for 3 years after 13 years of inconclusive warfare.

The broad brush employed by English clerical compilers of the ASC with annual entries, often taking Easter as the start of the year, do not provide details of Tostig's travels and we know Tostig 'would not readily share with anyone' and was not the subject of any later chronicle so his activities and motivation require some speculation.

Tostig "went to Denmark to see his kinsman King Swein and asked him to support his plan to reclaim what he felt was his rightful status. King Swein offered him power under himself in Denmark."

He spurned the offer of a Danish earldom and replied: "Will you not give me the strength and backing of your power to achieve my rightful status? With your might and my planning, [we can] win England as your mother's brother Cnut".

[64] The 'hairy star', now recognised as Halley's Comet, and from the ASC entry for 1066 we can date Easter as 16 (or 24 in the Julian calendar) April.

Swein does not rise to the challenge of an unfavourable comparison with Cnut *the Great* and replies 'I am so much less of a ruler than my kinsman Cnut that I am hardly able to hold Denmark.'[65]

As the debate continues and Tostig moderates his ambition not to displace his own brother but just to take 'the part of the kingdom that is most devoted to me'.

We can be reasonably confident that Tostig had already formulated his plan for a second, northern invasion because after this rejection he decides it is necessary to extend his mission to Norway. This was a bold move. With a parting insult to his cousin, he said he hoped Denmark's enemy would be more supportive than his own family.

This is how *The Agrip* records Tostig's mission to Norway.

"When Harald had ruled all Norway for 19 years after the death of Magnus, a man came from England, named Tostig. He was a jarl and the brother of Harold Godwinson, who then ruled England and though his right of birth was equal to Harold's he was deprived of everything. He asked support of Harald and promised him half of England if they should win it. Harald took his army there and they won all Northumbria."[66]

We are provided some more expansive details and a sequence of events with one source which reporting Tostig 'made his way back to Norway' and 'complained of his problems to him'. This suggests a second visit and implies that Tostig had visited Oslo on his way to Denmark. This cannot be ruled out but the geography makes it an unlikely sequence.[67] The Norway visit certainly follows the rejection of his request for help from his Danish cousin. Possibility Tostig required two visits to persuade Harald. Tostig might even have been desperate because the plan he was composing for two simultaneous invasions was now dependent on persuading King Harald. It was not an easy sell.

Persuading Harald

First Tostig played on memories of past glories, reminding Harald how "Hartha-Knutr, son of gamli Knutr,[Cnut] ruled England, and how an oath had been sworn between King Magnus and Hartha-Knutr, and next how

[65] A similar conversation between Svein and Tostig is reported in the *Heimskringla.*

[66] *Fagrskinna* Tr Alison Finlay 2004 edition 9004131728 Brill Chapter 42

[67] It is possible that while Harald consulted Tostig visited the Orkney Isle

King Magnus had become the rightful heir of Hartha-Knutr, and how he had shown great forbearance in not claiming the possessions and power that were in England as well as those in Denmark". This claim was tenuous but was a good opening gambit. The throne of England, Tostig suggested, was Harald's by right based on the earlier treaty.

King Harald warmed to his cause: "Now many wise men met there each spoke cheerfully to the other, the King spoke of the Jarl's great unhappiness in that he had been driven from his kingdom without cause."

Next, Tostig might have revealed that the Normans were already planning a second invasion in the south as such news would be sure to have reached Norway with ships and sailors being recruited by the Normans. King Harald was a masterful tactician and the survivor on a lifetime of battles who would have appreciated the enormous benefits of joint invasions.

Finally, Tostig boasted of the support that his return would attract safe in the knowledge that nobody could contradict him. Heimskringla suggests that the claim of support was justified: "It happened, as he had told the King at their first meeting, that in England many people would flock to them, being friends and relations of Earl Tostig, and thus the King's forces were much strengthened. After the battle now told of [at Fulford], all people in the nearest districts submitted to Harald, but some fled. Then the king advanced to take the castle [York], and laid his army at Stanfurdubryggja [Stamford Bridge];"[68]

Tostig concluded with an argument that speaks volumes about his character and a confidence bordering on arrogance. He presented his critique of his hosts failure to regain Denmark. Success, he explained, came through having the powerful lords on your side which, he pointed out, others had done but Harald had failed to do. Tostig explained that he would be able to deliver the lords of the land in support of the invasion. King Harald generally did not take well to criticism so perhaps secretly recognised some truth in Tostig's words and admired a kindred spirit – Two arrogant, tyrannical psychopaths.

The Norse sources do not record the uprising in the north the previous year against Tostig perhaps because his deposition had happened barely four months earlier and the winter months since his downfall afforded little opportunity for news and gossip to reach Norway. Instead he is portrayed in *Heimskringla* as the leader of King Edward's army who was treacherously

---

[68] *Heimskringla* 89. Of Earl Toste.

out-manoeuvred by his junior brother, Harold, who had control of the old king's money. The supplicant successfully portrayed himself as a military leader who had been robbed of his birthright by his brother.

The Sagas then suggest that there was a frank debate among the Norwegians where it was noted that the English could not really be trusted, nor would Norse troops be willing to serve under an English lord, and at one point the high quality of English opposition is noted. These reservations were probably recorded after the outcome of the expedition was known. Tostig was likely not present at these discussions which makes sense of the second visit mentioned when Harald delivers his decision to Tostig.

Harald would have grasped the strategic impact of attacks in the north and south of England, especially if these attacks were coordinated. Perhaps that element of Tostig's plan was now formalised. It is possible raised the possibility of the tactical benefit that the exceptional tides in September could provide. The exact timing of these tides would be the focus of one of Tostig's later coastal raids so that he could provide the exact timings.

Previously, with the participants uncertain, Tostig could not set a feasible timetable. The military logic of simultaneous invasions would now have been raised. Tostig's recorded actions after his return to Flanders suggest some careful and detailed planning had been undertaken in discussions with his new ally, the experienced Norse warrior while the latter explained the practicalities and timetable of mobilisation an army for this invasion.

King Harald would have been mindful of the expedition mounted in 1058 by his son although the D version of the ASC just reports that 'it is tedious to tell how it all happened'. This attack was an attempt by Earl Ælfgar to return 'with violence' after what is a suggested to be his unjust exile. Aelfgar had the backing of the Norwegians plus King Gruffudd to take the title of Earl of Mercia after the death of his father, Earl Leofric, the previous year. So the Norse were certainly privy to some of the politics of England. Apparently opposing Morcar, the son of their erstwhile ally, was seemingly not a problem but it is more likely that they were unaware of the Mercian takeover.

This earlier expedition might have been more of a rite of passage, planned by Harald, to test the mettle of his son with whom the king would soon 'share' the role of kingship. A new foreign adventure by the patriarch of the family would serve a personal, domestic, dynastic purpose. The old king's vengeful forays to settle old scores made him vulnerable and power had passed to the family of his second wife, who was mother of the new co-king.

Harald's plans

Having semi-retired, the task of mobilising an army was not a trivial task. "In the last part of winter when spring was about to come King Harald sent a command throughout his kingdom that the army should make ready, troops and ships, to leave the country in the summer, and appointed who was to go from each shire." Other sources talk of 'war-tokens' being sent to all the districts. Although sparsely populated, the distances to be covered by the messenger were multiples of those covered by Tostig on this mission. The timetable suggests the notification might have begun its long journey in late March, following the melting of the snow as it travelled north.

The sagas note 'that no better choice of men has been made ready for any single expedition from Norway.' From this one might surmise that the old King was calling on his veterans. Other sources make it clear that Harald left a significant army for his son, whom he had made co-king some years earlier. Removing his veterans might be seen as a service towards his son, trying to emerge from the shadow of his overbearing father. Veterans easily turn into rebels as a new younger order emerges.

We have become accustomed to states being able to mobilise their armies with a simple act or instruction but as William discovered in the 11th century is rather more complex, perhaps even more 'democratic'. As noted in the *Encomium Emma* 'the king, supported by the counsel of his chief men, and relying on the goodwill of his soldiers, ordered that a [large] fleet should be prepared' for King Sweyn's 1014 invasion of England. When support was withdrawn after Sweyn died, his son Cnut had to take them home to Denmark.

Norse sources make it clear that Tostig had already submitted to Harald, agreeing to accept him as his overlord, which might appear to put him in conflict with William although there is no suggestion that Tostig was included within the order of battle for the southern invasion. So one might have expected Tostig, in his role as de facto Count of Flanders, to mobilise a contingent in support of William's invasion as they were family.

Joining forces with William would ostensibly have also serve the purpose of confronting his brother and provided a much simpler plan for Tostig. Because Tostig did not bring his force to aid William's invasion we might perhaps have expected to find some hint of displeasure in the subsequent histories such as the various praise-poems that recorded William's conquest of England. This silence might suggest that his absence enjoyed William's support.to mastermind and report the other invasion[69]

Planning with William

Orderic Vitalis, writing *Gesta Normanorum Ducum* in the early twelfth century, believed that during his exile Earl Tostig had visited Duke William of Normandy in an attempt to forge an alliance against Harold.

"32 ... the Duke sent Earl Tostig to England, but Harold's fleet forcefully drove him away, so Tostig, prevented from entering England safely or returning to Normandy because of contrary wind, went instead to King Harald *Fairhair* of Norway and begged him for support as a suppliant. The King granted Tostig's request with pleasure....". This passage has Duke William as the supreme commander and suggests that Tostig planned to return to his master in Normandy but ended up in Norway because of the winds. Such a gross failure of navigation is not credible. This narrative is consistent with other French sources with their focus on William's role as the sole organizer of the invasions.

Writing in France, Orderic had no access to Norse sources or tales of Tostig's movement. However, the sequence cannot be excluded since Tostig had over two months waiting in Scotland and might have left it until this late stage to recruit the Norwegians for a northern invasion. This timetable is unlikely, but not impossible. It certainly supports the conjecture that William and Tostig conferred about the northern invasion suggesting again that William was party to this plan. Evidence that they were also working to an agreed invasion date is set out later.

Such a face-to-face meeting could easily have been organised between Tostig's wife Judith and William's wife Matilda who, as we noted, were raised together in an environment which required political acumen to survive. We are not told, but it is probable, that these women were literate and an exchange of letters could be accomplished within a week.

Judith could easily have confided the details of Tostig's meetings with the Norse kings and especially the very important details of the planned northern invasion to Matilda in writing after Tostig's return. It is however in keeping with the reported nature of their husbands that they would also

---

[69] It is perhaps another indication that William regarded Tostig as an ally in that the Domesday surveys record Tostig's landholdings while those of his brother Harold were not recognised.

want to meet in person to hear news of Tostig's plan and especially the agreed timing. The 'alpha' male, William, would have needed to be persuaded of the wisdom of engaging in any joint venture. As we have noted when Tostig met the Pope and again in meetings with King Harald, he proved persuasive even if his approach was far from tactful.

Tostig would have provided much useful intelligence as he possessed detailed knowledge of the English armies, their power, their leadership and their current disposition after his first raid. It was probably easy to persuade William of the advantages invasions launched simultaneously. Although we have only one suggestion for this meeting, there was every reason for both parties to keep it secret to prevent any speculation about coordinated timings.

The evidence for a plan, formulated by Tostig, to synchronise the invasion date is suggested by the timing of the move of the Norman fleet to St. Valéry-sur-Somme with the Norse landing in Northumbria is explored later. This date was set by the lunar calendar when Tostig's timings would fully exploit the exceptional tides during the northern invasion.[70] This points to Tostig as the author of the plan since he alone recognised how the tides could serve the northern invasion and that this set the timetable for the two invasions. The Norman invasion would also benefit from the fast tides due in September, a point William would certainly have checked with his mariners as planning progressed.

Tostig's raiding in late April is consistent with the conclusion of negotiations with King Harald in Norway 'in the last part of winter'. The choice of the family estates on the Isle of Wight as the first target for his raids could provide cover for a clandestine meeting with William. This was certainly the only opportunity the two men would have to meet before Tostig continued his disruptive raiding along the English coast. It is reasonable to expect that William was near Caen for the Easter assemblies during which Tostig's putative visit might have taken place.

While the plan for twin invasions would be common knowledge by mid-summer, their coordination would have been suspected had any meeting been in public. Furthermore, had news of such a meeting reached the ears of King Harald in Norway it would have raised suspicions in the mind of

[70] There have been several excellent expositions of the deception plan operated by William to disguise his departure. These pose problems in assessing any agreement made with Tostig.

Tostig's paranoid ally who it is recorded was not trusted by the Norwegian nobles.[71]

William was not finding it easy to persuade his inner circle of nobles that an invasion was feasible although the evidence suggests that preparations had begun on constructing the fleet. The only date we have is for a June assembly in Caen to dedicate the abbey of the Holy Trinity.

The French chroniclers, William of Poitiers and Wace, both credit William fitz Osbern, whose home was on the Welsh borders, with actually persuading William that the invasion was practical. William was to prove a master of deception and misinformation, so giving credit to another for his renewed optimism about the proposed invasion which reportedly persuaded the nobility to join his invasion. Citing a Norman noble with English connections rather than Tostig is not only in keeping with William's behaviour but served the need to keep the coordinated plan secret which was vital if it was to be effective.[72] During the summer, the Norman forces began to assemble and the June gathering is noted as the time when all agreed to back William's invasion plan.

Such a meeting might be seen as superfluous and risky for Tostig as it could have been communicated in writing. To mitigate some of these risks the meeting might have taken place on Tostig's ship to also help cloak any rendezvous. The security of his own ship allowed Tostig a quick get-away should the meeting not go well perhaps with William detaining him, if he rejected the important role Tostig had to play at Fulford.[73]

Crossing the Channel to Normandy immediately after attacking England would have helped dispelled any doubts about Tostig's intentions. After such a meeting with William, Tostig could exploit the coastal currents and ensure that his small fleet would not be spotted by English ships as he made his way west. Tostig recognised that tides and winds can force a change in travel plan for sailors, so returning along the French side would

---

[71] Fank Barlow suggests there was a meeting but William was 'not yet ready to get involved'. *The Godwins* #96

[72] Modern French historians such as Michel de Boüard have shown how skilfully William deployed spies and attempted to misinform those across the Channel about his intentions drawing parallels with the Allied deception plans for D-Day in 1944.

[73] Tostig would be aware of the detention of his bother Harold a few years before which forced him to swear an oath to support William, who still held one Godwinson brother hostage after the 'succession debacle' of 1051.

avoid any risk of being driven onto the English coast by a sudden storm. This route home would have provided opportunities for Tostig and William to meet secretly, provided their wives had arranged the rendezvous.

Matilda would run the troublesome Normandy while William was away and Judith would in time be a significant player in the appointment of Popes and the Holy Roman Emperor, so communicating and coordinating Tostig's plan for two simultaneous invasions could have been left to them. It is an indictment of the way history has been recorded that the interventions and activities of women are sidelined so we are left to wonder at just how very well the timing of 1066 unfolded to the benefit of William leaving it to story-tellers to attributing the beneficial timings to providential wind and weather.

The story of 1066 needs these powerful women to have the role facilitating the meeting and communicating progress with the planning. It is unthinkable that Tostig would have departed without imparting his proposal for simultaneous invasions which was such an obvious benefit to both men. It would have been sensible for a letter between Judith and Matilda, outlining Tostig's proposal, to have preceded any meeting between their husbands. It is also hard to believe that Judith would not have shared this information with her 'sister', Matilda. We cannot be sure who suggested a meeting especially as any meeting was likely clandestine for the reasons outlined, but the plan can be ascribed to Tostig, with some confidence.

From Tostig's perspective he was hedging his bets. As William was having a difficult time persuading his nobles to take part, the new information and the plan provided by Tostig would have been attractive. Whatever happened something seemingly allowed William to exude confidence, rather than just determinations, and this was evidently enough to finally muster a Norman invasion force. With just four people privy to the details of the plan, the secret source of this renewed confidence was safe.

Raiding

Tostig had the plan ready was giving it effect by making raids on England. He attacked the Isle of Wight, taking some plunder and provisions plus the ASC describes him mustering 'as many of his house troops as he could'. We know his hearthtroops had been killed in York when his rule in Northumbria was overthrown, so he was looking for new recruits who would swear loyalty to him. Subsequent events do not suggest that his appeal was very successful.

The first raid could perhaps be portrayed as a visit because it was to the family estates that are recorded in the Domesday survey of landownership. His return served several purposes. It put his brother and all England on notice that he was not going to accept his exile. His visit gave him some of the resources he would need for a sustained campaign. Possibly his trip had another purpose since these landholdings placed him near Normandy and it would send a clear message of intent to William.

Secure in the knowledge that England would now face two, coordinated invasions, Tostig's strategic raiding began. This was a way to unsettle the land he hoped in time to dominate, if not actually rule. England had enjoyed two generations of relative peace and it was fifty years since the last invasions by Sweyn and then by his son, Cnut. The era of coastal raiding that blighted the reign of Ethelred was a memory. Viking leaders now sometimes came just to visit their relatives. By June the locals would have been enjoying the early fruits of their farms with the 'hungry month' of May behind them.

After leaving the Isle of Wight, where Tostig collected money and provisions, but the chronicles make no mention of men, he raided along the Sussex and Kent coast, past Dover and into Sandwich Bay. This trajectory is consistent with a crossing to Normandy for a meeting and by first heading south the local defenders would not be alerted to further coastal raiding. Had he sailed along the coast, they would have seen him coming and made defensive preparations. Vanishing over the horizon, heading to Normandy, would allay fears about further raids.

The English chronicles later note that the Isle of Wight provided the base for the Harold's army which deployed to defend against the Norman invasion through the summer and into the autumn. They expected this developing threat from Normandy as William had announced it. Tostig's raid alerted Harold to the vulnerability of the extensive Godwinson landholdings. The complex tidal flows around the Isle of Wight might have suggested this as a good base to ensure that the English fleet could respond quickly to a landing along the coast and avoid the risk of being trapped by unfavourable tides.

Tostig's raiding army was limited to those few men he had might have enlisted from the Godwinson estates plus a much bigger contingent that he had brought from Flanders, which subsequent events tell us were not 'his sworn men' but loaned by his brother-in-law, Count Baldwin.

Tostig's numbers were later bolstered by the arrival of Cospig who seems to have been Tostig's deputy when he was earl in Northumbria. Cospig had passed the winter in the Orkneys as an exile. He now arrived with 17 ships, another pointer to some detailed planning undertaken by Tostig. Perhaps Tostig was provided with a ship for his return from Norway to avoid an embarrassing transit of Denmark. This would facilitate a visit to the Orkneys to meet Cospig and possibly to inform the Earls of the plan.

Tostig's numbers were still small, making them vulnerable to any attack by Harold's navy. To address this threat he went to the main English base at Sandwich. Its strategic location served to guard the south as well as the east coast. Sandwich avoided locating the ships within the tidal flow of the Thames Estuary, but nowhere in the chronicles are we provided with a consistent story of how these ships were employed or crewed. There is limited fishing in these shallow waters, so the supply of mariners was likely limited perhaps promoting the need for some naval training of new recruits at this base. Battles in the Norse lands around this time were not infrequently fought at sea. Therefore some practice was sensible. We can also deduce from subsequent events that there were boats ready to go to sea and some crew, or trainees, to man them.

Sandwich is adjacent to the Roman fort at Richborough, a thriving port for over two centuries. Sailors favoured the tides and winds which made this a harbour from earlier eras.
The Wantsum Channel gave access to the river Thames at Reculver where another Roman fort was built.

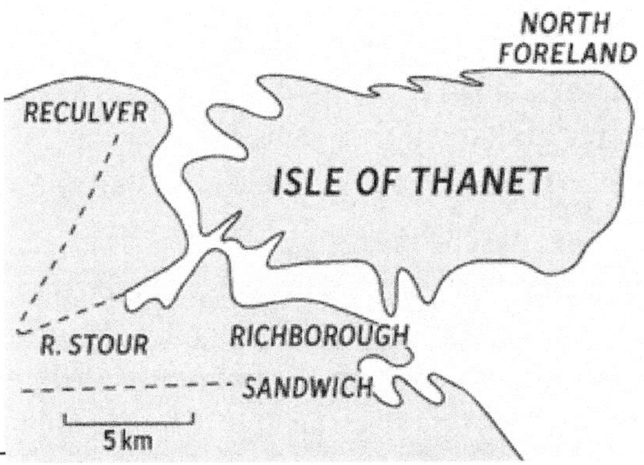

Sandwich was also a strategic choice for Tostig as it was surprisingly remote from London and if threatened he would be able to reach his exile base in Flanders with a favourable wind and tide within a day. The chronicles suggest Tostig spent some time in Sandwich, possibly hoping to provoke a response from his brother. Staying for a few weeks would certainly provide a suitable provocation. The time would be an opportunity to exchange news with his wife, Judith.

We later learn that their two sons survived the northern battles and perhaps Tostig used his proximity to sail home and collect them now that the detailed plans for the two invasions had been confirmed. He would need them if matters worked out as he planned. Leaving his lieutenants at Sandwich working to attract as large a force as possible and prepare it for their journey north, Tostig could safely cross the channel to Flanders and return within the timetable suggested by the chronicles.

The response of King Harold can be seen as either slow or measured. The ASC notes that Harold was aware of these raids and had probably been informed or deduced of the two invasions being planned. He was still in the process of making his defensive plans before mobilising and deploying his land and naval forces to best address the threats. There was no need to rush. Sandwich was on the isolated peninsula of Thanet and intelligence reports would have told him that the Norman invasion fleet would still be months before it was ready to sail.

As soon as Tostig became aware that a response was imminent, his stay in Sandwich came to an end, which was likely the reaction that Harold expected. ASC Version D notes that Tostig took 60 ships while the C version notes that sailors were taken from the town 'who were willing or unwilling' so Tostig and Cospig evidently had enough of their own men to enforce their will and press the local mariners into service. It made sense to take all of the seaworthy vessels since this would deprive Harold of the chance to chase him, a sensible tactical choice and another example of Tostig's military thinking.

Gaimar[74] notes attacks in 'Brunemue', probably the estuary of the river Burnham in Norfolk, which it has been suggested was aimed at his brother Gyrth, Earl of East Anglia, who had stayed loyal to his elder brother, Harold. Tostig might have been testing the water to see if he could destroy family unity. Attempting to divide and rule was worth a try, but it was a ploy and bound to fail. Gyrth had taken sides when he did not oppose the uprising and agreed to the exile plan for Tostig late the previous year. After this landing Tostig probably appreciated the family was united behind Harold.

Tostig might still hope his raids would disperse the defenders by attacking all along the coast, forcing troops to be spread along the coast ready to react to a renewed era of raids. The raids might even make some of the coastal levies reluctant to respond to the muster and prioritise the defence of their homes. In the immediate prelude to the battle we will note how Tostig was

[74] Translation from Ian Short *Gaimar History of the English* OUP 2009 9780199569427 #5158-5166

masterful at sowing doubts and thereby confusing or delaying the response of his opponents.

King Harold also had to consider the costs that would fall on him plus his earls and their thanes if he deployed the army too early. The country had learned how impossible it was to defend its long coast effectively against sea raiders. The early provocations of Tostig's coastal raids might have disrupted England's defence planning which was certainly what he intended. Harold's perspective might have been different. He could afford to wait until invasions were imminent and meanwhile leaving the locals with the resources to repel raids, a facility that would be lost once the army was mustered.

But raiding might have been a more subtle strategy as the Godwinsons themselves had raided the coast to force King Edward to negotiate. Even Morcar's father, Ælfgar, had employed the same tactic to reverse his own sentence of exile. With Tostig now conspiring to overthrow his brother, the raiding might have misdirected attention allowing speculation that Tostig was just following a recognised road to reinstatement. It is certain that Tostig would be sowing confusion. It is likely that for the sophisticated exile, the raiding intentionally served all of these purposes.

The response in the North to his raids however proved much more robust, perhaps because the armies of Mercia and Northumbria were better prepared after their rebellious campaign the previous autumn. Plus they had several weeks warning of what was likely heading their way knowing they were Tostig's likely target.

Raiding the Humber

The small settlements of East Anglia offered little piratical gain. Further north, the coast of modern Lincolnshire, was now 'enemy territory' as it was part of Earl Edwin's Mercia. Tostig's desultory raiding would continue and designed to serve multiple purposes.

First these raids mobilised the northern armies and kept them in the field which ensured that they could not be drawn to defend the south coast with Harold. This was perhaps a key component that Tostig had explained to William. If the full force of England's many armies had been deployed in the south, he knew that William's invasion stood very little chance of succeeding.

Keeping two of the strongest armies in the north was essential for the Norman invasion to succeed. King Harold II was probably aware of the plan for a northern invasion as there is no evidence that he tried to summon these two armies of the brother earls to move south. News of Tostig's fruitless trip to the Godwinsons' cousin in Denmark would also have reached England.

Second, raids would also have made Tostig aware of the size of the Mercian and Northumbrian armies and something of their organisation. He might also have recognised what the chroniclers later report that he would be facing the brothers 'who used their armies as one'.

Tostig's landings and the time spent in the Humber would provide opportunities for some vital reconnaissance that would prove critical to his subsequent plan. He could update himself on the tide times and how they would impact the ingenious plan that he was refining.

Finally, it is conceivable that Tostig even hoped that the isolated and insular nature of the fenlands of the Humber coast might permit the establishment and holding of a bridgehead from which to exert some menace and from where he could later launch his invasion when King Harald arrived with reinforcements.

With his force of perhaps 60 ships there might even have been an element of bluff designed to deter a concerted attack in this challenging landscape of mudflats and tidal channels. Any reports filtering back to King Harald in Norway would support the boasts Tostig had made earlier about the local support he enjoyed although he was too clever to have actually have promised such a bridgehead. It was July and he was one of only a handful of those who knew that the timing of the two invasions was still almost three months away.

John of Worcester in his account of these events notes that King Harald met Earl Tostig, 'according to previous arrangement, joined him with his fleet and, on a swift course, they entered the mouth of the river Humber..' This version might be taken to suggest Tostig had established or at least reconnoitred a base near the Humber rather than making the tactical withdrawal suggested by all the other evidence. This coastline is still being altered so much by erosion that suggesting any location is tentative but in the north lee-shore of Spurn Head a very large fleet of longships could find a harbour.

Popular historical narrative prefers a single and rather simple motivation for any action but Tostig's raiding into Lindsey and the mouth of the Humber served him well as subsequent events demonstrate. Studying the leaders, before and during the coming battles, demonstrates that they were all subtle and their actions intelligent as well as complex. So Tostig probably had many motives for his raiding and key among them was confusing his enemy. Even the seemingly chaotic way in which the raiding party is reported as scattering might have been designed by Tostig to suggest that he was now a spent force incapable of landing so that they would not pursue him or take seriously any talk of a Norse invasion.

There is however no doubting the robust response by the defenders to Tostig's raids. During the summer, Gaimar describes how Edwin come to the defence of Lindsey. The southern branch of the Humber, the River Trent, provided the boundary for what we recognise as Lincolnshire. Like the northward-flowing River Ouse, the Trent was bordered by floodplains which gave this early kingdom its name Lindsey, or literally 'Lind Island'.

Mercian earl's, with their capital on the west coast at Chester, still had the duty to protect their territory on the east coast.[75] The Earls knew the coastal attacks would yield little because the population and economic activity was located on higher ground inland and in the towns along the Trent. But they responded forcefully against the man they had ousted the previous year. An exile, even the King's brother, could legally be killed if he returned without royal approval.

The mighty Humber that drains a fifth of the territory of England gave its name to the land on the north bank. The English chronicles say Tostig was quickly driven off when he crossed the River Humber and landed in Northumbrian territory. This again would have raised fears among locals with memories of raids from the sea still the subject of folk tales and perhaps persuaded some thanes of the need to leave a contingent to repel or report coastal attacks, a reaction supported by two clashes we know about when the invasion eventually arrived.

The chronicles report that the brother earls drove Tostig out of Lindsey and also report that he was deserted by his Flemish allies, even suggesting that this was the cause of Tostig's retreat to Scotland. Tostig had certainly 'impressed' some seamen from Sandwich. In other words he had forced them rather like press gangs of later centuries who caught people to put them into the Royal Navy.

[75] The lands of the 'Five Boroughs' was an organisational relic of the 'Great Heathen Army' invasions in the previous century. Their independence was eclipsed in the reorganisations imposed by Cnut but seemingly joined the rebellion.

As noted, Tostig's raid on Sandwich had certainly temporarily deprived Harold of many ships with which to pursue his brother or deploy his army. Among his other motives for taking the English ships was perhaps to inflate the perceived size of his fleet that would be reported as it sailed along the coast since observers would assume the ships were full of warriors rather than just a skeleton crew and some reluctant sailors.

It is possible that the Sandwich contingent decided to escape which would not have been difficult. Once the warriors landed to raid inland, opportunities presented by the tide would allow the English ships to desert and float away. But given the evident tactical skills displayed by Tostig it is just as likely that Tostig accepted that they had served their purposed and let them 'escape'. He also had a continental contingent loaned to him by his brother-in-law, Count Baldwin from his exile base. Gaimar suggests his Flemish contingent departed 'not by arrangement'.

The latter might be speculation on the part of Gaimar to fit narrative that was subsequently accepted of Tostig as a failed rebel. The impending Norman invasion was in need of ships and sailors so perhaps Tostig had agreed to release the ships and soldiers from Flanders. This would leave Tostig just the 17 ships brought by his lieutenant Cospig.

The sailors returning to Sandwich might indeed have seized an opportunity to desert Tostig, but those from Flanders knew that awful punishment would await them if they deserted 'not by arrangement' so it is possible to interpret the sight of the fleet sailing in separate directions in different ways. Further reason to doubt Gaimar's version is that the ASC (C) numbers Flemish casualties alongside the Norse after Stamford Bridge.

Tostig would not survive to give his account of events but the pattern of the tidal flow along the coast favoured two separate departure times. Anybody sailing north rather than south would have waited for about 6 hours for the tide to turn. Non-mariners observing this might have interpreted and reported the different departure as a desertion.

This might have seemed like an easy victory for the young earls. By a show of force, Tostig had apparently been forced to retreat and his force scattered. But Gaimar's concluding remark allows one to interpret that Tostig did not feel under pressure and that this was indeed a tactical withdrawal. "Then, with those who remained behind, [Tostig's troops] made ready and left, setting off for Scotland to Malcolm who was in alliance with them. Earl Tostig paid him great honour and offered him costly presents."

This raiding provided an invaluable reconnaissance of the Humber and its capricious tides. Tostig would have obtained the updated timing of the exceptional 'Spring' tide and he would put this knowledge to devastating effect later. The north bank of the Humber would provide the embarkation point for Tostig some months later after his invasion and raiding in Holderness. The mud flats could make it impossible to embark his army if he got the timing or location slightly wrong. The time he spent in the Humber would remind him of the exceptional tides that flow along this river. The plan that Tostig had probably explained to King Harald for their invasion was how they would employ the tidal bore to convey them swiftly and effortlessly to York on the special September tides.

Discovering the strength of the opposing forces might have alarmed Tostig and provided a motivation to conceive the strategy that would split the Mercian and Northumbrian armies on the day of the battle. Even though he was out of sight during the late summer, his presence in Scotland ensured that the local armies remained alert and certainly could not venture south to reinforce Harold or return to their homes which for most of Edwin's army was on the distant west coast. Tostig would have several months to refine the subtle plan that would soon be revealed. He sailed to Scotland and did not raid the coast on the way, perhaps out of caution or not wanting to alienate those he hoped soon to rule again.

Scotland

By 1066 King Malcolm III was secure on the throne of Scotland after the overthrow of Macbeth and his step-son in 1058.

Tostig had skilfully organised two invasions that would perforce divide the defenders of England. He had also forced the armies to deploy into the field in advance of these invasions by raiding along the south and east coasts.

Earl Edwin might now have uncomfortably identified a possible threat to Mercia from Strathclyde because Tostig knew his army was deployed in the far east of the territory Mercia controlled. It was almost a tradition that those in Scotland would test their neighbours when they were perceived to be off-balance.

But nothing happened when Tostig brought the news to his host in Scotland that the Mercian army was on the east coast. Tostig had become Malcolm's 'sworn brother' in 1057 and escorted him to King Edward where he was privy to the oath 'to be peaceful' with England. Edward had been in effect the foster-father to Malcolm during Macbeth's rule.

It would certainly serve Tostig's plans if the Mercian army could be drawn back home to defend against an invasion by Malcolm. If a raid was proposed, Malcolm perhaps reminded Tostig of his oath, although this did not prevent a number of incursions south of the recognised border by the Scots in 1069, 1072 and 1080 until Malcolm made peace and withdrew, acknowledging each time the English king as his overlord.[76] One might even have expected Malcolm to take an active part in the Norwegian invasion or provide a contingent of soldiers to Tostig, but again a mix of domestic issues and recent oaths prevented Malcolm getting actively involved.

It is seemingly inconsistent with the strategic cunning displayed that a raid was not launched through Strathclyde into Mercia by Tostig himself. Tostig was too short of troops to launch a significant raid plus there was always some risks in further raiding and travel. Perhaps keeping his eye on the big prize Tostig remained on the east coast where he could more easily keep in touch with Norway and Flanders.

The inactivity that is implied by the surviving sources requires these explanations. If the coastal raiding had occupied the month of July, there were nearly two months to fill before the Norwegian army was scheduled to arrive. This was sufficient time for a trip back to Flanders or across to Norway but this cunning strategist appears to have decided that he could exert maximum pressure by remaining out of sight, a threatening presence.

Summary of the preliminary moves

The motive for Tostig have always been clear: He felt cheated by the Northumbrians and betrayed by his brother. His actions are consistent with a plan to pin the northern armies so they could not go south to address the threat from Normandy.

His new ally, King Harald, had relinquished effective control of Norway to his son and had used his semi-retirement to settle scores and in the process made more domestic enemies: It was probably only a matter of time before he was assassinated if he stayed in Norway. His Rus princess-bride had long ago been replaced by another in Harald's bed. The latter had provided Harald with two sons to whom he could pass the kingdom. So Elsveta's position was doubly insecure and her daughters vulnerable if she was

[76] But in 1093 after failing to agree terms with William Rufus it came to battle where Malcolm was killed and his eldest son mortally wounded.

widowed. Her family could not protect her from distant Kyiv. This final expedition to support Tostig nicely addressed their different needs.

The Kings, Malcolm of Scotland and Swein of Denmark, had valid political and strategic reasons not to support Tostig's plan. They had little to gain, and participation presented significant risks.

The ability to organise the northern invasion and coordinate with the Norman plan was provided by Tostig's scheming intellect coupled with some important inside information learned when he lived for 13 years at Fulford. His marriage to Judith, and Matilda's marriage to William, not only established a close marriage-bond but created a trustworthy channel of communications. Tostig's northern enterprise excused him from participation in the Norman invasion of someone who was effectively his brother-in-law.

Northern Invasion begins

In the short years following the peace with Denmark, King Harald commissioned the building of a longship of 35 oar-benches, or 70 oars, amounting to a combat contingent that would number at least 80. This expedition would provide the first outing to project this veteran's prestige.

During the summer, westerly winds are the norm. Autumn sees a transition to clear, cold arctic air bringing cloudless blue skies as the seasonal wind veers towards the north just in time to fill the sails of a Norse fleet. This pattern of the weather for early autumn is also noted in Yorkshire.[77] Such a wind would have favoured the journey south and made the departure point of The Solunds, near Bergen in Norway, a sensible one.[78]

A longship with the wind behind it could expect to cover 150 to 250 kilometres in a day on the open sea. This suggests that 10 days sailing should bring the invasion fleet together in the Firth of Forth.

King Harald's fleet set sail with perhaps 200 warships plus many supply vessels in late August or very early September. Only one writer[79] actually

[77] This 'Indian Summer' has been noted by several farmers who have joined the walks around the battlesite in recent years

[78] These same northerlies are reported in Norman sources as preventing them from leaving St. Valéry-sur-Somme.

[79] From Orderic Vitalis

gives us August as the month for the departure and this provides a sensible time for sailing, a few days in the islands on the way, plus some more time reorganising in Scotland before the start the invasion on the date provided in the historical record.

Time is needed not only for the crossing but for a stopover for Harald in the Shetlands while the rest of the fleet went to the Orkneys. Subsequent dates require the assembled Northern fleet to leave Scotland between 10th and 12th September, which is the same time that William's fleet completed its redeployment to the excellent harbour at St. Valéry-sur-Somme.

"When King Harald was clear for sea, and the wind became favourable, he sailed out into the ocean; and he himself landed in Shetland, but a part of his fleet in the Orkney Islands. King Harald stopped but a short time in Shetland before sailing to Orkney, from whence he took with him a great armed force, and the Earls Paul and Erlend, the sons of Earl Thorfin; but he left behind him here the Queen Elsvetta, and her daughters Maria and Ingegerd."[80]

Fagrskinna [Chapter 63] only mentions a single daughter being left and that 'Ingibjorg, daughter of Jarl Finnr Arnason' was taken south with Harald's fleet, probably as a guarantee of good behaviour towards his family.

The commanders of both invasions had provided for intermediate stopovers to allow slower ships to catch up. An invasion requires a concentrated and coherent force in order to be successful. Clearly this principle was well understood. While they lacked the communications technology that is essential for modern command and control, they had devised sophisticated plans that deserve our respect. The same near faultless planning and execution will be exhibited by the commanders at Fulford.

'Sufficient' time is of course essential. However a leisurely timetable risks allowing the defenders to make preparations. Such information would only be of real value if they knew where the invasion would land. The timetable was tight but adequate. The observation that this Norse fleet arrived in the Humber on the first day of favourable tides suggests that a contingency, to account for factors like the weather, had been built into the plan. But all had gone to plan and even a five-day delay would still allow them to exploit the special tides.

---

[80] *Heimskringla* 86. BATTLE AT SCARBOROUGH.

Rendezvous

The sources do not all agree about Tostig's reunion with Harald. Scotland is often mentioned. Later English chroniclers are less precise and talk of meeting at 'an agreed place', perhaps because they never knew the whereabouts of the rendezvous. The mouth of the River Forth, with some long sandy stretches near modern Edinburgh would provide a landing and suitable haven for Tostig during his months of waiting. King Harald had detoured to Orkney where another contingent was added to the invasion and there was space enough to land along these sandy beaches even given the highest estimates of the fleet size.[81]

The stopovers a safe base enroute made good tactical sense after crossing the open sea from Norway. The next stage of the journey employed predictable tidal flows and the cycle of onshore, offshore winds, which followed the coast. Keeping the fleet together would be simpler for this next phase. There are precise parallels with the Norman crossing, and its tactical pauses during their crossing, discussed later.

English sources are also ambiguous about who was in charge, but they are wrong. Tostig was definitely the junior partner in this invasion. Perhaps the early English historians were aware of Tostig's role as the instigator of this invasion perhaps explaining why they promoted him. However, his modest contribution to the invasion fleet, and role in the subsequent battle, confirm his subordinate status.

The wily old warrior, Harald, would have wanted to hear what else Tostig had learned and might at this stage been told of the detailed plan and the timeline. The limited evidence for allows time for such councils of war when the various leaders of the warrior groups would have their tasks assigned as they were about to launch a sophisticated campaign. King Harald would not meet them again until the day of the battle at Fulford.

Subsequent events show the armies and fleets was divided into three separate units. Haralds 'best troops', comprising up to 60 ships, would keep out of the action. Earl Tostig's contingent was the largest and would attack Scarborough, devastate Holderness before sailing to the harbour at Riccall.

The latter would be secured by the third, much smaller component, comprising the Orkney Earls with a contingent of Tostig's men to act as guides and commandos. The latter would sail ahead of the main fleet where

---

[81] These vary from 400 to 700 ships

their presence would provoke anxiety, but not panic, as they were after all, neighbours.

Dividing the fleets made the invasion easier to manage as anyone with experience of managing convoys or crowds will recognise. Three separate 'invasions' would also spread confusion among the defenders.

Landfall in England

"Then [Harald] sailed, leaving Scotland and England westward of him, and landed at a place called Klifland." All the Norse Kings' Sagas agree that the first landing was at 'Klifland', modern Cleveland. John of Worcester suggests the arrival 'with an extremely powerful fleet of more than five hundred great ships' at the mouth of the River Tyne was unexpected. The place and time of the landing might have come as an unwelcome surprise, but it is unlikely that they were unaware that the Norse invasion was imminent since the Northern earls had already deployed their armies to confront it.

Although the groups had their own tasks, it is likely that they were still together, landing when the tide turned against them and there are a limited number of beaches in this spectacular landscape. Reports reaching York would be of the entire invasion force.

Some Norse sources talk of plundered and the speedy subjection 'without opposition' which is consistent with the local army had already assembled in the south. The northern part of Northumbria was the kingdom of Bernicia, whose ancient capital was Bamburgh. However, the southern part of the land seems to have been provided with some coastal defence.

"Then [Harald] went south to Scarborough and laid siege to it, but it was difficult to storm and was well defended. They eventually reduced it with fire."[82] The Norse sources give us more detail and talk of the invaders climbing to the site where a Roman watchtower that had been built to warn of earlier invasions from what they termed the 'Saxon Shore'. The invaders made a great fire which they pitch-forked onto the houses below causing the town to burn and subsequently surrender. 'The Northmen killed many people there and took all the booty they could lay hold of. There was nothing left for the Englishmen now'.

After Scarborough there are reports of another battle. *The Orkneyinga Saga* says that the fleet 'lay off Hallarnes [Holderness]' while Heimskringla

---

[82] *Morkinskinna* #49 Extract from the chapter entitled 'How it came that King Harald journeyed to the West'

suggests that the approach to Holderness was overland, the apparent confusion arising because they are probably describing the movements of two separate units. The Orkney force had seemingly been sent ahead to secure the landing places, while Tostig was making a show of force by destroying property in the 1065-rebels' territory. The *Heimskringla* records the battle with these words; "[the army]...brought up at Hellornes [Holderness], where there came a force that had been assembled to oppose him, with which he had a battle, and gained the victory".

We have no English source for this battle and it is not easy to localise it since Holderness is a district which also has one of the fastest eroding coasts in England. There are some ancient settlements that survive on the higher ground inland which could be candidate for this clash. A possible scenario was that the landing was noted from the defender's higher location and a party was assembled to attack the beached ships. The coastal tidal drift limits the time that the invaders would be beached as they would want to sail on as soon as tidal drift conditions turned favourable. Any battle would be limited to keeping the local defenders at bay.

If Harald had been present, his skald would have ensured his significant role survived to be incorporated into subsequent histories and the tight timetable of events was dictated by tides rather than generals. This suggests that this action was undertaken by the Orcadian reconnaissance force since it is their written sources that record this 'battle'. It is likely that Tostig's vengeful rampaging army would have been responsible for a number of skirmishes or small battle as they moved south on foot, but these go unreported.

Speed is a weapon used by good commanders. The exceptional tidal surge along the Humber/Ouse would allow the invaders to move swiftly inland from the coast. However, deception is an equally important component of a winning strategy. The battles at Scarborough and a second mentioned in Holderness provided a diversion, probably designed to lure the defenders away from York towards the coast. The invasion could be in danger when their boats moved up the Ouse if their arrival was predicted as the boats were vulnerable from the banks. The attacks on the east coast would focus attention away from the river. Months of thought had been devoted to planning this operation. The initiative was with the invaders.

Earl Tostig would be expected to lead this landing party from Scarborough through Holderness as he exacted revenge on the thanes of this Wapentake who had expelled him the previous winter. He would want everyone to know that he was back and looking for vengeance. It would be tough for the local thanes to stay with the army in York while their estates were being ravaged. It speaks of the discipline and unity of purpose among the Northumbrians that there is no record that anybody 'broke ranks' to try and save their homestead.

Tostig's diversionary invasion would also explain the order of arrival at Fulford. Reports of this part of the invading army might have encouraged those defending York to believe that they could defeat this force as they were probably still unaware that the King of Norway remained out of sight, leading his fleet towards the mouth of the Humber, ready to ride the tide all the way to York. King Harald had simply bypassed Tostig after the former had landed at Scarborough to keep pace with the tidal timetable.

Tostig's actions might have been designed to tempt the defenders to leave York to chase him across Yorkshire. Had they done this, it might have allowed King Harald to bypass Fulford and land in the very heart of a weakly defended city. The chance to land back in York unopposed is very much the sort of military stunt that would have appealed to King Harald. But spies and the reconnaissance force sent ahead would discover that the disciplined Northumbrian army had stayed in York, so they would have to resort to the plan to do battle at Fulford.

Frustratingly, noting the words of Tostig's own sister that he did not confide his plans, we are forced to continue to speculate about what was in his mind. The sequence of events was however no coincidence or happy accident. Any modern commander would recognise the unfolding actions as components of an excellent plan.

St. Wilfrid's, Brayton

While reports of Tostig raiding in Holderness reached York within the day, Harald could have overtaken them by sailing down the coast and onto a location where his ships were just a single tidal surge from Fulford. It is likely that the veteran warrior, Harald, would have welcomed the ride to conserve his strength. Remaining at sea also served to allow his presence to go unreported. When the time was right, the river would carry Harald's ship to Tostig's old hall at Fulford the following day.

Harald's stopover at St. Wilfrid's had political significance which sent a message. It was the base where late in 1063, one of the local leaders who was suspected of disloyalty to Tostig was tricked into visiting his sister, Queen Edith, when the ASC tell us that Gamel and Ulf were murdered. This assassination was indicative of the rising northern opposition against

Tostig and a prelude to the rebellion late in 1065. Another rebel stronghold had been occupied.

The stopover served the very practical purpose of getting out of the flow of the river which would otherwise carry Harald's fleet back towards the coast as the river ebbed. They would have to wait for a tidal bore in daylight to complete the journey to Fulford, missing the surge that would pass during the hours of darkness.[83] The hall at St. Wilfrid's was set on a small tributary and a haven where they would not feel the full force of the tidal flood.

The English commanders might have had difficulty disentangling all of the available information arriving. They had reports of the depredations in Holderness, possibly reports of some activity at Riccall and perhaps even the landing at Brayton which would have created a complex picture as the different armies carried out their allocated tasks. This was doubtless the intention of the invaders, so it is difficult to blame the defenders for delaying any reaction.

The brother earls, Edwin and Morcar, wisely held their forces back, guarding the prize, York, resisting the temptation to charge off to the coast. The Mercian fleet and most of Edwin's army, we are told, were at Tadcaster. They too might have been tempted to react to reports of the landings at Riccall with a pre-emptive attack. However, the timing of the tide was against a forceful response because the ebb flow which might have carried them to Riccall was also during the hours of darkness with an inrush shortly after daybreak.

Had they been tempted, the distances are such that they could scarcely have reached the Ouse before the next tidal surge swept Harald past the watershed where the River Aire meets the Ouse. Rather than a battle, the Mercian fleet would be pushed right back towards Tadcaster while Harald's fleet floated on to Fulford. The tides were very much on Tostig's side.

The Orkney Earls had what in modern military terms could be termed a reconnaissance role.[84] They would check the route was clear. Perhaps one boat then drifted back on the ebb tide to say that the next bound along the

[83] The challenge presented moving a fleet at exceptional speed along a narrow river with bends and obstacles in the dark is not considered feasible and gives an arrival time at dawn which is not what is reported.

[84] The tidal surge passed Brayton around first light so they could have reached Fulford about 1800. A recce fleet, possibly Orcadians, could have secured the base at Riccall during the afternoon but could have arrived in dawn twilight if they risked a night journey.

river route was clear for those that followed. Landing beaches get crowded and congestion must be prevented as each ship arrived to find a berth. Such logistical details are not recorded. The movement of any large force is difficult and having the Orkney contingent established in advance to organise the landings and secure the area from interference is important and what is suggested by various sagas. Without such planning, collisions and overshooting would be inevitable.

The tidal bore

The timing and depth of the equinox tides plus the wide mouth of the River Humber and its orientation towards the east, funnels the tidal counter-flow which has to battle against the purposeful drainage-flow downstream. In most rivers the salty seawater penetrates some distance inland to turn the water brackish upstream but the outflow is never overcome by this tidal inflow.

Unless one has witnessed the rush of a tidal bore it is difficult to comprehend just how fast a breaking wave and churning muddy water can travel upstream. To watch a wide river go from near empty to flooding its banks in a matter of minutes inspires awe. At each bend in the river, the wave rises to try and break over the bank and flood the land beyond.

This surge served the invaders, preventing any defenders harassing the landing even if they had been able to anticipate the army's arrival. It is a force of nature best admired from a safe distance driving any soldiers sent to keep watch at bay. Any insolent defensive barrier strung across the river would be swept away and banks cleared of potential enemy as they were temporarily flooded.

The bore, and Ouse river boatmen still recognised the Scandinavian name 'The Aegir' for this phenomenon, is caused by a complex interplay of landscape shape, compass alignment and the lunar cycle. The average speed over the stretch from Goole to Fulford is 13KPH which is just over 7 Knots (about 8MPH) but the speed varies as the river narrows, where the flow can accelerate and where it widens the speed can slacken, especially noticeable on the inside of a bend.[85]

The same waterlogged landscape, flooded by a sequence of nine days of exceptional tides that would climax two days after the battle, made it

---

[85] The maximum permitted speed for boats on the tidal section of the Ouse waterway is 10knots suggesting that the inrushing tide flows close to that limit.

impossible for defenders to set an ambush. This timing does serious credit to Tostig's strategic planning. Without the assistance of this tide a procession of longships, rowing upstream at the best speed of their oarsmen, would be vulnerable from the banks. Moving at walking speed relative to the bank they would be easy prey for spears and arrows.

Any threat from a group of riverside defenders was minimised not just by their limited access as the land around flooded but also by the speed at which any longship was within range. Canal boats can still be witnessed moving like speedboats.

The ever-cautious Harald needed to be confident of the claims and planning presented by Tostig. The experienced survivor would have sent the smaller Orkney fleet ahead to check for obstacles or ambushes and secure the landing places. This Orkney contingent of perhaps 40 ships could occupy the main landing area as they approached the equinox in 1066. Harald and his fleet were a day behind, waiting for the daytime cycle of the tides. This advanced party however had another landing site to secure.

Landings

It is Gaimar who notes King Harald's route to the battle and his landing at Fulford on the eve of the battle. After his overnight stop at St. Wilfrid's in Brayton, just south of Selby, Harald's dawn departure would reach Fulford by the evening. This same source even tells us that they did not need to row upstream confirming that they took advantage of this tidal phenomenon.

One source states, while others imply that Harald reached Fulford the day before the battle. This was tactically challenging. His contingent would not have the protection of the main army. The plan was sensible because the King of Norway rode the tide that would deliver him as darkness fell. To arrive on the earlier tide would have invited the defenders of York to launch an attack. By the time the second tide of the day ebbed, it would be night.

Tostig would have months to think about how to plan the actions around Fulford Hall that had been his home just 10 months before. The 'quiet months' waiting in Scotland were perhaps occupied by employing the data gained during his summer raids so that all of the natural elements could be harnessed to the advantage of the invaders.

The very low tide which precedes the tidal bore can be calculated to be about 17.20 at Fulford: The bore would normally arrive within the hour.

These timings suggest that the landing could have taken place as the light faded on 19th September 1066.

The arrival at dusk would effectively prevent a hasty attack being mounted against the landing after which offensive action was impractical during the hours of darkness. The invaders would have enough light to land before the shroud of darkness protected them as they unloaded their ships and prepared for the coming battle.

The surging water of the bore would also deposit the longships high up the riverbank. This is a tricky manoeuvre but one which is facilitated because the river itself turned through almost a right-angle at Fulford. This backs the flow and provides some limited slack water on the inside bend where the boats would be beached. By leaning hard on their 'steer-boards' the ships would enter this slack water then use their momentum to ride up the bank.

Successive longships would be moving at a marginally more modest speed as they slowly fell behind the breaking wave at the front of the bore helping to space the ships and make the bank landing manageable. This was one of the first bores of the autumn so it was not the highest. These 'spring' bores would peak later before returning to their predictable, normal course.

The term 'beaching' is not quite correct as the surface was covered in smooth rounded stones, a natural glacial deposit that is locally known as a staithe. These banks have changed in recent decades with frequent flooding form the upper Ouse. The gentle slope of the banks once made this a popular swimming place for the locals in the 1980s. Cattle could wander to the river to drink. A few even sought greener pastures on the opposite bank. This land of sloping banks was the one that witnessed up to 60 longships drawn up on the stone embankments providing an ideal location for King Harald's army to land.

The need for two separate landing places is explained because Fulford does not provide unlimited landing space. About 60 longships could be drawn up the bank alongside each other on the smooth stones of the bank. The peak tide would facilitate this as the level of the high-water holds for many hours before it slowly ebbs. This would have greatly facilitated the alignment of the ships, which would be left safely beached as the level of the water fell.

Tostig's thoughtful planning, coupled with Harald's 40 years' experience of fighting, made it likely that an advanced party had already secured this landing area at Fulford. Some of Tostig's men would likely have gone ahead to ensure that the chosen landing place was secure by joining the Orkney Earls when they secured the harbour at Riccall.

A strong contingent of this advance party likely made their way to Fulford under cover of darkness with Tostig's troops acting as guides. Some warriors would be needed since Earl Morcar would probably have been a contingent at Fulford to guard the hall and their fate can be imagined. Just as at Riccall, some guides were in position to bring the landing ships to shore. Others were ready to counter any local opposition in those first vulnerable moments until more warriors landed.

With war pending, it is unlikely that there was much traffic on the roads because the population would have sought refuge some time ago. So a band of warriors could have moved with little chance of being reported. Their task was first to observe and then secure the next landing place at Fulford. They possibly only made their move when they heard the rumble of the approaching bore as it rolled round the wide bend at Bishopthorpe.

This warband sent to Fulford might have preferred covert observation rather than rushing straight in to occupy Fulford Hall. If they moved to early, it would be possible for an army that was based just 3km away in York to rush and eject them. If they moved just after the tide cut communications with the city at the nearby ford the guards could not be rescued. So as soon as this threat was past, and Fulford was isolated, they would have occupied the hall and placed guides on the bank to bring Harald's fleet safely to shore not long before the first ships arrived.

If they had been spotted, and their movement reported or captured, some Orcadians might not have alarmed the brother earls in the way that sighting soldiers sent by King Harald or Earl Tostig might have done

All this speculation highlights one problem faced by historians. To what extent can one legitimately add to the narrative that has survived in the sources. The sagas were written about the kings but then, as now, those doing much of the important work go unrecorded. The approach taken here is to try and recreate as realistically as possible the military events that would precede the battle rather than leave 'blanks', jumping between the reported actions of kings.

Historians are preoccupied with what leaders do. Tostig merits little mention in the Norse narrative of the battle and is ignored by the ASC. One is forced to speculate in order to complete the picture because a story is rarely recorded if a king is not present. However, such speculation calls for some justification. In this case of the landing site, military lore is clear; any good commander would want to secure the space before they planned to land their main army. While it is important that key events, location and timings must be supported by evidence, it is legitimate to compose a narrative. The reader must judge if the speculations are credible.

This reconnaissance and landing party might have had a vital intelligence gathering role. If the plan to draw the defending army out of York had succeeded, the way to York might be open. The advance party could have been tasked with discovering if York was only lightly guarded. In that case Harald might have been waved on and bypassed Fulford to land half an hour later along the extensive staithes in the very centre of York.

This is where some of Tostig's men, with their local knowledge, would have been invaluable. Any plan to occupy York is not even hinted at and only indulged here as we know it was the sort of stunt that the old campaigner, Harald, would have loved. Having learned that the army was still in York, the landing party at Fulford would be shouting to the approaching longships, guiding them to land at Fulford. They would stick to plan A.

On their way to Fulford, Harald's fleet had bypassed at least one tributary. The bore follows the line of least resistance at each watershed and continues along the wider River Ouse, sending a noticeable ripple along the other arm towards Tadcaster following a convoluted 12km of narrowing but navigable waterway to where the Mercian had their base.

Tadcaster was the base of the Mercian fleet who had come to defend their east coast lands. There were well trodden routes that followed the rivers into the hills of England's backbone beyond which lay the heartland of Mercia. Tadcaster was therefore a strategic blocking position that would discourage any invader from taking their ships inland. The Mercian army would be on the move soon after news of the landing at Fulford was received but they would move overland to York, not in their ships.

While Harald was landing at Fulford, "Earl Tostig with his fleet ....with a quick voyage ... entered the mouth of the River Humber and so sailing up the Ouse they landed at a place called Richale" according to the chronicles. Riccall had space for an almost unlimited number of ships and it provided a defensible location, should there be an army already deployed south of York. Tostig had exploited the same favourable flow up the river. At Riccall the river almost doubled back on itself before heading west, away from York, past which Harald's fleet had surged earlier.

At this bend the bank is breached creating a flood plain that would in future centuries be used to ret [soak] flax for spinning into linen, an industry noted in many placenames along the Ouse and its tributaries. At Riccall, Tostig's fleet were afforded additional protection since their haven could only be accessed via some exposed causeways. The tactically wise among the invaders would nevertheless be reassured that there were already strong Orcadian guards in place.

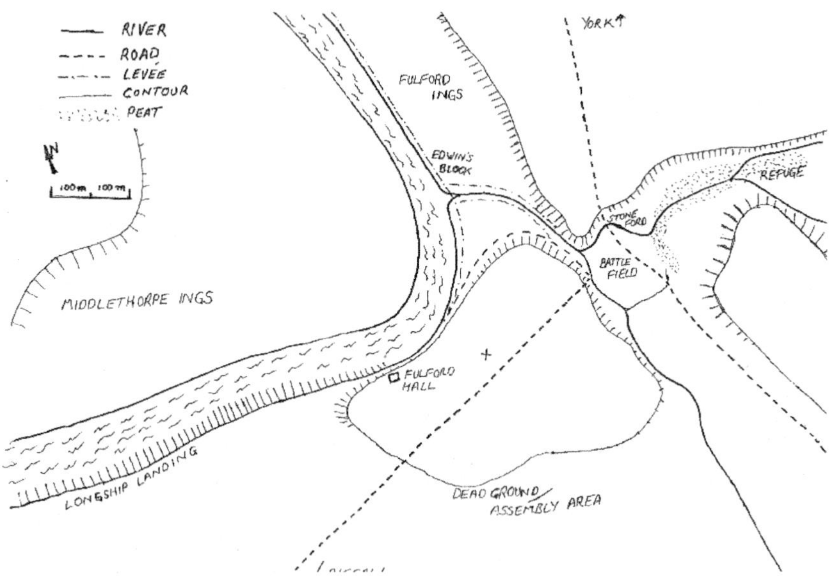

An overview of the battle area on the morning of the battle has most of the Mercian army on Middlethorpe Ings. Later Earl Edwin and a small contingent will deploy to the opposite bank to block the river crossing that will be exposed when the flood ebbs. His brother, Morcar, left some men guarding the stone-ford road to block that route to York. King Harald of Norway had occupied Fulford Hall while Tostig will bring the rest of the army from their landing at Riccall, three hours march to the south. At first they will keep out of sight in the dead ground south of the hall. Tidal flooding will keep the armies apart until after midday.

Water Fulford Hall

The Domesday survey of wealth and tenure, compiled 20 years after these events, tells us that Tostig held the hall at Water Fulford during the reign of Edward *the Confessor*. All subsequent land grants by King Harold were deemed illegitimate by the new regime. Tostig's local knowledge gained in the decade or more that he occupied this hall was the key to all actions and timings in the battle that would follow. Fulford, he knew, provided a defendable assembly area, and offered several other subtle tactical advantages that he would exploit during the battle.

Parts of this hall still stand within the modern Water Fulford Hall. One might image Tostig explaining boastfully to Harald that his servants would ensure that he was royally entertained and housed as soon as he reached Fulford. His actions in Holderness had already announced that things were neither forgotten nor forgiven. Occupying his hall sent the unmistakable message that Tostig was back.

It is unlikely that any of those unfortunates left to guard Tostig's old hall would have survived to carry a warning message. Darkness and the flooding brought by the tidal bore would have made any close observation by Morcar's men difficult, leaving the defenders quite literally in the dark.

Harald's evening arrival posed tactical problems

The Mercian army was half a day's march from York. Their ships would have provided a comfortable base during their extended stay away from their homes. Mercian territory extended from London, then north to the River Humber, before tracing a path northwest over the hills to the west coast north of modern Liverpool with Chester as its capital.

Boundaries were frequently ill-defined except where a major river could provide a recognised boundary. Centuries before King Offa had defined the border with the Welsh by constructing his dyke, a steeply embanked earthwork.

It is safe to assume that news of the landing at Fulford quickly reached Earl Morcar who would have sent some senior military to observe and report back. Darkness, and a wide, deep moat of tidal floodwater would have limited the information gathered from the other side of the ford at Fulford. Scouts on the west side of the River Ouse, viewing from Middlethorpe Ings, could have counted the fleet and assessed the force they were facing.

The defenders opposite the hall could count the ships in the fading light. They would have calculated that King Harald's army did not match either the Mercian or the Northumbrian armies for size. While an impressive fleet of ships were drawn up the bank, by estimating an average of 40 warriors per ship, their army certainly numbered under 3000. Was this the best Tostig had to offer, the observers might have thought. They could not know that this was only the first contingent with King Harald, not Tostig, at its head.

King Harald's arrival nevertheless posed a serious tactical challenge to the brother earls. In York, young Earl Morcar had to prepare for several scenarios. The high tide just before dawn might tempt the invaders to refloat their boats and continue into the city. Perhaps Morcar made some plans to block the river entering York and certainly deployed to defend the landing places which had, since prehistory, provided the city with its strategic role as an inland port in the wide, fertile Yorkshire vale.

Medieval York would later install a chain to control access along the river. It is possible the relics of the Roman outpost at Gate Fulford originally had some barrier to block the river and prevent boats sneaking past if they did not have proper authorisation, but any Roman barrier had been abandoned for six hundred years. A Roman-era picket barrier was identified which might have run from the riverside all the way inland to Walmgate Stray, an area of some low-lying grazing land crossed with multiple natural and man-cut channels in this wet hinterland. Such obstacles might slow a person sneaking in or out of town but would not stop an army.

It is unlikely that any effective river barrier could be improvised in the time available. Another defensive option was to deploy the local army along the river wherever the invaders could land but that was tactically unsound. Within the city there were many landing places for ships and they had no idea where the invaders might choose to land. They might simply bypass any obvious opposition so long as they were in their boats.

But Harald had other options: He might decide to attack York by crossing the river once the tide had fallen, perhaps crossing at night or very early the following afternoon. Some of their ships could be strapped together to bridge the river as the water ebbed. This low tide was the counterpart to the exceptional tidal bore that flooded the land. The draining ebb of the river reduced the Ouse to a trickle compared to its normal flow.

There were risks attached to this attack plan. The tide ebbs slowly for 8 hours during these floodtides and it is only in the last hour that the river would look almost empty. It would be easy to create a bridge of boats, but it would need continual adjustment as the tide fell and scrambling from one ship to the next would not make this an easy way to cross the river. Darkness would compound the problem had this approach been adopted.

An army on the other bank would add a formidable obstacle. It would be relatively easy to defeat such a scrambled crossing if a contingent was positioned to block any attempt to establish a bridgehead. Such guardians placed along the bank could raise the alarm if a threat developed allowing the defenders to be quickly reinforced to disrupt any attempted crossing to outflank York. But that section of the bank was completely unguarded. It was on the opposite bank to the Northumbrian army in York.

This was the dilemma faced by the defenders. If they left this route open, the Norse army could cross unmolested, and it would bring the attackers to the walls of York the following morning. However, deploying an army to oppose Harald's force at Fulford would mean that the defending Mercian and Northumbrian armies would be separated by the River Ouse. The only bridge between them was back in York.

The brothers would certainly have recognised the narrow stone ford-road connecting Water Fulford to York was a third attack option for the invaders. This direct route favoured the defenders as an attack could easily be blocked. Such places are often referred to by tacticians as 'choke points' through which an army must be funnelled before they can again deploy in the open fields. A modest force of Northumbrians could block a whole army if the invaders tried to attack here. A 'gloss' or addition to one version of the chronicle describes such a situation connected to the Stamford Bridge battle which notes how one warrior blocked the crossing of a bridge to protect the retreating Norse army. Morcar doubtless covered this approach by posting a substantial guard to block the ford after the landing at Water Fulford.

So the invaders that were visible to the defenders had three viable attack options. Whichever approach the Norse adopted, the defenders needed a plan that they could cover all these attacking options. Even if the armies of the defenders were divided by a river, from what they could see, either English army was a match for the force that had landed at Fulford.

The biggest threat, and the greatest unknown, was the whereabouts and intentions of the vengeful Tostig. They had received reports of raiding where Tostig had probably made sure he was recognised. Might his army be making his way towards York overland from the east coast? Or had he already landed and occupied his hall at Water Fulford? To compound their immediate problem with the recent landing, the defenders had to recognise that another army might still be heading towards York overland.

Four different scenarios had to be covered. The Earls had to devise deployments to counter each of these different threats.

It suited Tostig to sow such doubt and we might image that he did all within his power to confuse Earl Morcar. The Earls would have sent spies to warn of any landward approaches, but they had nothing to report because Tostig had a better plan. However, for the defenders, the absence of observation does not prove the threat is not there. Such uncertainty reinforced the necessity of keeping the Northumbrian army together and near to the city to cover the eventuality of attacks from the east or south. Any western approach could be covered by the Mercians.

With landings at Scarborough and now Fulford threatening his capital, Morcar did not intend to leave the city undefended. The Earls had not fallen into the first trap that Tostig had laid for them: They had not left the city weakly defended in a fruitless chase of the invaders pillaging Holderness. York was the prize the invaders sought to occupy and they would have to fight to possess it.

We now know that Tostig had made his way swiftly south to the mud flats in the mouth of the River Humber to rejoin his ships and then, riding the tide, to land at Riccall. The defenders did not know any of this so they had to redeploy their armies to counter all of the perceived threats.

Manoeuvres in the dark

The night before any battle can be a busy time for a soldier as commanders arrange their troops ready for action. The eve of the battle of Fulford saw every army, except Kings Harald's 'best men', on the move. Arguably warriors preferred to be busy as sleep might not come easily to men being tested in battle when the morning dawned.

The major move was for the Mercian army who had to march from their base at Tadcaster 15km away to occupy some high ground on the northwest bank, overlooking the Norse landing at Fulford. It would have been dark before the news to march reached them but they could be on the move quickly. Some doubtless had to march attired for battle. They would provide the vanguard and lead the army. The bulk of the troops would load their shields, armour and weapons onto carts as they had been camped for over two months giving plenty of time to prepare for any move.

An advance guard, probably those with horses, reached the north bank opposite Fulford Hall while the Norse were themselves settling in for the night. The ships, and in Norse saga one reads of them being called wooden forts in their skaldic poems, might provide a safe bedding place for many. But the landscape provided a large assembly area, behind the hall, in dead ground. This dip in the surface would keep them out of sight until they deployed for battle. Perhaps it was just the glow of their fires that was visible to the early Mercian arrivals who would have made a show of force and plenty of noise to send the message that this route into York would be opposed. Option one was now blocked to the invaders.

Nature, and the tidal bore, had provided King Harald's force with a very wide moat for their temporary protection. When flooded by the tidal surge, the Middlethorpe Ings are covered in water. Soil surveys suggests that this grazing land was firm although now covered knee-deep with water which would have discouraged the defenders from deploying too close to the riverbank in this wetland when they reached the area after a hard night march. Even when the tide fell, some water was trapped in ponds, and it would take a week for the land to dry out. However, there is a wide path along this bank, built up as the Ouse turned sharply to the east depositing some of its load of silt at this point. A good walkway beside the river, built by this debris, would reemerge soon after each tidal surge.

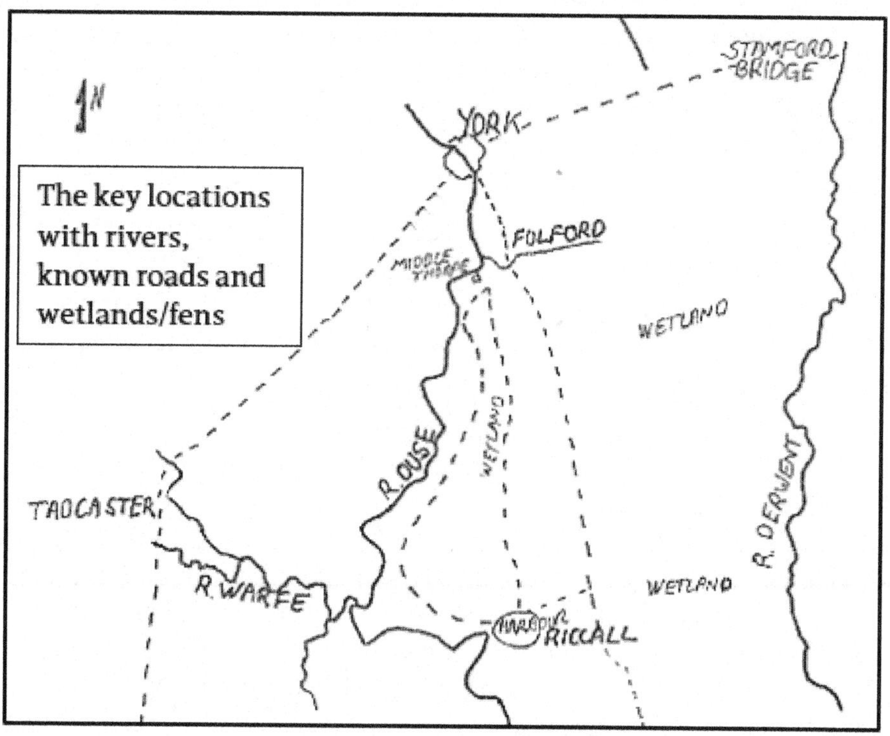

The key locations with rivers, known roads and wetlands/fens

It would have been the early hours of the morning before the foot soldiers of the Mercian army covered the 15km but quickly assembled ready to defend this vulnerable bank of the Ouse. Their battle might actually come before it was light because this interval gave the invaders their chance to bridge the river. Armour and arms would be collected, and each band would be sent to their position.

The warmth generated by the forced march would soon dissipate in the darkness giving them an uncomfortable few hours lined along the spit of dry land that widened as it nears the riverbank, watching the silent ships opposite. Their feet would be wet as they edged forward following the ebbing tide.

It would be perhaps four or five in the morning before it became clear that Harald's band of warriors would not try to force a crossing here. However, their vigil would continue until the next tide had surged in. Few warriors would ever have witnessed the sight of an almost empty river filling to flood its banks in minutes. The arrival of the surge obliged a retreat to higher ground, 300 metres away from the river. The flood also washed away any chance of a Norse crossing.

By the time the Mercians reached a place where they could rest after a cold sleepless night it was also evident that the ships were not going to ride the following surge into York. Some seamen attended the moorings to keep their ships secure as the tide surged past. But the army was not boarding to try and force a river entry on the dawn tide, closing another potential attack option.

The Mercians were a match for the invading army who were still quietly camped in the dead ground. The invaders also had Fulford Hall at their disposal with their ships providing shelter for others, and it is likely the specialist seamen stayed with their ship. Harald's army might be the only one that actually rested that autumn night.

Meanwhile inside the city, groups under the command of their thanes, would be moving to prepare defences at the few places where the riverbank was suitable for ships to land. The city owed its location in part to the navigability of the river and to the existence of landing spaces along the banks where glacial material had lined the banks with stone. At York, the river was also narrow enough, at a breach in the glacial moraine, for a bridge to be constructed. The line of the River Ouse is to the west of an esker[86] which deposited the material linking the city to Fulford. Beyond Fulford a field of isolated sand and stone deposits runs away to the south.

---

[86] See annex C Geology for a description of the relevant land formations.

Some defenders might have been deployed to fortify and guard the city gates built in Roman times. One strong band of warriors were deployed away from the city, at the flooded muddy ford. These soldiers were needed to put on a show of force especially at first light to discourage the invaders attempting to capture the ford. They were also there to stop any attempted infiltration when the tide was low.

With the Northumbrian defenders deployed to guard against the different threats few had any rest as they prepared themselves and their positions.

Riccall is one of the few places where the tidal rush along the Ouse can be exited. For most of its course the river follows some gentle bends with flooded meadows either side. An island of gravel which was one of many esker-field deposits, now almost lost to industrial extraction, provided a breakwater as the river took another of its dramatic sharp turns dictated by the ancient geology, this time towards the west and away from their destination.

The invaders base at Riccall was also a busy place although it is unlikely that the brother Earls were properly aware of this threat yet. After Riccall, the tide takes several hours to follow a long detour to the west into Mercian territory before heading back towards York and Fulford. By leaving the flow with the largest contingent of the army at Riccall, Earl Tostig had these precious extra hours of daylight the day before to bring their ships safely into the harbour on the eve of the battle.

One can calculate that it was dark by the time all the well-spaced fleet were safely berthed at Riccall. With a minute spacing between each ship, 400 would take over 6 hours to enter the haven at Riccall while King Harald had bypassed this harbour and followed the long bends in the Ouse leading to Fulford where his 60 longships could have landed in the final hours of daylight.

The bore offered a free ride for four hours but the last ships to reach Riccall would need their oars to overcome the gently ebbing flow that wanted to push them back down the river. The logistics of this river move are impressive and one can only wonder at how this was calculated and communicated to each ship's captain. This had been a well-timed and choreographed invasion which the tide-times and subsequent events allow us to confidently describe.

We do not hear of any longships being swept past Riccall and on to Fulford which is a testament to the organisation and the skill of the seamen. A few weeks later, some of the Norman invaders would not be so fortunate and would miss the landing zone and be massacred when they came to shore in the wrong place.

The night would have been busy with preparation since the army needed to be on the move with the first streaks of dawn light, around 05.30, at that time of year.

Some physical contexts for the battle

Before describing the battle action itself, this section provides the physical factors that impacted the battle and drive the decisions of the combatants.

Weather

The only written evidence we have describes the weather five days after Fulford. This suggests that the sky was clear and warm. This is an early autumn pattern that is frequently noted on England's east coast with an unusually stable warm spell of weather. A stable pattern of squally storms occasionally afflicts farmers through late September but the literature favours the former dry and warm pattern in 1066.

Light

A new moon would be seen two days after the battle, so there was no moonlight the night before the battle. On a clear night, there is just about sufficient light from a full moon to walk safely along a track. Moonlight would have helped those making their way to Hastings to meet the southern invasion.[87]

The Norse army would have to wait for sunrise just before six before making any move. The sky lights up slowly by the second half of September in the north. It would not be light enough to stride with confidence until it was light at about 7 o'clock. Early departures would have been stumbling about.

Sunset at this latitude comes at 17:47 and it is completely dark before 19:00 in the evening. These figures dictate the window during which the events related to the battle could take place. There could be not post-battle pursuits because it was too dark.

Tidal conditions

In 1066 York was a tidal port. The date of the battle was approaching the exceptional seasonal tides that would peak five days after the battle. However, the flood levels on the day of the battle were already 85% the height of their Monday peak.[88] Tidal predictions are subject to some variability as recent rainfall, atmospheric pressure, wind direction and silting within the river affect detailed timings. Tide estimating for Fulford is

[87] The benefit of moonlight was tested by the author when walking in period clothing the route to Waltham Abbey. Progress was slow.

[88] This timing is relevant and consistent with the extensive debris that was recovered from the site during the archaeological project.

further complicated by the construction of a weir in 1757 and later locks downstream at Naburn.

The basis for these figures were very kindly computed for the port of Goole by the Hydrographer to the Royal Navy whose help is acknowledged and very much appreciated.[89] The necessary height and time adjustment for the flow along the River Ouse to Fulford is discussed in *Finding Fulford*. Research suggests that the general pattern of tidal surges has been stable for centuries.[90]

In September the sun and moon interact to produce an equinoctial 'spring' flow. These are the lowest and highest tides of the year. During the very low tides, which are the counterpart of the higher than usual tides, the infamous clay huts that can capsize a ship, are exposed along the Ouse. These are remnants of geological processes about 13,000 years ago when the last ice sheet retreated and drained along the line of the River Ouse. Navigating the river when the tide was ebbing was perilous, constraining movement. The invaders wisely planned their journey when the river was in flood.

It is also important to recognise the unusual way the tide rises and falls during these weeks of exceptional tides. It is not a steady rise but a dramatic surge. In an hour, the muddy banks are covered to 80% of the eventual depth by churning water. The transition is dramatic. If the River Ouse is observed today just below Naburn, the rise in the water level in the minutes after the tidal front arrives, still inspires one with awe.

The measurements, observations and calculations allow the river tide to be modelled. The exceptional tide would start to arrive at Fulford about six on the morning of the battle and peak about nine. It would then fall slowly until late afternoon when the maximum land would be exposed just after five when the light also began to fail on the day of the battle. By seven it would not only be dark but the locations of the battle action would again be covered in water. It can be estimated that the ford-road at the heart of the action and the 'pool' described in Norse literature would be covered by three metres of muddy, surging tidal water.

The impact of the tidal flood on the course of the battle cannot be overstated. Early in the project the course of the action could be described with some confidence even before the impact of the tide was recognized. It

[89] Tidal calculation at historic dates in the past can be calculated using their on-line calculator.

[90] Based on Colin Briden's two articles on the tidal Ouse.

was however an attempt to understand how the same landscape was described with such different terms that provoked the tidal investigation. The calculated timing and depth of the tide not only explained how the same landscape could be described in different ways which corresponded to how tides transformed the surface during the day. Addressing the described actions was not only consistent with the tides but contributed to understanding the sequence. It was one of the 'eureka' moments encountered during the project.

The full relevance of the tide to the conduct of the battle is addressed in the narrative of the battle. In summary, the exceptional September tide filled the beck and flooded the Ings and land to the east, creating the fen-like landscape described in the early sources. The ebbing tide would have rendered the stone surface and especially the area adjacent to the road through the ford accessible as the literature suggests.

The asymmetry of the ebb and flow is also noteworthy since the river seems to remain 'full' for almost 5 hours preventing the sides engaging. The water level remains almost still as if it was resting after its energetic arrival. The normal pulse between tides is about 6 hours but in the upper reaches of the River Ouse the time from the arrival of the bore until the ebb is over 8 hours.

These figures significantly constrain the time during which the action can take place as combat cannot commence until the water is low enough for one side or the other to cross. It was the local knowledge of the Northumbrians would temporarily be able to gain the initiative by using the Roman-era stone-ford crossing.

Sunrise

The sun was visible above the horizon shortly after six o' clock on the 20th of September but daylight creeps in slowly in Autumnal Yorkshire. The surging tide had already filled the ford preventing any pre-emptive attacks by either side. The English scouts standing on the northern straighter and steeper shoulder of land leading down into the water-filled ford doubtless strained their eyes attempting to interpret the size and composition of the opposition, ready to report on the intentions of the unwelcome arrival on the opposite bank that had landed at Fulford the previous afternoon.

The lie of the land likely prevented Morcar's scouts from providing much useful intelligence. Just like the Mercians on the opposite bank who had the ships in clear view, Harald's army was mostly concealed behind the rising land with only the hall near the crest visible to both.

There was no sign that the invaders were organising for battle perhaps because they recognized the flood tide would separate the armies until noon. It was an anxious wait for the defenders but much less so for the invaders who knew the plan. Were they facing Tostig's or Harald's army or was it just a large group sent to secure the area? It would be another two to three hours after sunrise before the armies would reveal themselves.

Pitched battle

Battle was not the only option available in this period. A force that was clearly inferior might accept terms and submit. But we read that King Harald's invaders 'offered battle', or in a different saga 'elected to give battle' and the challenge was evidently accepted by the native armies. Civil disputes and disagreement on English soil in early decades of the 11th century were often settled by negotiation and without shedding much blood. Earlier the derided Danegeld was paid to invaders limiting their raiding and avoiding unpredictable and expensive battles.

Something was different about the coming clash at Fulford as there is no evidence of any parlay. No embassies were exchanged. King Harald did not send to demand submission or ask for hostages. All parties apparently accepted that the matter would have to be resolved with weapons. There could be little doubt that Earl Tostig was not looking for a negotiated settlement. The leading thanes had rebelled and killed all of Tostig's men the previous year so could expect no mercy if defeated.

Unlike the battle at Stamford Bridge, just 5 days after Fulford, there were negotiations before and even during that battle. Submission to another overlord made little difference to most people. Taxes would go to a different person but redrawing power and influence probably had limited impact on ordinary folk and local leaders would often be left in post, provided they remained loyal. This more subtle era of power politics was soon to end.

Rebellion was always different. The people of the north were fighting for a principle. It was something intangible, but we might recognise it as their local freedom. The old Celtic order of hierarchy was being disrupted by the introduction of administrative ways from the south. Tostig appears to have tried to impose a more centralised taxation and administration which would now be seen as normal but this removed power, and especially the power to collect tax, from local lords. Tostig's attempt to replace local with central control undermined local power and this was worth fighting for. It is doubtful if Harald and Tostig recognised or discussed the tyrannical tendency they shared which favoured centralised, arbitrary power.

Tostig's local knowledge

The environment seems to favour the invaders in subsequent events rather than the defenders. Arguably, Tostig knew the ground and the way the tides worked well because this had been his home for over a decade. It is possible that this was fortuitous but their choice to offer battle at Fulford strongly suggests this was based on Tostig's advice.

Harald would not have wasted his time since arriving and would have done his own appreciation of how to turn the landscape to his advantage and it does seem that he took charge of managing the battle tactically. Harald was the boss.

From his base at Riccall Tostig had the luxury of knowing that the land to the south of the beck was now secure with his ally in occupation at Fulford. There was no need to send scouts ahead or to move tactically and this would allow the Riccall army to move as quickly as possible.

All is fair in war! The opposition would not be expected to stand back while an army assembled. Harald, and the flood surge, had secured the battlefield from any possible interference from the defenders until the water ebbed. They were safe to move freely to their muster point at Fulford.

Generals would normally want to bring their armies to the conflict in formation to discourage any pre-emptive or opportunistic early assault. The deep moat at the ford precluded any attack so they could move from Riccall to Fulford in open formation. This was a luxury for the invaders.

From the defender's perspective, they would love to rout any early arrivals. Tostig's military planning had been thorough. The battle site is what we refer to as a pitched battle because one side had chosen the location. It was occupied by Harald who was, for now, enjoying the protection of the flood water. To add to all these strategic advantages, Tostig's reinforcements from Riccall could wait in dead ground until their leaders set them in their battle positions.

The local topology once again favoured the invaders when it came to observation. It might have taken several hours to appreciate the scale of the build-up at the ford and to recognise that it was indeed another army with both Harald and Tostig deploying armies for battle at the ford. It suited the invaders to keep the defenders guessing so it is likely that the early troops were told to stay in the available dead ground, denying the defenders guarding the crossing, any knowledge of this build-up or, as we will discover later, providing targets for the Mercian archers.

Initiative

The initiative remained with the attackers as is often the case because the defenders do not know where they will be attacked. Forewarned of the landings, the earls and their experienced commanders had in the days or possibly weeks beforehand doubtless spent time selecting ground that would favour them in any battles to come.

Recognising that Germany Beck was the best place to block any advance from the south, they had resisted the temptation to deploy their army beyond this natural obstacle. But until Tostig was confidently sighted and his approach route identified they could not deploy to guard this defensive position. Relinquishing their control of the city and moving to Fulford early risked leaving the city open to an unopposed occupation, this time possibly overland from the east. Such a two-pronged assault by the invaders still had to be considered although one of the defender's armies was now deployed to stop an attack from the west.

However, this Mercian army was now on the 'wrong' bank if the attacks materialized from the south and along the east bank.

We now know that the battle took place at the muddy ford but the wily warriors, Tostig and Harald, would be looking for any gaps in the disposition of defenders to exploit and give them an easy win right up until the time that battle was joined. Tostig might still have had those loyal or beholden to him who could try to send him word if anything was left undefended.

Reconnaissance parties were doubtless still looking for the other invaders. The landing at Scarborough and attacks in Holderness suggested that Tostig was approaching from the east. The defenders might well have thought that Harald's landing was actually designed to induce them to deploy their army to Fulford and seen this as a trap to leave the city undefended. The defenders were faced with such challenging dilemmas as the day of the battle dawned.

The overnight deployment of the Mercians had blocked any western approach by a forced river crossing at Fulford. The ford to the south was secure, at least temporarily, thanks to the flood. The strategic planning by Tostig and Harald had confronted the Northumbrians with another dilemma and the brother earls were wisely covering all options, but at the cost of dividing their armies.

The guessing game would only truly be over when Tostig and Harald revealed themselves and deployed their armies for battle. They had no need to rush as the flood water would keep the foes apart until midday. It would serve the attackers purposes to have the armies of the brother earls out of position with most of the Northumbrian army still positioned to defend York.

The only obstacle blocking the invader's path was the group guarding the ford. Daylight had revealed Harald's men had not moved. They would not take the western option or indeed try to rush the city in their boats as the high tide filled the River Ouse all the way into York. With the defenders still out of position, the prospect of a quick victory beckoned. They knew that only Germany Beck's wide, deep tidal moat, stopped the invaders advancing on York.

For the defenders at least some of their enemies' options were now closing. It was now clear that Harald intended to remain on his bank and attack along the east bank of the river. There would be no bridging the river with boats at low tide. Neither had they ridden the flood at dawn to carry the invaders right into the city. The guessing game that the invaders had posed to the defenders was still not over as one major unknown remained. Where was Tostig?

Two concerns might have troubled the young brother earls as the hours rolled round towards midday. First there were the groups of warriors that could be glimpsed arriving from Riccall before being concealed by the dead ground behind Fulford Hall. Second was some lingering doubt about the identity of the force that had arrived at Fulford by boat as they seemed to be inactive.

Tostig's arrival at Fulford

It is possible that the boastful Tostig wanted to reveal his presence, but he was the junior commander. Tostig may have chosen the place, or pitch, for the battle which Harald had occupied the night before. The King had been in position for over 12 hours, time enough to study the landscape and formulate his own tactical plans. He might even have recognised that the tale told months before by Tostig to a sceptical audience about this exceptional opportunity offered by the tide to win an easy victory was actually true. The old tyrant was not noted for sharing any credit with others, attested in many surviving accounts, so after his own reconnaissance Harald would now take charge of the battle plan.

The state and layout of the tracks from Riccall is not entirely known but the paved road uncovered at the ford itself might suggest that the Romans extended it some distance south. Good roads are essential to move armies. Moving in step offers considerable advantages in terms of the rate at which a body of soldiers move. Roman armies recognised this and marched in step, but we have no records that either Norse or English armies at this time marched as a unit so it is not easy to calculate the rate of flow of warriors to Fulford.

Boots also churn up any soft land, further slowing progress and forcing detours. Groups are observed to move at half the speed of individuals travelling alone. A crowd produces an invisible pressure on those around them that slows the overall progress of the group. Calculations help inform any estimates, but the details are a matter of conjecture. These suggest that it would take about 4 hours for the first troops to walk from Riccall and there would be a three-hour gap between the first and last soldiers arriving. Tostig's army would not reach three quarters of its potential strength until midday.

Earl Tostig, like any good general, would not want to risk provoking premature attack before he was ready. He would display such caution five days later at Stamford Bridge when he did not reveal that he had a parlay with his brother until challenged by Harald. He wanted to play for time and delay the battle in the hope of reinforcement from Riccall. Now at Fulford, he would stay out of sight and keep his enemy guessing.

While the first troops, setting out at first light, could have reached Fulford about 10 in the morning, the poor road would limit the flow and it would be a few hours before a sizeable force was assembled.[91] Walking two abreast, 40 to 50 warriors could pass each minute suggesting over 2000 warriors arrived each hour. A disciplined formation, marching in step would significantly increase the flow of warriors.

---

[91] If one estimates 40 warriors flowing past a point each minute, the flow would bring 2400 fighters each hour to the battle. So two hours should see a force of over four thousand assembled with the rate slowing as the track was churned by those who had gone before.

Realisation emerges

The guessing game was nearing an end as the invaders revealed their armies for assessment by the defenders. The attackers had posed so many alternative threats from different directions that might have still hoped these had led to the wrong disposition of the defences.

The nursery rhythm, 'The Grand Old Duke of York' embodies the contempt soldiers feel towards commanders who keep redeploying them. To their credit the young earls had not taken the various baited traps. This meant that they were still able to bring the full Northumbrian army to the ford before the tide ebbed. But they would have to hurry.

Perhaps the earls should have questioned why an invasion force that they easily outnumbered had already let two opportunities to attack pass. Were they being lured into another trap by these sophisticated invaders?

Failure of their scouts to locate Tostig's rampaging army did not mean this threat did not exist. They could not yet be certain that his army had made its way to the Humber to rejoin their ships and exploit the rapid, free ride offered by the tidal bore to reach Riccall so quickly.

It is likely that it was an observant Mercian warrior who recognised that the size of the opposition was swelling. Morcar's men defending the ford had their view blocked by the rising land on which Water Fulford Hall stands. But a warrior standing on the higher ground on the west bank, where the Mercian's had established their base, could observe not only the growing size of the opposing army but also oversee the tracks arriving from Riccall. It was full of warriors armed for battle. What they were witnessing was Tostig's army arriving and the opposing army expanding in its assembly area.

Translating these observations into an action plan was far from simple. The Mercians had rushed from Tadcaster the previous evening. They had performed their task and made their preparations for battle although they had not been called into action which would have come as a relief to many. However, the Mercians gain meant that all the pressure had been transferred to the Northumbrians on the east bank.

It was possibly only their earl, Edwin, who really understood the emerging threat because his brother had not yet arranged his army to meet this growing force at the ford. It probably took some time for the impact of what they were observing to be appreciated. Unfortunately communicating this intelligence to the defenders at the ford was a problem even though the river and flooded land separated them by only 500m. Again it was the lie of the land that prevented them perhaps shouting warnings across the river. They were too far away, out of sight and separated by a river and flood water.

Earl Edwin, the older brother, must have returned to the city to report the growing size of the army and discuss the implications. Scouts from the Mercian base at Tadcaster might have arrived with reports of the enormous fleet that had arrived at Riccall. Such an important message would be unlikely to be left to a lieutenant. Possibly around the same time some of Morcar's men guarding the ford also shared their suspicions that Tostig's army was assembling near the ford. Perhaps a few too many of the invaders came out of the dead ground to look at the landscape. The sight of a banner or shouted taunts from one of Tostig's men might have pointed to what was happening in the ground south of Water Fulford Hall. Interpretation of such military intelligence was difficult then, as now, because so much was ambiguous.

So the realisation of how and where the battle was planned might have been gradual but by mid-morning the invader's plan must have been clear. The battle was set to take place at the weakly defended ford. It would fall to Morcar to confront Harald's and Tostig's full force provided he could assemble his army to make it a contest.

Only when the other 'wing', or 'arm' as the translated Norse sources variously term Tostig's force actually deployed, would the guards at the ford be certain that they were facing a second sizeable army. It was led by the man who had been their earl ten months before.

Redeployment

Once again, it was time for the English defenders to respond rapidly. Two redeployments were necessary. The defenders at the ford had to be reinforced. The narrow path along the river also had to be blocked as they must prevent the Norse getting round the end of their line to attack the ford from behind in a classic outflanking move.

It is possible that it was the Mercians who first appreciated this risk of being outflanked. They had been guarding the west bank of the Ouse for a full cycle of the tides. Shortly before first light, as they stood-to in case the invaders planned a move, they would have witnessed how the path beside the river emerged from the ebbing water. This raised path is a natural construction formed when the coarse sand from centuries of successive floods is deposited from the flow. This builds a natural embankment known as a levée. Recent excavations suggest that the surface of this path was reinforced with broken pottery over the centuries to improve the surface of this practical, natural riverside path.

When the tide had ebbed, this path would open a way to cross the beck and then get behind the Northumbrians guarding the ford. The weapons, arms, leadership and training of the time were all designed so that they could fight the enemy in front of their shieldwall. This outflanking option had to be blocked. The boastful Tostig might have explained to Harald the difficulty the defenders would have occupying such a blocking position, and he was right.

Whether Edwin took the initiative to redeploy some of his men to the opposite bank or if it was jointly agreed that the Mercians should undertake this task is not known. As with so much of the detailed narrative, the actions must be deduced from the descriptions and the physical evidence identified. Another reason for assuming that Edwin made this decision is that Morcar could himself have more easily dispatched a contingent of his soldiers to defend the flank. But from his side of the river the threat was difficult to appreciate. The fact that he did not do this might suggest that the elder brother told him of the weakness that had been exposed and also informed him that he was already redeploying to block it.

Flanks are a necessary preoccupation of every commander. Tostig had doubtless been aware of the opportunity that this could present and the astute Harald would also have had a chance to actually observe the operation of a cycle of tides which would likely have been explained to him either in Norway or Scotland. The old warrior would appreciate the tactical avenues the tides opened and appreciated that any outflanking move would be completely invisible to those defending the ford. The newcomers to this landscape, the Mercians, might also have noted this riverside crossing and recognised the danger it represented for their Northumbrian allies.

The footsore Mercian army that had rushed from Tadcaster the night before was now in the wrong place. They had ensured that the easy option of crossing the river was blocked and there is ample evidence of their aggressive intent that would be manifest in the showers of arrows they rained on the invaders later. The new threat they had to address was from a charge along the emerging bank beside the river once that route was exposed by the falling tide.

The dilemma for the tired Mercian defenders who had been on the move or alert to repel an attack through the night, was whether they should all abandon their blocking position on the Middlethorpe Ings to move to defend the path beside the river or split the army. An attack along the east bank could be imminent but the Mercians knew the tide would cycle and again allow the invaders to cross the Ouse and threaten York from the west. They needed to guard two places, and their reaction was effectively decided by what was possible.

It would take several hours for any foot soldiers to rush back into the city, cross the narrow bridge and then join the rush to Fulford, a journey of about 7km. Because the invaders had kept them guessing, it is unlikely that they were aware of the need to redeploy until mid-morning when the defenders finally understood the size and disposition of the armies they were facing. So marching the whole Mercian army to the new location, frustratingly barely a hundred metres away, would take too long and arrive too late to be of any use as the timing of the low tide would expose the riverside path before they could redeploy there.

Only those Mercians with horses would be able to move from the west bank to the east in time to block the path by the river that was slowly emerging from the ebbing flood. Horses could halve the transit time. The path beside the river itself was much too narrow for horses so the final section would have to be on foot along the narrow levée. The modern landscape still allows one to identify where they must have dismounted and began their move forward on foot.

The Norse sources report in somewhat derogatory terms about this redeployment. The Mercian movement along the levée is noted; 'all their troops in line' which might reasonably be interpreted as the necessity for the troops to walk in single file between the river and the flooded Ings. The path by the river is 5 to 10 metres wide. On this occasion the landscape actually worked in favour of the English since the invaders could only see the small contingent of Mercian struggling to get into position on the riverbank. They could not observe the full force of Morcar's army as it raced from York to the muddy ford.

The Mercian blocking force therefore made their slow but steady progress picking their steps with care as they waded forward with the deep river on their right. Care was required since the river would swallow any warrior decked in armour who slipped down the riverbank. Although sliding off the levée the other way, into the Ings, would not be fatal but would slow progress.

These Norse descriptions can be matched to the conditions that fits the known time, tide and landscape. It can be estimated that the Mercians must have been standing ankle-deep in water when they arrived at the place where the beck entered the river. From here the Mercians would see Harald's longships drawn high up on the bank and their comrades still stranded on the opposite bank. This was a bold and astute move which the boastful Tostig might well have portrayed as impossible in his own planning.

This small Mercian force should have reached, and effectively blocked, the crossing of the beck beside the river perhaps an hour after leaving the army on the west bank. The timetable dictated by the tides allows some respite before the route was open for attack. Perhaps the horses might have been taken back to bring a second wave of reinforcements, but we get no reports of this. The very narrow front that had to be defended did not call for large numbers, only some heroes, who could hold the line against the full forces of a Viking charge.

Rush to battle

It was earlier conjectured that a significant portion of Morcar's Northumbrian army was held in York leaving a sufficient force deployed to defend the ford. The ford road, like the path beside the river, offered the attackers only a narrow front, as there were 'deep pools' either side. So a modest deployment could hope to block a much bigger force in this waterlogged landscape. The defenders stood on the higher, firm ground with a narrow front to defend so this was an excellent defensive position. However, there is a cruel military logic which dictates that victory normally goes to the biggest army, even when one side has a strong defensive position.

No leader wants to divide his force and once the enemy's disposition was clear, Morcar and his advisors would want to assemble the whole Northumbrian army in a single location with their earl at its head. They knew it would take about an hour to accomplish this. It would be well after midday before the tide exposed the ford. It was time to gather the whole army for battle at Fulford.

Halfway to the ford from the city was the collection of farmsteads named as Sutton (South Farm) when mapmakers first recorded the location. This was much later recorded as Gate Fulford. This was where the path taken by the Mercians would follow a road down to the river to get into their blocking position beside the river.[92] The Mercians and Northumbrians would go their separate ways at this junction; perhaps the brothers took their leave at this point.

The rising land prevented any Norse seeing the Northumbrian army as they moved along the line of the modern A19, where the high ground built on the glacial esker traps the river flood water and contains the Ings. Some Norse skalds had mockingly reported the brave Mercians struggling to get into position while the full force of the Northumbrian army was quickly moving to Fulford, but out of sight.

The coat of iron rings that would soon protect the wearer from sword slashes and limit the penetration from spear thrusts, is not only heavy but sets a natural cadence to the speed at which the wearer can move. Running involves moving up and down which would have been uncomfortable, exhausting and stressful on the legs. A brisk walk was not just a sensible compromise but necessary when fully armed for battle.

A fully equipped warrior would certainly not want to run and we learn that when Norse warriors rushed to Harald's rescue at Stamford Bridge 'more died because of the heat than at the hands of the Saxons'. But an hour would allow those in York to join the force astride the road on the higher ground on the north side of the still flooded ford.

Morcar's Northumbrian army already occupied an impressive natural defensive position that did not require a complicated deployment plan. A thousand men could provide a deep shieldwall which would cover the 100m gap that would be revealed when the tide had fully ebbed.[93] The flood water would serve to corral the invaders who could not approach the ford as a coherent shieldwall because of the folds and steep slopes into the beck. Nature had constructed excellent defences especially when the river was in flood.

---

[92] Excavations on the south side of this road revealed a section of a palisade wall which probably extended from the river to the road and logic would suggest continued to the wetlands further east. This looks more like a control boundary rather than a military defence wall.

[93] It would be foolhardy to be within the beck basin when the river was 'empty' or at its lowest ebb since the inrushing bore would not be far behind which would overwhelm anybody in its path. Swimming when clad in chainmail armour is not an option.

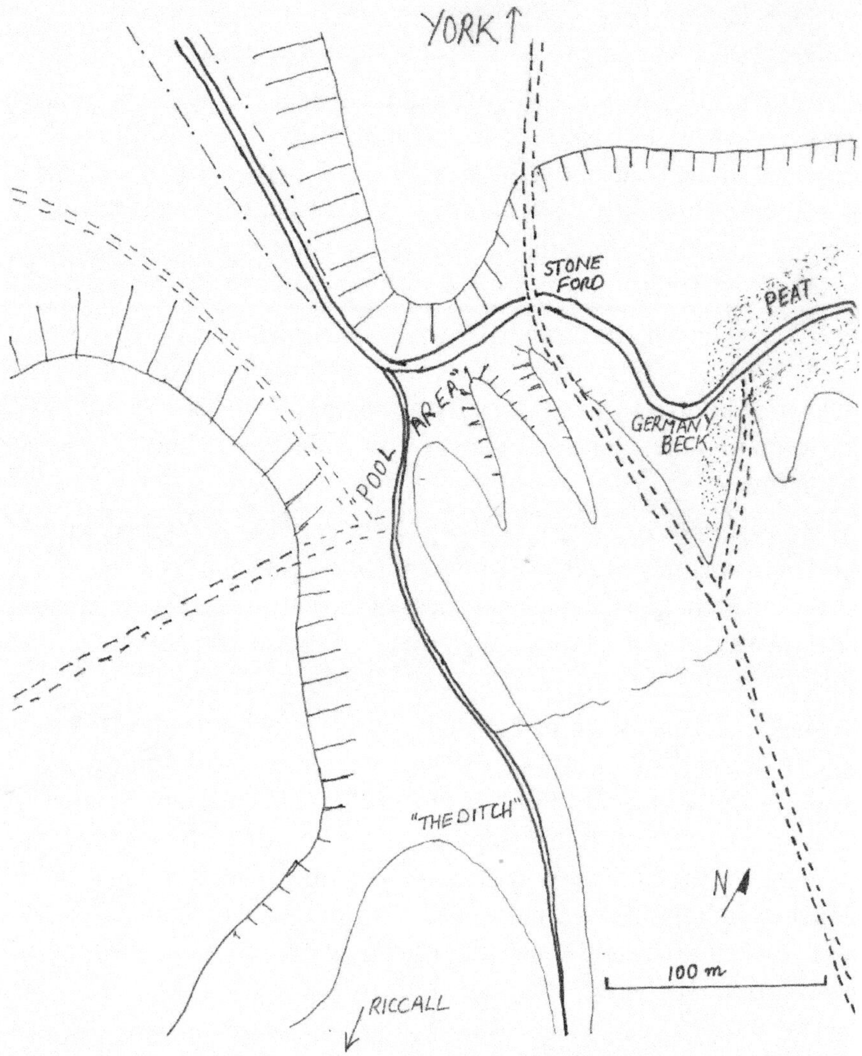

The landscape at the heart of the battle can best be described as 'lumpy'. Two becks drain the water from this glacial landscape to the river. One is Germany Beck with its stone ford which will be at the heart of the battle action. The other is nameless but referred to as a 'ditch' which was full of water when Tostig deployed what the sources call the invaders 'weaker army'.

So this ditch represents a tactically significant feature viewed from a military perspective even at seasons when the tide did not penetrate this far. This natural obstacle doubtless provoked the construction of the embanked fording place which at 10m wide, which could allow a marching Roman cohort to access the land to the south of the beck.[94]

This water course, known as Germany Beck displays separate personalities during the peak tides in spring and autumn. The beck normally flowed in its course that was one or two metres wide and rarely more than 50cm deep but often just a trickle. It drains an extensive area where University of York now stands. The fenland maintains some flow of water into this stream all year round.

However, when in flood it can be 20 to 40 metres wide and filled to a depth of up to 3 metres. The arriving tidal bore transforms it within half an hour from a trickling drain to a static pool only falling slowly over 8 hours. Such a transformation must have been impressive and was well known to local inhabitants.[95]

Earl Morcar and a contingent of his mounted could have reached the ford ahead of the main body, giving them time to prepare and organise for the impending battle. As the opening phase of the battle reveals, he employed this time well, preparing the troops already at the ford to assault his nemesis, Tostig.

It is likely that there was a reasonable road leading either side of the stone ford crossing of the beck and Morcar's men probably moved at the best speed their armour would allow. In an era when time was appreciated rather than being 'told' by a timepiece, they wanted to arrive at the ford before the ebbing tide exposed the crossing. Modern observations of the frequent floods in this area allow one to estimate that it would be early afternoon before the ford-road would be exposed to assault. It seems however that Morcar was impatient for battle.

Earl Edwin had also won his race to close an avenue of attack that would soon be exposed. Prominent among his small force beside the river was Earl Waltheof who we noted earlier all the Norse and Icelandic sources name as leader of this contingent. While the ultimate leadership of the Mercians was undoubtedly vested in Edwin, the surviving reports strongly suggest that Waltheof was the prominent military leader at the riverbank. One cannot exclude the possibility that this young warrior had actually led the first contingent to rush to block this potential gap in their defences

---

[94] A military response would have been impossible on the earlier stepping stone-crossings that were identified below the Roman surface during excavations.

[95] The building of a lock at Naburn in 1757

while Edwin followed with reinforcements after a farewell meeting with his brother.

Morcar's right flank was now protected by the River Ouse, the flooded Ings and his brother. His left flank was perhaps even more secure with two layers of unassailable natural defences. Not only was the land on the invaders side covered in water that would remain wet for many weeks, but beyond the section that Morcar had covered with his shieldwall was a natural two metre wall of glacial-compacted sand and stone up which one might scramble but not walk, which is still visible in the modern landscape.

A bed of peat, many metres deep, had since about the 6th century been smothered by these surging tides so the peat no longer grew. The peat layer was now covered with a metre of fine alluvium. Recent excavation on the site revealed a 5/6th century crossing of this bog made from leafy branches on a solid bed of logs. The long-lost crossing rested on the top of the peat. It seems that it was not easy to cross the slippery mud that periodically penetrated and by the 11th century this mud had become much deeper, burying the wood crossing, 80 metres upstream of the stone ford. Any attack from the south that was launched here would get bogged down in this wide ditch.[96]

The steep bank continues towards another peat bog where there is even an ancient laid hedge, probably dateable to the time of the battle. This thicket was certainly strong enough to stop soldiers even if they waded across at least 100 m of waterlogged field or slid down the steep bank on their side to reach this spot.

Ironically, when the table were reversed later in the battle and Morcar was in retreat, the protection afforded by these obstacles would be tested as it provided a refuge for the Northumbrians. The natural fortifications of Morcar's left flank would prove the salvation for him and some of his army as it offered a place 'where there was no opposition' as one Norse source notes, once the northern, dry side had been lost to the Norse army.

In 1066, the area around the ford was marginal land where some bio-archaeological studies suggest limited grazing. Later records suggest cutting of the peat and wood cutting. There is no suggestion of housing,

---

[96] Extensive excavations surrounding this wood crossing revealed no debris that could be linked to the battle which supports the interpretation of the action presented here. This section of land is almost unchanged since 1066.

with the exception of Fulford Hall on the high ground to the south of the ford.[97]

Three kilometres north of the ford were the city walls of York which included the stone walls of the fort that had been extended when the city spilled beyond the Roman bounds. A defensible boundary could nevertheless have been prepared to withstand a siege had that been the plan. Morcar had almost a year to prepare. With King Harold preoccupied defending the south coast, such a defensive strategy might have appealed but we do not have any evidence that defence inside the city was ever considered as an option.

Siege and defensive tactics were not entirely unknown, but to judge from the written record, they were uncommon. In military terms, castles provide an effective way to dominate hostile countryside but had not yet been widely adopted. A decisive battle appeared the preferred option.

The continental habit of building imposing strongholds throughout the countryside was uncommon in the territory of England until after the Norman conquest. It might also have been intolerable for the new, young earl to remain behind the fortification while the enemy was free to ravage the country. Earl Morcar was doubtless beholden to the thanes who had invited him to become earl and there seems to be no doubts that a confrontation was the only way to settle matters.

One might speculate that King Harold had sent word as soon as news reached him of the invasion telling them that he was heading north with troops to repel the invaders as they had likely agreed in the Spring. Big armies are better than small ones. However, there is no evidence that such a message was received, or it might have arrived too late.

A military plan to concentrate England's armies and overwhelm the Norse invaders was sensible although history leaves us no account of different options being considered. The remarkable speed with which the northern invasion had arrived at the gates of York perhaps rendered any previous plans obsolete. Harold could not realistically have responded any quicker and this again points to invasion being planned precisely to prevent the armies of England uniting.

There is scope for speculating that William's redeployment to St. Valéry-sur-Somme from their ports in Normandy helped persuade Harold that he

[97] There is significant ceramic and other finds suggesting that the settlement of Water Fulford occupied the high ground south of the beck in the 13-16 centuries.

could head north. Harold had already abandoned his defence of the coast opposite Normandy as it was now deployed in the wrong place. William's move and some confused reports about the impact of a storm in the Channel, might have encouraged Harold to believe there was time go to the aid of his brothers-in-law. The first consequence of the pending battle was that Harold felt there was either a time-window, military advantage or a regal obligation to take his cavalry north.

Invaders deploy

Back at Fulford, it was time for Harald to issue his orders. He had not wanted to provoke an attack before the full force was assembled. It is not too fanciful to suggest that Harald held a council of war and gave his instructions to the assembled warriors. We learn of him using the blast of a horn during the battle to control what this experienced fighter might have already identified as the key action that would be required to turn the battle. The plan and the signals had to be agreed. The soldiers were then told by their leaders exactly how they should respond when they heard a blast on the war horn as reported in the sagas. Once that was done it was time to deploy.

The strange asymmetry with a four-hour flood and eight-hour ebb, produces several hours when the water is almost still. The tranquillity of the water in the hours after the high tide was matched by the inactivity around the ford. The invaders' deployment could have been anytime between ten and noon. However Tostig's army, flowing in from their Riccall base, would not have been there in strength until about eleven and it is likely that this was the time when orders were given. By that time the dead ground where they were concealed from sight must have been congested with a crowd of at least four thousand all ready for battle.

All of the records provided after the battle seem to imply that Harald had a unique plan for this battle but it is more likely that, like any good general, he was ready to respond appropriately as the battle developed. His habit in the Byzantine battles where he served as the commander of the Varangian Guards was to watch and wait, not committing a significant part of his army, until the enemy offered him an opportunity to defeat it.

We are told (Morkinskinna 49) "King Harald. landed and drew up his troops on the riverbank, with one wing toward the river and the other toward the still water of a deep pool", which describes the ford area in the hours preceding battle. Any Norse army beside the river were visible to the Mercians while the other 'wing' reported here would be out of their sight.

The reverse situation pertained for the Northumbrians, and it is this inability to oversee the whole battlefield which would soon be crucial.

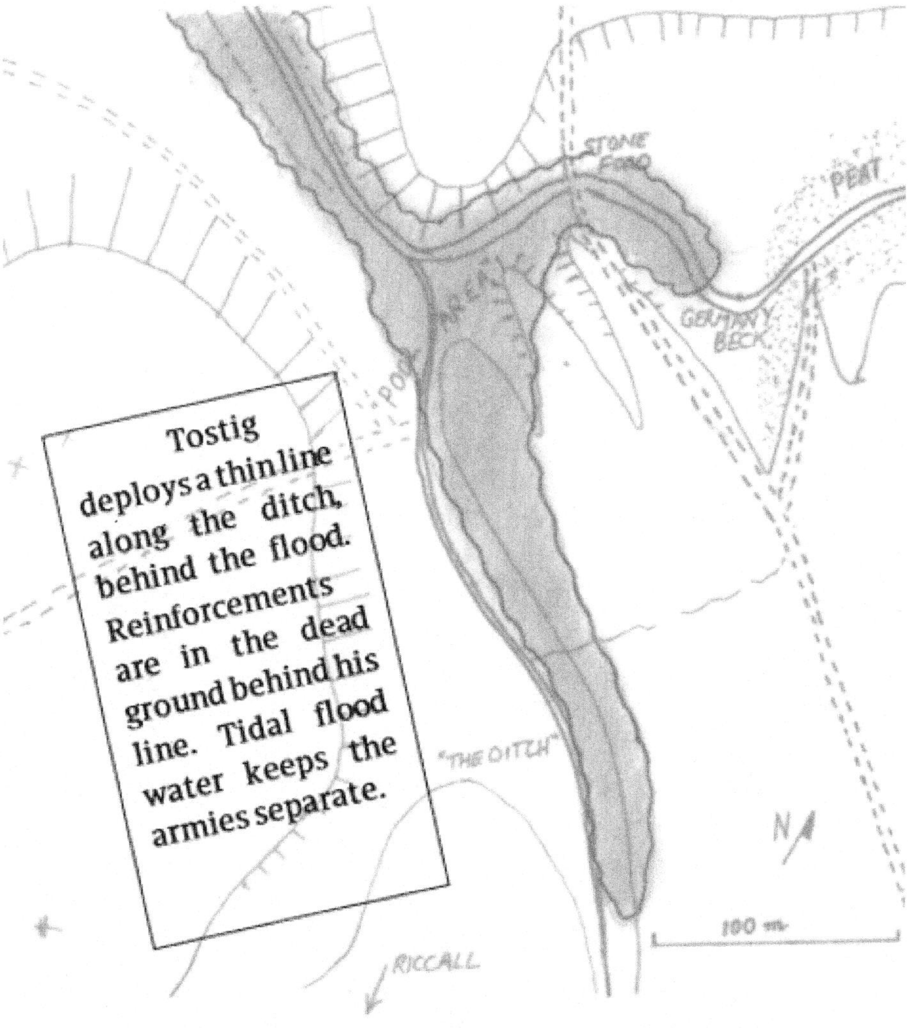

Another source explains the deployment in this way: 'The king's standard was close to the river, where his battle array was densest, while it was thinnest by the pool.' We are also offered the observation that the troops at the pool 'were least reliable' noting that 'when the attack was made, that wing gave way'. Whether deploying the less reliable troops, and having the thinnest line there, was a ploy, an excuse, or simply an observation cannot be known.

All these can be argued but subsequent events favour this as a tactical trick. Since there was no need to make excuses after the victory it does suggest that the writer of this verse was privy to information that is not reported by others and the informant was presumably part of Harald's contingent.

These references to the deep pool can be uniquely identified as the location of the ford. The pool then drained across the waterlogged fenland to enter the river where the Mercians had assembled to prevent the enemy crossing. The descriptions of the water do vary but reporting whether it was rising and falling, a stream, pool or lake, plus the various ways the landscape is described provides a rough time stamp for the battle actions and each help define the location of each reporter.

A good plan would involve temping the Northumbrians to attack across the ford as the alternative was to assault the strong position with its narrow front on the defenders' side. The invaders recognised that this would require a long and bloody battle where they risked being swamped when the tide surged back if they did not break through. If a weak-looking force headed by Tostig could tempt Morcar to attack, it would serve to draw the whole Northumbrian army onto the Norse-occupied, south bank.

We cannot rule out that the skalds were indeed making an excuse by portraying the events that unfolded as part of Harald's battle plan but there were tactical advantages that would accrue from allowing themselves to be driven back. On balance the events favour the suggestion that this was indeed part of Harald's clever trap. The weak deployment was probably a ploy.

An assemblage of arrowheads found when the site was investigated permits some speculation of the atmosphere in the build-up to the battle. We noted that the armies arriving from Riccall and Harald's landing army had an extensive area of sunken ground that could not have been overlooked by their enemy. An added incentive was the desire to stay out of range of archers, ironically depriving the defenders of any appreciation of the growing threat. The find-location of one arrow suggests that the Mercian archers could achieve a range of over 100 metres which would have corralled the invaders in the dead ground behind Fulford Hall.

One might imagine the feelings experienced by the overnight guard that Morcar had placed on the north side of the ford as the undulating ground began to fill with enemy warriors. They knew the slowly ebbing tide would bring them to battle within a few hours. Previously some small comfort lay in their ignorance of the size of the army opposing which could not be fully appreciated. Now they knew this was indeed a new army brought by Tostig rather than the containable force that had landed the previous evening.

They would have doubtless dispatched urgent messages to inform their earl of their assessment, emphasising the vulnerability even given their excellent defensive position. This probably only served to reinforce the observation delivered by his brother, Edwin, whose men had earlier realised that significant reinforcements were arriving from Riccall.

The role played by the limitations that communications play in battles of this era should be appreciated. The use of banners, perpetuated in British Army tradition of 'trooping the colour' to make sure soldiers would recognise their rally-point. Bugle calls and messenger had their value but they allowed for limited control in battle. Generals would favour a vantage point from where they could overlook all of the action. The problem that would determine the outcome of this battle was that the defenders, unlike King Harald, could only see half of the battlefield.

The force guarding the stone ford crossing would have been relieved by the arrival of Morcar with the news that the whole force was enroute from the city. One might speculate that the reorganisation was something of a relief as this distraction denied them time to ponder what was about to happen. Morcar had a long flat ledge, overlooking the beck, to array his army as they arrived from York.

Tostig's deployment was more complex. It is no trivial task to organise and move several thousand troops across uneven land in order to ensure they are in position to play the part conceived for them.

Although the sources do not explicitly say Tostig's group was expected to give ground as the weaker army, Harald was setting up a possible win-win situation for the invaders as he could sweep round behind the Northumbrians either by forcing a crossing of the beck where the Mercians had redeployed beside the river, or just surging round the rise where the hall was situated. The evidence from the arrowhead scatter is that this wily warrior did both.

Nowhere does Harald confide his plan to us but his deployments are strongly suggestive that he had already choreographed a number of battle plans that could play out over the next few hours.

Midday

As the middle of the day approached, the tide was halfway through the eight-hour ebb. For nearly four hours the water had seemed to stand still but now a gentle ebb was evident, in a pattern repeated to this day,[98] slowly exposing more of the bank. The pace of draining water would accelerate in a pattern similar, but not as dramatic, as the tidal bore itself. In the half hour before the next tidal surge arrived, the Ouse would appear almost empty with a narrow, stream gushing towards the oncoming wall of water. But that was still several hours away.

One Norse source describing events tells us that the water in the pool was 'still', reflecting that point in the tide cycle in the hours before the ebb-flow became noticeable. This might suggest that it was as late as two hours after midday before the battle began.

Much of the water was still to drain along the rivers and becks although the water trapped on the Ings would remain and be topped up by the next tide that was due in the early evening. The water filling the ford was now visibly flowing into the ebbing Ouse. Even Harald might have been impressed by the actions of this extraordinary tide that Tostig had suggested could offer them an easy victory.

One hundred metres separated the opposing shieldwalls arrayed for battle although still separated by water which was now visibly falling. They would be near enough to shout insults and war cries. Tradition suggests that the chant favoured by defenders confronting earlier Viking invasions was the single word, 'out'.

The scene was set for the first of the three battles that would decide the fate not only of King Harold Godwinson, England but the Anglo-Saxon nation.

Morcar's charge

Heimskringla gives us the clearest description of how the battle began. It was Morcar's force that 'advanced downwards along the ditch' into 'the arm of the Northmen's line which was at the ditch' that gave way and 'the banner of Earl Morcar advanced then bravely' and 'the Englishmen followed, thinking the Northmen would fly'.

It is worth picking this accurate, if economical description apart to place it within the understood landscape and timetable.

---

[98] Visible below the lock at Naburn.

Tostig's deployment would look impressive as it spread along the ditch that flowed into Germany Beck. His left flank was protected by the slowly draining pool. The gentle slope on which Tostig's army was deployed would display the depth, or shallowness, of his army to the Northumbrians. It apparently lacked depth.

Tostig had seen the flooded land surface many times and recognised the complex folds concealed below the water. Because his army did not share this knowledge of the local landscape, any hasty advance could disrupt the continuity of his shieldwall deployed along the edge of the undulating natural amphitheatre south and west of the ford and almost perpendicular to the ford-road. Edging forward aggressively as the water receded made little tactical sense.

The literature makes no mention of any movement by the invaders after this deployment, but we have noted that these early sources provide limited tactical details. We are given a start state and told how it ends. So the tactical movements must be surmised which the landscape permits, with reasonable confidence.

However, staying along this ditch supports the suggestion that the 'weak' line was part of the ploy to invite the attackers onto their side of the beck. They did not follow the retreating water toward the uncertain terrain concealed by the 'pool'. Tostig's apparent failure to press forward was part of his plan. He had aligned his troops on the ground where he wanted to fight the battle.

Morcar's perspective, and assessment, from the opposite bank was quite different. From the slight height advantage afforded from his location, Morcar might now have noted Tostig's shallow line was being bolstered by troops arriving from their base at Riccall. The thin line of shields was growing in depth if not in length. The longer he delayed, the larger the opposing army grew. This was certainly an incentive to attack sooner rather than delay. If the opposing army could be driven off while the flooding protected his own flanks. There was even the prospect of the English earls actually encircling Harald.

The dilemma for Morcar was not only the reinforcements. In a few hours, his right flank beside the river would be vulnerable as the tide ebbed. For now, however, the water not only protected his brother beside the Ouse but blocked at least half of Tostig's line who faced the ditch. A plan to go and attack the exposed part of the enemy was tempting.

Timing in battle is important and momentum multiplies the potency of any army when it is moving forward. So far, the initiative had all been with the invaders. The morale of the Northumbrians, observing a shieldwall that they were confident they could break, would be high especially as the army of Harald and his best men beside the river were both out of sight and probably out of everybody's calculations for now. It suited the experienced warrior to tempt the young earl to cross the beck and charge.

Watching from his own vantage point near Water Fulford Hall, Harald had the best view of the battlefield. He was able to observe his enemies: Led by Edwin, some were advancing steadily beside the river to try and secure that flank, plus he could see that the full army of the Northumbrian was now guarding the north bank at the ebbing ford. He was a general of unmatched experience in Europe. His well-tried winning way was to get his enemy committed before unleashing his strong reserve the moment he discovered a weak spot.

He waited to see if the young earl could be tempted to cross the ford and attack. Failing that he could tell Tostig to advance across the ditch and charge into the ford, once it drained, and then launch his own outflanking attack beside the river to encircle the Northumbrians. Morcar probably also recognised that his enemy would in due course have some attacking options of their own.

Morcar had his overnight ford-guard, who were ready and fresh, to lead an attack. They were now reinforced by the sweaty warriors who had recently rushed from the city ready to follow. These new arrivals might have enjoyed a short pause to catch their breath, grab a drink and take in the situation. The numbers appeared favourable to Morcar who had about 4000 refreshed, trained and equipped troops. It looked as if Tostig currently had a smaller army that was thinly spread who had themselves dashed for three hours from Riccall that same morning.

Two options were available to Morcar: He could stand on the higher ground and wait for his enemy to attack through the muddy ditch and battle uphill. As noted, this was a truly excellent defensive position with exceptional flank protection, at least for now. We have no reports of wise heads suggesting that if they stayed in that position, it would be very hard to dislodge them. Even if the Mercians guarding the riverbank were swept aside, the Northumbrians would be well placed to counter this outflanking advance once it reached them defending the high ground. And the fresh flood would imperil any attacker who did not make it back to high ground.

This would seem in strictly military terms to be Morcar's best option but it risked opening the river route into York to his enemy.

His other option was to charge across the ford as a column and burst through the enemy by overwhelming them at their weakest point, on their right flank, before rolling them up as more Northumbrians crossed the ford. In assessing the options, the vulnerability of the riverbank being defended by his brother might have been an issue because a successful charge by Morcar could actually counter Harald and Tostig's whole plan to outflank them. What if they could surge through Tostig's line and force the invaders back to the boats? The Mercians could then help finish the invaders off once the tide ebbed. This had some risks but was not an unreasonable plan, given what they could see.

In the light of the excellent tactical judgement shown so far, the defenders possibly did consider the 'stand your ground' option and rejected it. Perhaps those who had rebelled wanted a quick resolution with Tostig so were prepared to adopt a 'death or glory' stratagem. Attack was a risky but a sound military option based on what the Northumbrians had gathered about the size of their opposition and the way the landscape would evolve as the water emptied into the Ouse.

Attacking would seize the initiative from the invaders and Morcar would regain some ability to dictate the course of events. His army had done too much waiting about between rushed redeployments over the previous days. With local advantage, the Northumbrians knew about the stone base of the crossing and its embanked ford, constructed in Roman times. Wading through water, even if it was only ankle-deep, would unquestionably reduce their mobility, potentially rendering those crossing vulnerable. But a fold in the land and the distance Tostig stood back from the beck worked to the advantage of the defenders. Perhaps this was part of the deliberate trap Tostig had set. In these unique circumstances, it seemed like a reasonable tactical decision to take the initiative and cross before the invaders mustered the confidence to close on the ford once the land drained.

Another topographic feature worked in favour of Morcar's men. The approach road on the enemy's south side of the ford does not lead towards the centre but close to one end of Tostig's line. This 'loose end' was Tostig's right flank and also furthest away from the dead ground where fresh soldiers could be fed in after their march from Riccall. It was a tempting target, and the Northumbrian charge would exploit this weakness in Tostig's shieldwall deployment that was spread at least 300 metres across the embankment. The full might of a charge would quickly break any line, even one that was 10 men deep. Inertia and momentum would be with the attackers. After they breached the wall they would wheel to the right and start to 'roll up' the invaders line before Tostig had time to realign.

A fold in the land where the Romans had built their road would afford Morcar's charge another element of surprise as it would not be overlooked while they assembled to attack. Nor would Tostig's line be able to wheel towards the attack at one end of their line as two similar folds in the landscape were still filled with water.[99] However their actions would soon be visible to those positioned at the right end of Tostig's line. It is possible that they responded by wading across the ditch to their front to go and meet this threat, but they likely just stood their ground.

So after splashing though the ford and assembling perhaps 500 warriors, almost unseen, battle commenced. The charge worked. Morcar's momentum carried them forward. And ' the Northmen's [Tostig's] line at the ditch gave way' and the Englishmen followed 'thinking the Northmen would fly.' The flow of Northumbrian warriors would crash into the line which had been compromised. This was not a head-on clash between shieldwalls but was an attack that came to the invaders from their right side. So 'the banner of Earl Morcar advanced then bravely.' This advancing banner was not just an incentive but the basis of all training and the Northumbrian soldiers had an obligation to follow.

Morcar had momentum and with enough troops behind him, this assault had the energy necessary to keep moving forward. The slope along which Tostig had deployed initially favoured the defenders, but it would have been relatively easy to use the 'step' drill with the shieldwall advancing rhythmically as a unit, to push the invaders back. The relentless short steps of the whole wall created a force that was hard to resist. To stand your ground risked being unbalanced and to stumble or fall in this situation would be fatal.

If progress slowed, the English might also have launched a series of small surges. The wild boar, a close relative of the domesticated pig, was well-known for breaking cover and charging those threatening it. The momentum of the charge would knock the hunter back even as the beast, hopefully, impaled itself on his spear. This formation relied on momentum

[99] This seems to have been the preferred route for those riding horses in subsequent centuries as many 12/14C horseshoes were lost in the muddy ford.

to burst through the shieldwall. These wedge-shape groups could have assaulted the invaders line that had now been outflanked.

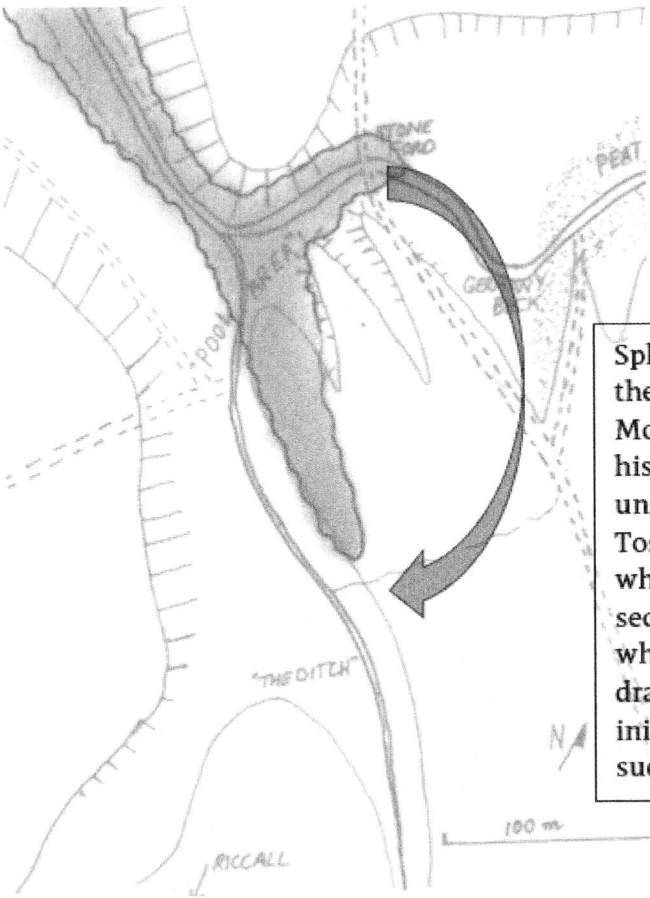

Splashing across the stone ford-road, Morcar could move his army, almost unseen, to attack Tostig's right flank which was the only section of his line where the ditch had drained. Their initial charge was successful.

When the charge succeeded in breaking the opponent's shieldwall warriors could attack the unprotected interior where spears and axes required both hands, leaving their shield slung over their back. The hope was to make a full breach in the line and then expand to attack from the rear while fresh Northumbrian troops arrived to keep the enemy front line focused on that danger.

To defeat this stratagem the enemy had to envelop the attackers.[100] As the road out of the ford had brought the attack on the righthand end of Tostig's line, he was likely some distance from the opening action and one might imagine those around him starting to forming a new line, a second shieldwall, which was oriented to meet the threat from their side. But much of his army could not immediately engage as they stood overlooking the pool. Their movements were restricted and they could only turn to meet the developing threat.

There was likely some noticeable degree of confused movement along the Norse line as they adapted to the new alignments. Morcar's warriors, watching the invaders peeling away from the pool to form a new right flank, might have interpreted this as them fleeing the battle which is noted in reports. In fact they were likely rushing to hold the line and contain Morcar's charge but on the Fulford landscape they would have been out of sight while they redeployed.

The rising ground onto which the Norse were retreating would start to favour them as they neared the original centre of Tostig's line where the high point allowed him to observe and to be seen. This compression and realignment increased Tostig's line's density significantly.

There are metrics which can be employed to assess the way crowds move. These reveal that groups move much slower compared to mobility of an individual. This successful opening phase for the Northumbrians would have lasted perhaps 30 minutes which is the time it would take for Morcar's army to cross and for Tostig's line to be stabilised by realignment.

The arc of Morcar's advance now began to stretch the advancing shieldwall of the Northumbrians, widening the front and reducing the momentum as the depth of their wall thinned. The geometry of the land surface, which has since been levelled to provide a sports field, was challenging for both sides as an advance of just 40 metres doubled the length of the line in contact on the undulating terrain where three 'fingers' of land seemed to reach towards the beck.

In the normal push and hack of close-quarter fighting among fresh warriors, the integrity of a wall of shields could hold. Only much later, when tiredness and lack of replacements became a factor, would the shieldwall develop gaps. But at this early stage, the shieldwall was quickly

---

[100] The charge by Harold's brother Gyrth and Leofwine at Hastings illustrates how a breakthrough can quickly lead to isolation when a capable general can deploy a counter attack.

repaired and both sides moved tactically to ensure their opposing walls remained intact. After the initial drive it was only the weight of numbers which could drive one side forward.

The first English chronicle of the battle, Symeon agrees that '..at the first onset of the fight [the Northumbrians] overthrew many;..' The armies were now fully engaged. The lines were drawn and a trial of strength began. Courage and determination would normally determine the outcome. At Fulford, as we have seen, the water and the landscape would play a significant role in determining victory.

Each exhausting and possibly lethal mêlée might last a few minutes with each one denting the opponent's line. These probing attacks would go on as each side sought to break the continuity of the opposing shield wall. This style of attritional warfare is attested in the fortuitous survival of one epic poem describing the Battle of Maldon which continues until one side is unable to re-form the line after which fighting becomes innumerable micro battles for group and personal survival.

Fighting is an exhausting business. Those at the front of the shieldwall could be expected to maintain contact for no more than five or ten minutes before pausing for breath. So after a rush at the opposing shieldwall, those at the front might attempt to change places with those behind unless both sides needed a pause and for a short time, the pressure abated. If their shield had been hacked by sword or axe it would be imperative to move behind those who could afford some protection and seek a replacement with ample evidence that such spares were available.

There was plenty of killing and wounding work for those just behind the front shields, especially during any pauses when the intense pressure was relieved. They could stab in many directions exploiting the long shafts of their battle spear which required both hands to thrust into any tempting gaps. The axe was another two-handed weapon and both of these weapons relied on others' shields for protection; A swinging axe would provide some respite for those in the front as the opposition swayed to keep out of range.

This was a trial of strength and stamina. Whatever difference existed between the armies might be noted in the combat experience. The English had enjoyed a generation of peace, were at a disadvantage compared to the invaders who were probably mostly battle-hardened during the Danish wars. After perhaps an hour of gory progress, the leading English fighters would be tired if still exhilarated because of their earlier progress. But the Norse formation was still holding, perhaps reinforced by fresh arrivals from

Riccall. It was now literally an uphill battle for the attackers whose line had to lengthen as they pressed the invaders back while the falling tide exposed their right flank.

Observers

Morcar's early progress was unseen by Earl Edwin and his Mercian contingent guarding the river flank. Their focus was on consolidating their hold on the riverbank after completing their redeployment from the west to the east bank of the Ouse. They probably knew little of the initial success at the ford although the noise of battle would have filtered over the landscape to them. There was no way for the brothers to see the other or receive timely messages. The flooded Ings now stood between the brothers.

The ebbing tide continued to transform their landscape. Islands emerged that joined to form causeways and then a broad walkway along the riverbank. They could see that a matching, broader path was emerging on the invaders side of the beck and experienced Mercian leaders knew that the land would soon allow a charge, if that was Harald's plan.

The environment would again favour the attacker as momentum was with those charging forward. The small contingent of Mercians were in no position to take the initiative and they would have to prepare to stand their ground. Their best hope was to get close to the 'V' shaped ditch where Germany Beck drained into the Ouse as any charge would lose momentum when they emerged from the beck having waded through the ebbing water in the beck as it flowed into the Ouse.

Although the whole land surface of the Ings has risen by nearly 2 metres since the time of the battle, the shape has changed little. The place where the beck flows into the Ouse has migrated just 20 metres upstream (roughly north) and the present banks are steeper than those revealed when the area was excavated to replace the foul-water drain that runs from the city to the treatment plant at Naburn. The beck itself used to flow diagonally across the field although in the 19th century it was diverted around the edge of the landholding in what was called a 'Dutch River'.

Meanwhile Harald was also observing events, exploiting an advantage denied to the other commanders on the field that day to observe the entire battle. He might have smiled to see that much of the Mercian army was still stranded on the wrong side of the river and perhaps grudgingly recognised the effective way that some of Edwin's contingent had redeployed to block the riverbank. He had observed the size and deployment of Morcar's force as well as the way Tostig was now holding his army together after the initial shock of the Northumbrian charge. The way Morcar's attack had fallen on the right flank of Tostig's line might have been more effective than expected but, ironically, its success had drawn the enemy onto the ground of his choosing.

One might speculate that King Harald and his army still kept their low profile during this time. He knew his enemy could not easily plan for what they could not see. The time and place to deploy his reserve was approaching. Fresh soldiers are what he required for the moves that he was planning.

Generals always hope to find and exploit a weakness in their enemy. Morcar had successfully exploited a weak spot but Tostig had stabilised it after falling back. The genius of King Harald is that he appears to have actually orchestrated this distraction to fully engage his adversary and blind them to how quickly the fortunes of battle can be changed. Harald's ploy of a weak-looking line had engineered such an exposure.

Harald was nevertheless aware that Tostig's line had been under pressure for some time and Norse sources confirm that the English thought the Norse line might be put to flight. But those same sources inform us that behind Tostig's line, out of sight near the river, were Harald's fresh 'best men'.

We cannot know how many options Harald was weighing. A breakthrough by Morcar, that would follow any collapse of Tostig's shieldwall, would seriously threaten his own force. Many generals might have rushed to reinforce Tostig's line immediately with their veteran troops and this was a conventional tactical option. He could have employed the tactical advantage of surprise using fresh troops to outflank either edge of Morcar's army. But that was not the course of action he chose.

It is a mark of the experience of Harald that he did not follow the obvious courses. Having divided the English armies, he was looking to decapitate the opposition not just to defeat them. He did not want a slogging match as the locals could call-up reserves whereas his casualties could not quickly be replaced. A decisive, if hard won victory over Morcar would still leave the Mercians undefeated, requiring another battle and Harald had a plan to make today the decisive victory over both earls.

Extending Tostig's predicament also suited Harald for a number of reasons, political and tactical. Tostig would be put in his proper place when Harald 'rescued' him because everybody would recognise who had saved and won the battle. Harald, the consummate tactician, wanted to allow all of the Northumbrian army to cross the beck, leaving no troops to block his planned encirclement and it would take a full hour at the very least for 4000 warriors to cross at the narrow ford road. All the time that the battle continued Morcar's men were exhausting their energy and resilience. Patience was something only a confident general like Harald could exercise.

Harald hated coming second. In his old age he is reported to have become an even worse loser. His plan might seem like a gamble but that is the nature of warfare and it was the game he had successfully played all his life. Rushing to help Tostig was the response of a cautious commander who would not want to risk a breakthrough that might then threaten his own army. He was waiting for the tide to fall so he could spring his own traps with two outflanking attacks.

But Harald was not entirely the master of events. His actions were still constrained by the complex interactions of tide and landscape. For much of the day these elements had enforced a patient approach. The falling tide also allowed the front occupied by the Mercians beside the river to stretch a little inland. The Mercians were being reinforced and soon they might even be strong enough to block the crossing and to occupy the levée that ran beside the beck. This was the route which he planned in order to capture the north end of the stone ford and isolate Morcar's army.

Fine margins can decide battles. Some observers might have doubted the military wisdom of throwing his special troops against some opposition beside the river that posed no actual threat. Harald however chose these options because it was the one that could defeat both of the brother earls opposing him.

Preparations at the bank

Blocking the riverbank had been a challenge for Edwin. The issue was one of quality rather than quantity. The Mercian shieldwall had only to be wide enough to block the levée beside the River Ouse. A mere ten or twenty warriors might plug this gap standing shoulder to shoulder with their shields overlapping, at least until the tide ebbed. However, it would have been foolish to deploy such a small force as it would invite destruction because all knew the strength of a shieldwall lies in its depth. The shieldwall would need to cover a greater front as the day wore on and a little more dry land was exposed.

We noted earlier that the sources seem confused between Earl Edwin and Earl Waltheof and for clarity, the actions and orders are attributed to the senior earl, Edwin, who we know commanded the Mercians. Waltheof would have had little time since his appointment as Earl of Huntingdon, just months before, to recruit a force of his personal hearthtroops. It is suggested here that Waltheof was prominent and possibly in the front line of the defence. We later learn that one contingent of this blocking force escaped back to York and that was led by Earl Waltheof. From this we might deduce that he was either guarding the Ings-flank or at the rear.

Edwin would certainly have sent his housecarls and they would typically number over 100 for one of the premier earls in England who had been mobilised for a full year by this time. Local logistics suggest horsepower was employed to shuttle warriors and their weapons from the west to the east bank to effect the lateral move of less than 100m, but which required a trip of about 6km with the final kilometre through the waterlogged Ings.

This fenland flood plain extends all the way to the city but there is one place, where a Roman era palisade has recently been identified on dry, higher ground which extends almost to the riverbank. Edwin's force could assemble here but the journey along the bank to reinforce the blockade at the crossing would have to be on foot. The first troops could begin their move not much before 10 that morning at which time the levée allowed progress in single file but two hours later they could progress at least two abreast as the level of the water fell. The narrow, well beaten popular path beside the river had centuries worth of pottery fragments as a pavement which prevented the pounding feet making it impassable in peace or war.

Edwin might have had his last meeting with his brother at this point where, in later centuries, the settlement called Gate Fulford would be established. While Morcar was moving his army along the high ground towards the ford, Edwin led his small force down to, and then along, the river. The saga descriptions of the army moving in single file, 'down along' the river describes the only way they could reach their position at the ford.

It might have felt like an inglorious way to move to such a key position, but stepping carefully along the levée was vital. To slip down the riverbank would be fatal and wading through the water-filled ings was both hard-going and would churn the mud quickly rendering it impassable to those following. It would have taken about 20 minutes to carefully tread this narrow path to reach their position. This was a well-disciplined move otherwise it would have failed and quite simply got bogged down.

The narrow section of shieldwall that they needed to form had the steep riverbank to protect its right flank while the Ings providing an obstacle to any troops trying to get past them inland on their left flank. To their front was the steep embankment of the Ouse watershed with the beck. This shieldwall 'plug' might have edged slowly forward as the tide ebbed with a painful slowness until they overlooked the place where the beck flowed into the river. Some Mercian warriors doubtless deployed along this inland levée as soon as the tide allowed, extending the shield wall. These brave soldiers, and we speculate that Waltheof was one leader, would be particularly vulnerable. If those plugging the riverbank were forced to step back even a few metres, they could be attacked from the side.

The site and form of this junction was investigated when the foul-water drains that serve to take York's effluent to the Naburn treatment works was built.[101] Its location has changed little although the land sloped more gently on both sides to provide a path into town. No evidence of any stepping stones was noted although it is feasible that this ford was given a solid base from time to time.

This modest shieldwall might actually prove a difficult roadblock to destroy but it was only necessary for Harald's invaders to displace it. Rather in the way of a sporting scrum, with the sides locked together, it would only require the Mercians to be forced 10 meters back to open the way for other invaders to start along another levée to get behind Morcar's advancing army, 300m east at the ford, across which Morcar's men had successfully surged. The defenders recognised this but there was little more they could do to prepare to resist any forceful charge. Perhaps they fixed some spears in the ground to slow the charge. Perhaps they improvised a barrier from material that had been flushed along by the bore. Such details go unreported.

[101] Sadly, although the shape of the land surface was confirmed, the opportunity to undertake some relevant archaeology was blocked, with the contractor's archaeologists regularly noting they had found "no evidence for the battle" without specifying what evidence they were 'expecting'. This obstruction extended to preventing inspection of the metal finds. The final irony was that the microfilm of the finds is hermetically sealed and there is no protocol to open and inspect the photographic record of these finds. The real purpose of heritage investigation does not seem to be understood by those charged with its governance.

A few spear thrusts at the legs of the defenders by Harald's 'storm troops'[102] when they started up the bank might have been all that was required to unbalance the leading Mercian shields. Just as Morcar had achieved his initial success with a charge, it would soon be the turn of the invaders to demonstrate the temporary advantage that momentum offers to those charging into battle. The Mercians might slow them and dissipate some of the force but ultimately would have been forced to yield this foothold.

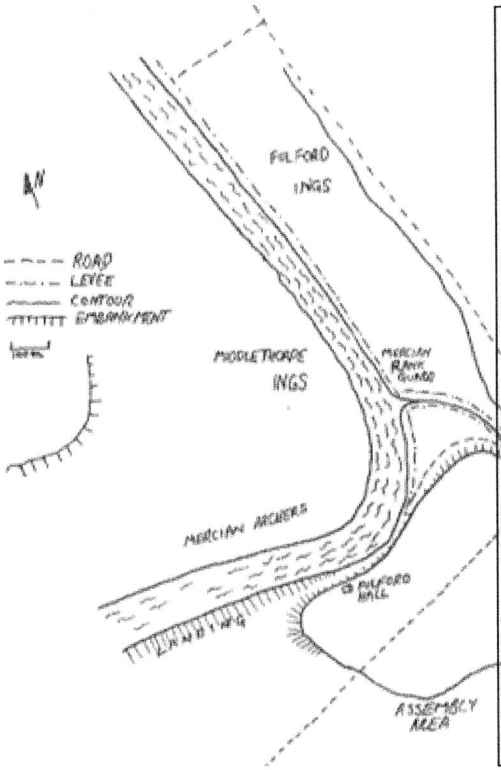

Earl Edwin led some Mercian troops, previously deployed on the west bank of Ouse, to block the opposite riverside path that would be exposed when the tide fell.

The Norse sources record this small force moving in single file, wading along the path between the flooded river and the boggy Ings to reach their position.

This crossing would allow the Norse to occupy the ford and cut off any retreat of the Northumbrian army after King Harald's counterattack.

Mercian archers poured arrows onto the Norse army when they made their charge.

But this was in the future. Now there was just that awful fear-filled wait for events to unfold. In front of them they could probably see some isolated invaders but standing 100m back at the bend in the river. Around this right-angle bend they could see the fleet of ships drawn up the bank. They might have hoped that by occupying the riverbank, and blocking this obvious attack vector, the invaders would turn their attention elsewhere.

The Mercian move the previous evening to block any crossing to the north bank had possibly produced the hoped-for effect as the invaders had not

[102] Earl Orre who led this charge across the beck has the abortive relief mission at Stamford Bridge named in his honour, 'Orre's Storm'.

taken that option. The invaders had not tried to outflank the city or to use their ships to occupy the city. Perhaps deterrence might work again. They might have hoped that their job was done because most commanders would not launch their best troops against what seemed like a sideshow. Deploying the whole army of the invaders to oppose Morcar was the obvious reaction and they might selfishly have hoped that would be the invaders next move.

Across the river they could also hear the shouts of encouragement from the rest of the Mercian army and it is certain that the sounds of Morcar's battle reached them. Their comrades on the other bank might have told them that things appeared to be going well as they had a slightly better, but not a clear view, of the whole battle. However, those in the thick of the fighting perhaps appreciated that the initiative was slowly passing from the ascendant Northumbrians as Tostig was able to bring more of his troops to bear and arrest Morcar's charge.

Afternoon

"They [The Norse Invaders] met at that river which is the upper Ouse[103], and there the hardest fight arises, and is kept up till 'nones' [mid-afternoon in this context]." Morcar's battle beyond the ford had developed into a bloody clash dictated by the ferocity of his men, who stood to lose everything if Tostig triumphed.

The experienced Harald who had observed the battle developing was now ready to make his move. The tide that would rush back at dusk would not wait. The cycle of tides he had observed for a day would now transform the landscape to his advantage. *Heimskringla*, which reports the battle from Harald's perspective, notes that the English had come to the ditch along which Tostig had arrayed his 'weaker arm' and that had worked well to the old warriors advantage.

The turning point

As a prelude to his counter-attack Harald 'ordered a war-blast to be blown and urged them on.' Now, all along the line, the Norsemen stood their ground and any remaining reinforcements moved forward to bolster Tostig's shieldwall.

The use of such signals is also reported in *Heimskringla* when King Olaf, Harald's much older half-brother, 'ordered the whole army to be gathered

[103] It is possible that this term is referring to Germany Beck, which flows into the Ouse.

by the war trumpets into battle array' suggesting the war-horn was routinely employed to signal to the army at that time. We are nowhere told if there was a well-rehearsed set of signals analogous to the trumpet calls employed for battlefield communications by later European armies, but for a signal to be effective its meaning must have either been rehearsed or already be well understood.[104]

The effect of such a signal along the whole length of Tostig's line was designed to arrest the progress of Morcar's charge. Stability was a necessary prelude to any counterattack by Harald's elite force. This stiffening of the line served several purposes. English warriors would now have their whole attention focused to their front to ensure their personal survival. Such a surge would also prevent any English war bands going to aid parts of the line that were under pressure. Harald needed to be sure this line would hold otherwise he risked Morcar's charge getting behind his own troops. The arrival of fresh troops to do battle with the tiring Northumbrians should help ensure Morcar's men would make no more progress.

There could be no fresh Northumbrian reinforcements available to be fed into their overstretched line that had rushed over the ford to match these fresh arrivals of Norsemen from Riccall, and estimates suggest the numbers were balanced. Indeed, a named unit who came from near modern Bergen we are later told were given the task of pursuing Morcar during his retreat, possibly hinting that they were given this job as they had fresh legs, being among the last to arrive at Fulford from the Riccall base.

This sequence of events was not haphazard nor exploiting a sudden opportunity. The complexity and random occurrences of any battle prevent precise planning but Harald had set traps. He had offered an attractive 'sacrifice' to Morcar hoping that he would accept it. The elation of success perhaps made Morcar unaware, or bravely mindless, of any force Harald might still hold in reserve.

Those compiling the Kings' Sagas three centuries later knew the outcome. This is one simple expression of the entire battle sequence: "When King Harald saw that the English array had come to the ditch against him, he ordered the charge to be sounded, and urged on his men. He ordered the

[104] **Surviving images of Roman 'trumpets' whose horn would emit its blast well above the heads of embattled legionnaires seems designed for battlefield communication.**

banner which was called the Land-ravager to be carried before him, and made so severe an assault that all had to give way before it;" [105]

There is no explicit mention of the battle with the Mercians beside the river bank in this particular saga version and the explanation offered is because no skald participated in the charge across the river. Others do record a two-pronged attack into the flank of the advancing English. In reconstructing the battle one must work with what is recorded and grateful that, for this battle, omissions of specifics from one account are rectified by details provided in the work of other saga-editions. A single saga cannot be relied on to tell the whole story and at Fulford some remarkable finds even survived to corroborate the two attacks that will decide the fate of this battle.

Arrows

Most of the Mercians, still stranded on the west bank, were able to provide more than just a unique narrative for us and perhaps give some shouts of moral support to their comrades on the opposite bank. It is an extraordinary aspect of this battle that so many warriors were unwilling spectators to actions taking place just metres away, across the river.

These spectators had not been entirely inactive. The whole area where the boats had landed, as well as the rising land on the south of the beck, yielded a remarkable haul of tanged arrow heads. These weapons would have kept the invaders at bay and deterred them from encroaching on the riverbank.

Any Norse invaders who approached the river were well within the range of archers on the north bank. Whether it was a part of the plan or simply a frustrated response to their isolation and inability to move to the other bank in time, the residual Mercian army could rain arrows on any warriors advancing towards Germany Beck. Ironically, it was perhaps this rain of iron arrows that obliged the invaders to keep out of sight and denying the defenders a full appreciation of the forces mustering against them.

Several arrowheads were found 200m, and one 300m from the north bank[106]. Perhaps the most powerful bows and the strongest archers were employed to arc their missiles into areas where the Norse might have hoped for some refuge from the direct fire of these deadly arrowheads.

---

[105] *Heimskringla 88*. THE BATTLE AT THE HUMBER.

[106] The range was just over 100 metre if the archer had moved around the bend in the river to shoot, which seems more likely.

These lobbed arrows were indirect missiles designed to disconcert the invaders. Firing at maximum range, they were at least making some contribution to the battle at the ford even though these soldiers had been sidelined.

As soon as any Norse warriors assembled for their attack along the riverbank however, they would be 50 to 70 metres from these Mercian archers and in need of their shields for protection from the arrow storm. Those who had ventured into this danger zone earlier in the day had doubtless discovered the force of bowmen that had assembled. These Mercians had laid their normal arms aside and equipped themselves with bows. Responding to the blast of the war horn would put Harald's reserve within range of aimed, rather than lobbed, shots as the Norse reserve prepared to charge into battle.

The flight time of an arrow means the twang of the bow will arrive before the projectile. At hunting ranges, typically less than 20m, there would be little time for an animal to react, but across the span of the River Ouse there would be just enough time to raise a shield against a sniper-arrowshot. The greater the distance, the more the archer has to loft his arrow. Over short distances, the trajectory is relatively flat but when working at ranges over 100m, the arrow would be shot skywards. At Stamford Bridge, Harald would order his men to raise their shields, suggesting the use of such volleys of arrows was expected.

A single archer can harass but when employed as a tactical battle-weapon, arrows need to be released in volleys. When the target is massed in close formation it does not afford an individual warrior the chance to take evasive action plus there is no obvious safe space if there is a shower of arrows incoming except beneath some interlocked shields. The light wooden boards of the shield would stop a lofted arrow and the Bayeux Tapestry depicts many shields still peppered with missiles.

There were two surviving concentrations of arrowhead finds. One close to the hall and the other on the rising ground where Morcar had been forcing Tostig's line back. The assembly area of Harald's reserves beside the Ouse bank, below the hall, was an obvious target for volleys of arrows and this storm would continue until the enemy were out of sight, out of range or the supply of missiles was exhausted.

The identified find-concentrations do not imply that these were the only areas targeted. Archaeologists have to be content with what has actually survived and in a place where it can actually be found. Twice the ground between the two assemblages identified has been excavated in the last century to lay foul-water drains to the nearby treatment plant at Naburn. The regular flooding has deposited fine alluvial material at the average rate of 1.6mm per year raising the surface by at least 1.5m since the time of the battle. Such a depth puts them well below the level where small objects can be detected by even the most sensitive equipment so it is only in areas near the flood-line or disturbed by the pipe excavations that arrows have been found.[107]

Not all the arrowheads would have remained in situ. Some would have been gathered during or after the battle and possibly those with broken points were ignored, leaving the evidence for us to find nearly a millennium later.[108] But another ghoulish explanation is that the area devoid of arrowhead finds was covered with soldiers who 'prevented' the arrows getting lost in the ground nearly 1000 years ago.

It is possible that some missiles broke on impact and that might indeed have been a feature of their design because the later socketed arrows are recorded as being harvested and returned during a battle. However, copies of these thin blades survived impact so it is possible that the tip damage was a result of the tips being broken when they were removed from shields.

Unlike both of the subsequent battles in 1066, nowhere in the literature is the use of arrows noted at Fulford. This is ironic because Fulford is so far the only site to reveal that arrows were employed. Unlike the historians composing the Norse, Kings' Sagas, English scribes do not have the rich source of contemporary stories, set to verse, to employ. This might explain why the actions of the ordinary English warriors, who were employing their bows, go largely unrecorded.

We have some insightful observations of this turning point in the battle provided by Heming, an exiled Norse warrior who was possibly one of Earl Waltheof's men. He had been left stranded on west bank. He was therefore one of those in a position not only to observe the battle but to employ his bow against the Norse invaders.

---

[107] The possibility that these various disturbances brought the finds to the surface cannot be excluded.
[108] The process of rusting away is a common experience but this damp environment promoted concretion where the iron reacts to bind sand and stones into a cocoon encasing the object. The final shape once the object is 'sealed' looks quite unlike an arrow and for such thin pieces of iron can consume all the surviving metal, leaving only an imprint of the original arrow.

Some years before, it was Heming's skill with the bow that had upstaged King Harald in a competition and led to his departure for exile. In his saga, he actually takes credit for loosing the arrow that slashed Harald *Hardrada*'s throat during the battle at Stamford Bridge. Although this is impossible to verify, there is poetic justice in this claim.

The perspective of the battle now shifts to the riverbank and the way the invaders forced their way across the beck to get behind the advancing English. Edwin and his small contingent of Mercians would now be tested.

Storming the riverbank

The Mercians would inevitably have given ground: They 'made so hard an attack that all were driven back.' The key was how quickly they could recover the situation. Norse sources record that "Morcar's brother had had his standard brought along the river, downwards against the army of Harald" confirming that it was Edwin's Mercians who were defending the river although they never mention Edwin by name. This army is also not named in Norse sources although it is defined as not being the local army.

Since the invaders were downstream compared to the defenders, the fall of tide happened slightly but significantly minutes earlier for the invaders. Battle can be won and lost on such small margins. Unlike the narrow levée, the surface at the bend that lay on the invaders side was significantly wider because the pulse of each surging tide had deposited extra material as it changed direction at this dramatic right-angled bend in the river's course. The Norse army would not have to walk in single file but could storm the crossing on a surface that spanned about 40m between riverbank and waterlogged Ings.

" [Harald] had the standard 'Land-waster' carried forward". The location of Harald's standard would be a signal and rally-point for his warriors throughout the battle. The reputation of Norse banners evidently impressed the author of *Encomium Emma*, King Cnut's second wife and mother of the late King Edward, which records that.

"Now they had a banner possessed of a wonderfully strange nature, which though I believe it may seem incredible to the reader, nevertheless, because it is true, I will introduce the matter into my true history. For although it was woven of the plainest bright and white silk and had no figure embroidered on it yet always in time of war a raven seemed as it were to appear on it, in times of war a raven was always seen as if embroidered on it, in the hour of its owners' victory opening its beak and beating its wings, restless in its feet, but very quiet and drooping in its whole body in defeat."[109]

A well-drilled army can move quickly and decisively. Film and fiction support portrayals of armies that move as units and respond to commands, but these must have been practiced. Reality might have been a little more disordered but Harald had made a plan and there had been plenty of time to communicate it to the troops. Now the progress of his banner would steer the waiting warriors in the right direction if they had any doubts about where they should be.

The warriors storming the crossing beside the river bank were Harald's experienced fighters and they had learned to follow instructions to survive and normally be victorious. They had kept their heads low during the morning, probably exchanging soldierly speculations about what would happen next. They knew it was normal for their leader to hang back only to launch them to great effect once an opportunity presented itself. Their battle they hoped would be short but sweet.

Harald had a few surviving veterans who had fought with him in Bulgaria, Sicily or the Holy Land. They were now probably his commanders. He also had a younger generation who had experienced the long campaign against the Danes which had not produced any resounding victories. Indeed he had needed to employ cunning and not a few tactical retreats to extricate his army in recent battles against their powerful Danish neighbours.

The ships that had spared their bodies a long march on the day of the battle which probably meant that the eve of the battle was spent in some comfort as they could have their chest of personal items to fine tune the tools of their warrior trade before the battle. Axes were honed with a keen edge; spears were brought to a sharp point that would pierce any fabric or flesh it stabbed while those with swords would surely have had some rituals to prepare them for action. Everybody wanted to have a second shield. Arriving by ship gave them the luxury of having a supply of spare shields to hand, one gripped in their left hand and the other suspended over their

---

[109] *Encomium Emma* ed A Campbell 052162307 1998. Emma's Encomium addresses credibility, as does Snorri's *Heimskringla*. An example of reliability issue arises with Scotland's Fairy Flag. The provenance of the Land-waster and the Faire Flag allows them to be related quite possibly as one and the same. A discussion can be found in annex E.

shoulder which would prove its value against the arrow storm. They had passed a comfortable night, been fed, had no need to rise in the dark and been spared a three-hour dash from the Riccall base.

An archer can shoot no more than half a dozen missiles in a minute. Everything we learn about this battle suggests the leaders and their soldiers were good at their job so we might suppose that the stock of missiles had not been squandered and that they were ready to unleash volleys when the right moment arrived. Perhaps two minutes of volley fire before returning to 'sniper' shots.

Combat has its own cruel logic. For those who had to endure this withering arrow storm, it made sense to close with the enemy as quickly as possible because at that stage the hail of missiles would abate. But from the moment this charge broke cover until they were at the crossing, arrows were being shot at them from the riverbank to their left. It made very good sense for any attacker to close with the enemy as quickly as possible.

Those who had a spare shield could have arranged it to intercept these flying blades while some possibly lifted their shield to intercept lofted arrows. The benefit of carrying their protective shield on their left would not be lost on these experienced fighters as they pressed forward to get close to their enemy so that the archers would stop shooting for fear of hitting their own comrades.

The battle at the bank

The Nordic sources all talk about King Harald leading the charge. It might have taken less than a minute from the time the charge broke cover until the full weight hit Earl Edwin and his Mercian guards blocking their access to the north bank of the beck. Any stragglers in this charge would have to endure the rain of arrows from the opposite bank.

We have the benefit of a unique observer of events unfolding beside the river. *Hemings Saga*, is part of the Orkney tradition and describes the remarkable adventures of the Norwegian son of a nobleman. This relates how Heming fled into exile after defeating the irascible King Harald in a series of martial challenges.

The credibility of this saga was assessed earlier. Making sense of its observations was a stumbling block as Heming could not have witnessed the events he described except from a viewpoint of the west bank of the Ouse. He was at the time believed to be a Norse warrior and it was the Mercians who occupied the west bank. Only later it transpired that the historic Heming did indeed take service under King Edward *the confessor* and seemingly joined Earl Waltheof after Edward's death. We set out earlier the complex politics of 1065 that saw Waltheof, a noble native of Northumbria, fighting with the Mercians.

So Heming was among those with the Mercian army who evidently did not redeploy to defend the east bank. He is therefore able to offer us a well-informed commentary on events effectively from the situation of a close observer. He is on the 'wrong' side, fighting other Norwegians, and stranded on the wrong side of the river but barely 50 metres from the action. While the shape and outcome of this battle can be compiled from the various Kings' Sagas, this additional record permits us to actually describe the turning points of this battle from the unusual perspective of the losers.

Heming contradicts the Kings' Sagas and notes that it was Eystein, Harald's top commander and scheduled to become his son-in-law, who led the charge. Heming does not want to give any credit to his nemesis, and the charge would work better left to a younger man, especially one who was out to impress. Heming also credits Eystein Orre with spotting that Morcar had broken through Tostig's line and he earns one more notable mention in the subsequent Yorkshire battle. The force that rushed from Riccall to unsuccessfully come to the rescue of Harald at Stamford Bridge is referred to in the Sagas as 'Orre's Storm'. He died at Stamford Bridge.[110]

Heming's observations match what it would be possible for him to see from his west-bank vantage point[111] and they corroborate the events recorded by the 'official' saga historians. Had he actually been a soldier within the ranks of Harald's army, as his origins initially suggested, his viewpoint and observations would have been limited and he would not have been able to provide this report of the actions. Few battles are likely to benefit from such a reporter who was so near but unable to take part in the

---

[110] Several sagas note that Orre's betrothed coincidentally died on the same day. She was with her mother in the Orkney isles. They attribute this coincidence to a soulful connection with her father although romantics might prefer to believe that her heart was broken remotely by the death of her betrothed instead.

[111] As the River Ouse turns through a right angle at Fulford, overlooked from the hall, puts observers on the north bank but at the junction with Germany Beck the Ouse flows north where once again it has an east and a west bank.

action. What he reports was observable only from the west bank occupied by the Mercians.[112]

One consequence worth noting that flowed from so many of the Mercian army being bystanders at Fulford was that this army was intact when King Harold II arrived from the south on Sunday.[113] Heming indeed provides details of his and the Mercian actions at Stamford Bridge, even claiming his role in dispatching King Harald with two shots from his bow.

Heming had an unrestricted view when Harald's army crossed Germany Beck to get behind the advancing Earl Morcar. His viewpoint in the known landscape makes it credible that Heming could also have observed the about-face and rear-guard action by Morcar's men although some of what he reports must be from what he was told as, for example, he could not have been in the presence of the King who had exiled him, and against whom he was fighting, to hear some conversations he reports. However, as Edwin was released to go into York it is likely that Heming could have obtained the report directly from him, again lending credibility to his record of events.

Heming's report of the action when the bank was stormed tells us that 'Eystein [Orre] had gone through the array of the English and killed Aki the tall.' This tells us the blocking force was not able to resist the charge. This is close to the shape of battle set out in other sagas with Morcar advancing against Tostig before Earl Eystein Orre leads the outflanking move. From the sharp bend in the Ouse where the north bank becomes the west bank, Heming's view of the critical action would have been unobstructed. This record uniquely captures the turning point, written from a soldier's viewpoint, rather than by a skald accompanying Harald. This source is therefore accepted as containing elements of an eyewitness to some critical parts of the battle.

The identity of Aki the tall cannot be determined: King Harold (of England) is recorded as being the only brother-in-law of Morcar and Edwin but Heming records Aki as another royal brother-in-law. Aki might have been

---

[112] There is scope for a little confusion in the later English sources who refer to the north bank. There is indeed a section of the Ouse that fits this description and it is the section where the longships were berthed. However, for most of its journey south to the Humber, the Ouse has an east and a west bank.

[113] Having walked the medieval route between Waltham Abbey and York, it is not credible that a body of foot-soldiers could have assembled in the south and marched north within the timetable allowed to participate at Stamford Bridge.

a fellow exile known to Heming since the name is Norse, deriving from a diminutive of the word *father*. It is improbable that an exile could have married well enough to be considered a brother-in-law of one of the earls. But the under-reporting of women from the historical record does not preclude the existence of an unrecorded marriage to another sister. The only known sister of the earls was Ældgyth who had married King Harold earlier in the year.

Aki could have married a Mercian noblewoman so would have been among those with a horse and therefore capable of responding to the emerging threat of encirclement faced by Morcar at the ford. It is again relevant to note that his fate would have been clearly visible to Heming because the Mercians were on the bank of the flooded River Ouse and not engaged in the battle. For now we must simply accept this fatal, fleeting appearance of Aki the tall. He was obviously known to Heming.

Waltheof's significant part in the battle defending the riverbank is well reported. Fagrskinna tell us that "Jarl Valbjofr of Hundatun [Waltheof of Huntingdon] came against them with an overwhelming force, which had been gathering together all the autumn." Earl Waltheof would have brought his limited force to defend his native Northumbria and might have joined the Mercians to avoid tension between him and Morcar, believing that he rather than the imported Mercian noble, should be the earl. This would have put him in the heart of the action, increasing his visibility and the chance that subsequent skalds and scribes might have confused or conflated the two earls fighting near the river.

Interestingly, the surviving arrow evidence suggests that Harald's reserve was deployed in two directions. The key one headed for Edwin's blocking force to open the way to York and to occupy the stone ford. The other charged to bolster the left flank of Tostig's army where the troops lining the 'pool' had been drawn into checking Morcar's charge.

Harald's fresh veterans would have been hard to resist as they drove these two new wedges between the Mercian and the Northumbrian armies. Their first target was achieved so they could now move along the beck-bank to try to occupy the ford and possibly cut off any retreat. The second wedge, if the other arrow-scatter is indicative, was along the south bank of the beck to add heft to the left flank of Tostig's army and turn the tide of battle.

Crossing the beck

Turning points in battle are clear in retrospect but defeat normally unfolds in stages.

In one sense the battle to block the riverside path was not lost since the written evidence suggests that this contest continued. The Mercians were not overwhelmed or destroyed. But in the context of the battle they had lost. The momentum of Harald's men, led by Orre, had captured the river bank crossing. The defenders recoiled and in that moment they 'lost'. Invaders following Orre could now move along the emerging paths beside both banks of the beck that would lead them to the ford 300 metres away and get behind Morcar's army who had earlier 'advanced bravely'.

While Harald's fresh veterans made their way in line along the beck bank towards the ford, the isolated band of Mercians on the more substantial river levée fought on in the manner of the famous Horatio, who defended the nascent Rome by defending a bridge. But the outcome shows that they were unable to mount a counter-attack and stem the flow of warriors either by the river bank or along the beck where it was conjectured that a small contingent, possibly including Waltheof, might have deployed.

It is unlikely that Harald actually joined this outflanking move since the main battle was still elsewhere and his job was to ensure that the surge of Morcar's men was held until their escape route had been sealed. Once the riverside charge had succeeded in dislodging the defenders, he would have likely turned his attention elsewhere, not least to get out of range of the arrows from the opposite bank.

This perilous development at the riverbank would have gone unnoticed by the Northumbrians at the ford since they had left the high ground of their erstwhile stronghold on their north side and crossed the beck to the marginally lower ground on the other bank. The land surface or a screen of trees need only rise two metres to block their view. They were in any case now facing the renewed counter-attack by Tostig which was, as Harald had intended, the focus of Northumbrian warriors full attention and he appreciated the role of the landscape in limiting information available to Morcar. He knew it was good to keep your enemy guessing.

The Ings extends halfway back towards York. The Norwegians might have charged the Mercian 'plug' repeatedly to force it back. The Mercians could yield a kilometre or more before there was any risk to their own flank. All the way they were protected by the Ouse and the Ings. They were probably relatively safe because the focus of the battle was now on the destruction of

Morcar's much bigger 'local army', as one saga calls it, to distinguish it from the Mercians who had come from the west to assist. If the 'Land-ravager' had moved away it would have relieved the pressure on the riverbank. Even if Earl Edwin could have fought his way back to the beck, which is unlikely, the Norwegians were already across in strength and preparing to surround the unsuspecting English at the ford.

Edwin's Mercians were now a sideshow for the battle at the ford. One source indicates that this force surrendered perhaps after a fighting retreat but possibly because their retreat route to York had eventually been blocked after several hours battling. Once some of the Norse reached the high ground they could move unopposed towards York and halfway would have encountered the access to the river where a small contingent was possibly positioned to carry messages. The last message that they would carry to Edwin was that his route back to dry land had been cut off and they were surrounded.

While the focus and the outcome of battles lies with the main army it is reasonable to credit all of the generals in the field that day with a level of tactical sophistication based on the manoeuvres and assessments already manifest. The lines of communication would have been defended so that commanders on the front line could keep in touch with developments around the battlefield.

Back at the ford some defenders, left as a rearguard, quickly appreciated their predicament and might have assembled a group to guard the levée at the place where the flat landscape of the Ings meets the rocky promontory of the esker that linked Fulford back to the city. This force was likely small, perhaps only 20 warriors, as most Northumbrians would have joined the advance. It is also reasonable to conjecture that such a force was indeed formed because without its timely intervention the ford would have been occupied and any possible retreat for Morcar cut off.

We cannot know precisely where this levée path actually emerged since the beck has been channelled but it is likely that the Vikings who formed one prong of Harald's counter-attack approached along the south bank of Germany Beck and had to wade knee deep in water along this still submerged path just before reaching the rise towards the stone ford crossing. Perhaps Morcar's commanders had sensibly left a contingent to cover this approach knowing that it would be exposed by the ebbing tide, and this rearguard was now called into action.

This Norse prong of the river-bank counterattack now faced a steep climb. As they approached the top they might have been briefly rewarded with a view of the battlefield that had previously been denied to them. This glimpse would be enough for them to understand their role. They could block any chance of Morcar retreating back to York. However their priority was on the matching small force left at the ford intent upon defending it who had the advantage of height as the land rises like a wall.

To make tactical sense of the events of the next half hour one must assume that these defenders were successful at holding up the invaders who had the significant and steep natural obstacles to overcome. So long as the invaders could be confined to the beck bank and not fan out over open ground, it would not require a large force to contain this breakthrough. The 'front' of this important sideshow could not have been more than four or five warriors wide, and it was likely only the press of the arriving Norse that forced the defenders very slowly backwards. But assembling a sufficient force for this assault would take time.

Unlike the level in the water channels, where the falling tide exposed fresh land every minute, the Ings held onto the flood water so that the path beside the beck did not get significantly wider although some athletic invaders might have gone onto the ings to try and bypass the defenders. The water could not drain into either Germany Beck or the River Ouse.

Earl Edwin might have wanted to get a message to his brother who was less than 400 metres to the east. But Edwin's Mercians were effectively isolated from Morcar's Northumbrians. While some prepared to fight gallantly to retain control of the rive flank, a few set off to update Morcar.

Wading along the half-exposed levée, it might have taken 15 minutes for the first Norse warriors to threaten the ford. These harbingers of a Norse swarm would need a little time to assemble a force. Meanwhile the men of the Northumbrian rearguard had time to organise and position themselves for battle. Within 30 minutes of crossing the beck a sufficient group of Harald's best were assembled, poised for action, now on the north bank of the beck, behind most Northumbrians.

The timetable offers just enough time for Morcar to react after a messenger arrived with the unwelcome news that his right flank and rear were compromised. After describing Morcar's initial success, one Norse history goes on to identify the two separate battles that have now developed "King Harald with his troop advanced so hard that (the enemy), gave way before him in two directions."[114] Another source identifies the separate armies with Earl Waltheof (Mercians) and the 'local' army (Northumbrians).

Morcar in the thick of the mêlée evidently recognised immediately that they would not be able to drive Tostig's reinforced army from the field so must retreat. That retreat might already have begun due to the press of the Norse warriors and the timely arrival of the disastrous news that the ford was about to be occupied, perhaps accelerated plans to fall back. At their back was a swamp that would soon be submerged again. They must avoid being forced into that trap. The ford was their only way out.

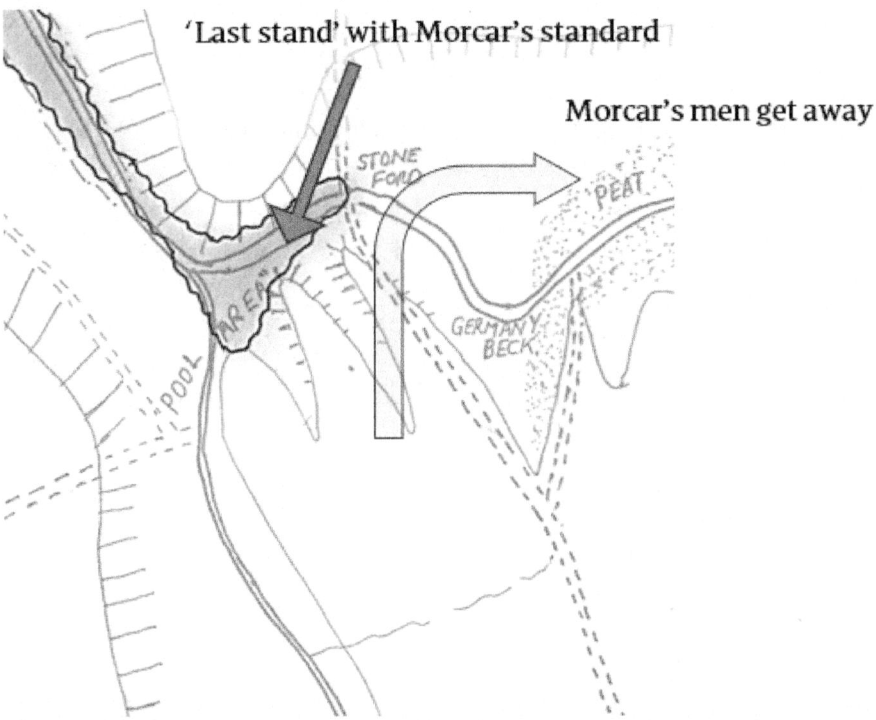

The tide falls fast in the final hours of the ebb which allowed Tostig's army to fully engage, reinforced by some of Harald's men, on their left flank. This forced Morcar's army to retreat to the ford where most escaped east along Germany Beck while a brave force held back the invaders at the ford where there is a narrow gap on either bank.

[114] *Fagrskinna* Tr Alison Finlay 2004 edition 9004131728 Brill Chapter 63

Surrounding the men in the ford

Retreat is a particularly dangerous phase in any battle. If controlled and conducted carefully, it is possible to extract troops with few casualties. Just as a shieldwall can use 'step drill' to press the enemy, it can take organised steps away from the line and disengage. This drill would permit the wounded to retire and be replaced during a battle. Lulls form a part of the experience of the individual fighter as both sides drew breath. Perhaps a hand on the shoulder or the simple command 'back' would open a gap between the lines.

Retreat is not the same as running away. Turning your back towards your enemy presented them with almost every advantage. Instead of being able to see where your enemy is moving, turning away blinds you to pursuing threats. When running away, shields cannot parry any blows, so the fleeing enemy presents an open target to hurl any available missile, unseen by those in flight. Instead of their own weapons threatening the enemy, they became an encumbrance if you ran away.

At the battle of Brunanburgh it is recorded in the Anglo-Saxon Chronicle that 'the west Saxons hewed the fugitive from behind terribly with their sharpened blades'. So long as soldiers remained in a formation facing the enemy, they were a threat and in the context of such bloody battles, they were 'safe'. The dangers increase if a retreat becomes disordered and turns into a rout. Rout is a situation that can turn defeat into a slaughter.

If the army maintained its cohesion it could avoid that fate. One soldier surrounded by three enemies is bound to die as he cannot face them all. Two soldiers have a chance as they can protect each other's back. Yet again this crude military logic can be extended to show that it makes sense to stick together. Anglo-Saxons and Norse warriors would have well understood this lethal logic.

With his enemy threatening to fill the ford with troops, "... Earl Morcar sees that, he orders his men face about and defend themselves well and manfully." This observation provided by a friendly observer not engaged in the action on the far bank of the Ouse suggests, perhaps using literary shorthand, that Morcar himself became aware of the loss of his riverside flank. The young earl was likely in the thick of the action as he had much to prove. It is likely that he left command and control to some older heads.

Instead of advancing, Heming tells us that he 'redirects his army to get back to the ford'. This demonstrates a measure of discipline and control as well as an acute tactical sense. If the Northumbrians had stood their ground they would have been trapped between two armies with a swamp at their back.

They were tired, outnumbered and now outflanked so it takes courage and leadership to accept defeat and retreat to the ford. This meant giving up the costly ground gained. It must have been a tough decision for the warriors to surrender ground when an hour earlier they looked like they were in a winning position. Dither or delay would have allowed their only way out to be cut off. All the evidence is that they quickly fell back to the ford, a retreat of 50 metres. The road back into the ford was at the furthest point from the charge of Harald's fresh forces where before they had been facing warriors who were just as fatigued.

They chameleon-like landscape offered them a thin slice of good fortune in their retreat. By now it was mid-afternoon and the local landscape was changing fast. The pool below the road was now almost drained so that the normal channel of the beck was visible. This was a muddy basin but one that could be forded and likely earned this place its descriptive name, *foule forde*. The layers of mud subsequently deposited here were the source of 15 horseshoes, datable to the succeeding centuries where the banks were better suited to horses than people.

While opening a wider escape route for the retreating Northumbrians we must assume that the ditch that had provided the axis for the invaders shieldwall was still impassable adjacent to the beck itself. Had that route been open then the part of Harald's counterattack sent to occupy the ford along the south bank would have quickly seized control of the ford. The understood landscape did not however obstruct Morcar's retreating army from entering the beck, now ebbing fast but filled knee deep with water.

There was an alternative way to cross to the north bank. With the small rearguard force just about holding the ford, the retreating Northumbrians might have had a helping hand down the steep approach bank which could be transformed into a line of spear points when the enemy arrived which would deter and critically delay their descent. Occupying high ground has some obvious advantages but the steep, slippery bank into the pool can in the context of this battle make low-lying land rather difficult to assault. Few Norse would likely volunteer to hurl themselves against such a spear-wall. It perhaps bought a short respite.

One small area, near the bank at this location, was an unusual deposit which archaeologists often call a 'lens' that contained many fragments of possibly human bones which sadly defied all attempts to date them. This small area was in the lee of one promontory so that the water slowed here explaining why material might not be flushed from here. Near this same area is the source of all of the sword fragments recovered. It is not fanciful to imagine that this was the site of the last stand of Morcar's loyal hearth-troops.

The other side of the stone ford road could hardly be more geologically different compared to the muddy pool just described. Below the alluvial mud brought by each flood was a flat stone surface which is often termed 'boulder clay' deposited during an earlier glaciation but subsequently exposed by the flood and flush along the beck. Much of the clay, itself a product of eons of minerals being dissolved, had been incorporated into the 'grinding paste' of rounded rocks at the base of a glacier. Larger rocks even bear the striations on their flattened base which were engraved as they were forced along against other rocks.

This stone surface was easier to access and provided space for some quick reorganisation as the enemy did not yet have access or oversight here. From the known outcome we can surmise that Morcar moved with his housecarls possibly using the ford road to join those holding the muddy pool. We know this because that is where we are told his banner was found. This would have provided a visual signal for the others to rally and reinforce the retreat message. Whether words were exchanged we cannot know but the housecarls with Morcar's banner temporarily stemmed any trickle of enemy into the ford.

As long as they held out there was an escape route along the ditch of Germany Beck leading away from the river where the water would soon be only ankle deep at the crossing but ebbing fast so the force of water was not significant.

The final line describing the turning point of the battle suggests the collapse of the defence. "And at last, flight broke out among his men, and they fled out into the river and Earl Morcar is slain and the most part of his folk. Many too sunk beneath the stream." This is the enemy's assessment and needs to be untangled to understand Morcar's perspective.

'Flight' seems to be the only word available to describe leaving a battlesite, perhaps reflecting the limited military vocabulary at the time. The exit of Morcar along the ditch that forms Germany Beck might be more fairly described as a tactical retreat even if it was hasty. Morcar might have hoped to make another stand although many of his men would probably have recognised that the battle was already effectively lost.

The victors in their description overlook the way the retreat was speedily organised as soon as their opponent's position had been fatally compromised as it was irrelevant to their reporting and the heroic outcome for them. Morcar must have brought his army speedily to the ford, the timetable allows barely half an hour, which they occupied and defended despite being almost surrounded by Norse soldiers.

If Harald's attack that crossed the beck been able to occupy the ford it would have prevented the Northumbrians from escaping. They could have provided the 'anvil' against which Tostig could beat his adversary. There can be little doubting that the old warrior, Harald, planned this fate for the army which Tostig had persuaded him to invade and to defeat. Edwin's Mercians seem to have slowed them just enough to prevent the annihilation of his brother's Northumbrians, possibly also restricting the flow of warriors towards the ford.

The expanded rearguard now fought to hold back the enemy and this retained the focus of Tostig so long as Morcar's banner flew. As so often happened in this battle-landscape, a determined band of warriors could 'plug' access to the ford. It made sense for those not fated to join this brave band to exit inland along the beck-ditch as quickly as possible. The tide would rush back soon, and all would drown if the Norse extended their control along the high banks as the fresh arrivals from the riverbank would already be making their presence noted.

The emptying 'pool' now revealed itself as two separate depressions. The one nearest the ford-road was too small to contain more than a hundred warriors which is the one that has so far been archaeologically investigated. It was defensible and there was an easy and obvious escape route up along the beck for the rest of Morcar's men.

All of the Norse sources mistakenly claim that Earl Morcar was killed and one might assume that Morcar's banner along with most of his housecarls were eventually seen to fall, providing the story that was taken home and eventually recorded in the Norse Sagas. The destruction of the victors of Fulford five days later at Stamford Bridge would have prevented them from discovering Morcar had survived to become a leader of opposition to the Normans.

Perhaps Earl Morcar's housecarls also recognised that Morcar's banner would be the focus of the Norse attacks and certainly provided the focus for Tostig who wanted to destroy the person who had replaced him. If the brave housecarls held Morcar's banner high, they could do their sworn job and actually give their earl a chance to escape. All the invaders' aggression would focus on the troops surrounding the banner since this was where convention dictated, they would find the young earl.

The weight of Norwegian numbers would eventually overwhelm these brave housecarls, but the plan worked. Crucially, Tostig was certain that the man who he maintained had usurped his land and title was dead, which effectively brought the battle to an end. Their stubborn sacrifice had given time for Morcar and a significant number of his army to escape.

There are mentions of this battle lasting all day. If this is true, the rearguard must have held out trapped in their muddy pool for nearly an hour. This is an impressive feat of arms but credible since the location would make them difficult to dislodge unless a supply of arrows or throwing spears was available.

One can interpret the words of the Norse historians as describing the returning flood putting an end to resistance even describing the ghoulish image of bodies looking like stepping stones. When this area was excavated an informal estimate suggested that about 80 bodies lying flat could cover the area described as this part of the pool. One might suppose that an image of the warriors making their final stand being overwhelmed by a wave from the inrushing tide would have been recorded. Therefore it is more likely that any of the rearguard still standing would have tried to make a break, running up and down the beck before being drowned, as one later English source describes their ending.

There are many references, even in English sources, to the flight of the English but the landscape and archaeology permit this alternative, tactical interpretation. The fate of the Northumbrians, providing a rearguard was sealed. They were surrounded as soon as the ditch was vacated by the 'fleeing' soldiers led by their earl. They did not try to escape and to buy time, they stood their ground. It might have taken time to destroy this band of surrounded warriors, but their action allowed most to escape. Heming's concluding remark on the battle says, "Many too sunk beneath the stream" providing the single suggestion that it was indeed the inrushing tides that sealed their fate at the ford.

When the saga tells us that one could walk 'dry-foot' across the bodies, it might be an accurate description especially the morning after the battle. A high tide would have come and gone with the rushing tide perhaps having sufficient force to align the bodies. The weight of the armour might have ensured that they were not flushed towards the river especially as it is the arriving bore, rather than the ebb, which possesses the significant force and this would have pushed them inland against the embanked ford-road.

The location of this section of the pool has two constrictions where the flow changes direction and many battle finds were located where the beck was diverted. These features would have helped to contain the bodies. Half a dozen tidal surges of muddy water up to the ford over the next few days, might have enhanced the macabre spectacle by importing grey alluvium to surround the bodies to make them look even more like stepping-stones, set into the ground.

A later English chronicler, John of Worcester using a source that is lost to us, provides this commentary. The English 'fought so bravely at the onset that many of the enemy were overthrown; but after a long contest the English were unable to withstand the attacks of the Norwegians and fled with great loss.'

He adds, 'More were drowned in the river than slain on the field.' This observation might be true if the battle continued until the next, higher tidal surge which would happen as daylight failed, and all the preceding events suggest the fight lasted that long. The inrushing tide might indeed have brought the conflict to an end as this chronicler suggests. It is hard to believe that warriors would not have taken to their heels as the water rose, advancing at walking speed, at the end of its eight-hour ebb.

Anyone observing the battle once the action was over might easily draw the conclusion that the victims had drowned. It is more likely that they lay where they had been killed, holding back the invaders. The water rose even higher on the days after the battle. Each surge would force scavengers and the organised recyclers, discussed later, to abandon the field of conflict until the tide retreated.

Another speculation is admissible and related to the sword fragments found. Most of these were sword tips which had been stuck into the muddy stone base here. Two of the sword tips show clear signs of having been broken off, not with the stroke of another weapon, but by forcefully fatiguing the blade. It seems that for some reason these blades were worked back and forth until the tips broke. Ritualistic, metallurgical and practical reasons can be advanced to explain what was found here.

As the place where the bravest of the Northumbrians died perhaps their swords were broken to honour them, although there are no contemporary records of this practice. In earlier centuries small pieces of iron were forge-welded together to provide a blade that was strong but flexible and often with an attractive, almost magical, surface pattern left by the welding and twisting. By the 10th century swords could be beaten from a single bloom avoiding the need to join many pieces of metal.

By the time of the battle so-called Damascus steel was already preferred for swords. These had a lenticular (lens shaped) profile while all the sword tips found were flat, and with a fuller, based on the found fragments. These were 'beaten swords' made from a single large 'bloom' of iron. Was the fatigue testing designed to see if the sword possessed the necessary flexibility? Or did the swords get stuck in the muddy base beside a notable body, perhaps even to lock it in place against the next tidal rush. Did the tips simply break as the sword was subsequently withdrawn having been wedged between stones in the base of the pool?

Those used to seeing thick slabs of steel beaten into the shape of swords carried by modern actors should know that the real thing was just a few millimetres thick and perfectly capable of removing a head or leg at a stroke. It has been a privilege to handle them. Did the fragments once mark the spot where their owner was killed?

As far as the invaders were concerned the battle was over. 'King Harald led the attack with his troops and joined battle so fiercely that the enemy was split and the local army began to flee' which again provides a little more information noting, correctly, that it was the local, or Northumbrian, army that fled. The Mercian army had indeed been split from the Northumbrians after Harald's counter-attack with the flooded Ings between them. This is confirmed by the later observation, 'Earl Waltheof fought the king more toward the river. He fled up along the river, and the troops with him were the only ones to escape.'

Retreat to the haven

For Earl Morcar, now reduced to perhaps half an army, the situation was perilous. He had skilfully extracted them and kept some cohesion for an organised retreat.

A hundred metre dash along a peat-filled ditch through an area that was untouched so far by the battle, brought Morcar's men to a place where the beck splits. *Morkinskinna* reports that the Northumbrians 'retreated to a place where there was no armed opposition, in the swampy ground around the pool.'

It is most unusual to find a place on a battlefield inaccessible to the enemy. But there is an area where it was postulated before this source became available that Morcar might briefly have rallied his army. This area had so much battle debris, later recognised as the main metal recycling site after the battle, it was clear that something had happened nearby. The area has steep natural walls surrounding it as well as ancient hedges preventing side access. This 'swampy ground', a basin filled with peat, can only be accessed even now at either end.

One Norse description concludes their description of events noting that the pursuing Norse, on reaching the ditch that is Germany Beck, 'jumped out into it' to pursue the fleeing troops. Over much of the ditch the banks are steep, providing the excellent flank protection discussed earlier, making an orderly descent tricky. It is seldom sensible to attach too much to the way a single word is translated but jumping out into the ditch is what some would have to do to escape. The alternative was an undignified slide down the steep sides, making a leap preferable. This also suggests that even as they retreated, a few Norse warriors were beginning to harass their retreat.

This short respite might have allowed Morcar to reorganise and prevent a complete rout. This same source provides the detail that it was the unit from Fjaler, an area north of Bergen, who pursued the Northumbrians during their retreat along the ditch. Either Morcar was still battling or perhaps the men of Fjaler were among the last to arrive so were assigned the job of pursuing stragglers.

The archaeology uncovered here is unclear because no excavations were allowed and detailed investigations on the fields around was prevented, so the action here might yet be better understood. What did emerge was a remarkable amount of iron recycling debris. The debris found might support the suggestion that, Morcar and the rest of his army departed, possibly disposing of all but their essential weaponry.

The battle might have been five hours old when the light began to fail on that later September day. The water in the ford would be at its lowest about 5pm. One can estimate that the refuge would soon be filled to a depth of over two metres when the tide surged back in, based on the regular modern flooding.

It is not unreasonable to suppose that initially several thousand Northumbrians rallied here but ultimately escaped from the battle. Perhaps as the light began to fail, Morcar might have formally released his exhausted army to flee but it is possible some had already voted with their feet. There were woods to the east and beyond them roads leading in all directions. A little to the south there was an extensive wetland where they could effectively disperse and hide overnight before making their way home to await events. The direction of the retreat would lead them towards the village of Heslington. Some doubtless made their way to York but Morcar would not be among them as to meet Tostig was to invite certain death.

It is possible to portray Morcar's escape as cowardice but this would be unjust. The esteem in which he is subsequently held as the historic leader of resistance in the Fens, a role attributed in most stories to Hereward the Wake, would have been sacrificed if he had deserted the battlefield. The success of the ploy of his loyal hearthtroops meant that the Norse sources are unanimous in pronouncing the death of the earl. Those fated to die holding back the Norse while most escaped, probably knew that a fate worse than death awaited them if they fell alive into the hands of the man they had expelled almost a year before.

Fate of the Mercians

Edwin's Mercians had already become a sideshow for the battle at the ford. One source suggests that at some stage after the bank-side flank was lost some, led by Waltheof, were able to escape. The levée beside the river was still the only dry exit.

Since Waltheof was not among Edwin's housecarls, he was not obliged to stay. As an earl himself, it would not be inglorious to lead some of his men in a getaway. They must have held out until early evening when the tide had ebbed as this afforded the best chance to escape across the damp Ings. The natural deposition of silt creates a barely perceptible slope as it runs away from the river. The finest material flows furthest leaving bogs that are still filled with bulrushes before land rises 20 metres above the Ings. Although the natural embankments kept the Ings wet after each flood, there would be several ways to exit along channels of dryish ground created by those who brought their animals to graze this common land before and after the autumn inundations.

An assemblage of 13 skeletons was excavated from the cemetery of St. Andrewgate. These can be dated to the time of this battle and half display the type of fatal wounds one might expect in battle. Although there is only one ambiguous mention of a battle at the city wall, it is possible that Waltheof led his contingent back to the city where they fought to prevent the invaders from forcing access, perhaps preventing some looting of the city. However two skeletons have traumatic wounds inflicted from behind suggesting that they might have been killed when retreating but their wounds might be overkill having already been felled.

There is nothing to suggest that these bodies were special or recovered from the battle by families as the graves had multiple occupants, suggesting haste, rather than ceremony. They had probably died in the vicinity, perhaps bravely preventing any overzealous Norsemen from entering the city to seek their reward. These putative saviours of the city were rewarded with a burial in consecrated land.

Surrender

The single report detailing Edwin's surrender is confusing as the historical wires get crossed because Waltheof had usurped the place of Edwin as a leader in Heming's saga and other accounts tell us that Waltheof escaped. So it is certainly Earl Edwin's surrender that is being reported. One source makes it clear that Edwin surrendered providing us with an interesting footnote.

Evidently after the fighting is over, Tostig rejoined the victorious King Harald having assured himself that Earl Morcar lay among the bodies now submerged by the tide at the ford. It is not unreasonable to suggest that the Mercians had held out as long as possible but reports of the death and defeat of his brother and the risk of drowning when the tide surged back led the Mercians to seek sanctuary and that meant moving to the higher ground around Fulford Hall, and that required surrender.

The reported exchanges tell the story well, even if the translation has dated. (Edwin's name has been substituted for Waltheof in the following exchanges.) Addressing the vengeful Tostig, the king says:

"'You would kill those that you capture but I will have my way with him.' Then the King said to Edwin, 'I will give thee peace if thou wilt swear never to fight against me, and to send me word the same day if you know that treachery is plotted against me.'"

"'I will not swear that' says Edwin 'to save my life but I will stand by my brother[in law] Harold, so long as I may; but I will send you word if I know that treachery is plotted against you, if that will save my life; but I will swear no oath; for it looks to me as though Tostig does not mean me to have much inheritance.' The King left Edwin quite free to go free."

It is a habit of tyrants to make such capricious decisions. History would come to know *Hardrada,* in its Norse form 'Hard ruler', as a tyrant. It was a crafty move on the part of Edwin to note what Tostig planned since this allowed *Hardrada* to make it very clear who was in charge. Tostig was indeed not pleased. The argument continued.

“Tostig says, ‘A senseless deed to let that man loose who you think so good that he needs to give you no oath!’

‘I believe’ said the king, ‘that his word is better than your sworn oath.’ And with these few words he firmly put Tostig in his place. The latter quickly recovered and started proposing plans.

“Tostig said, ‘Let us go with our army to London, and let us waste the land with fire and sword, and give no peace to any man, neither women nor children.’”

The tension, and the lack of trust between King Harald and Tostig, is evident and the saga goes on to make it clear the plan to set out for London was not followed, nor were the many other options Tostig proposed.

The battle was over. The two Earls had survived. Casualties had been high. The way to York was open. Tostig could reclaim the Northumbrian earldom from the rebels.

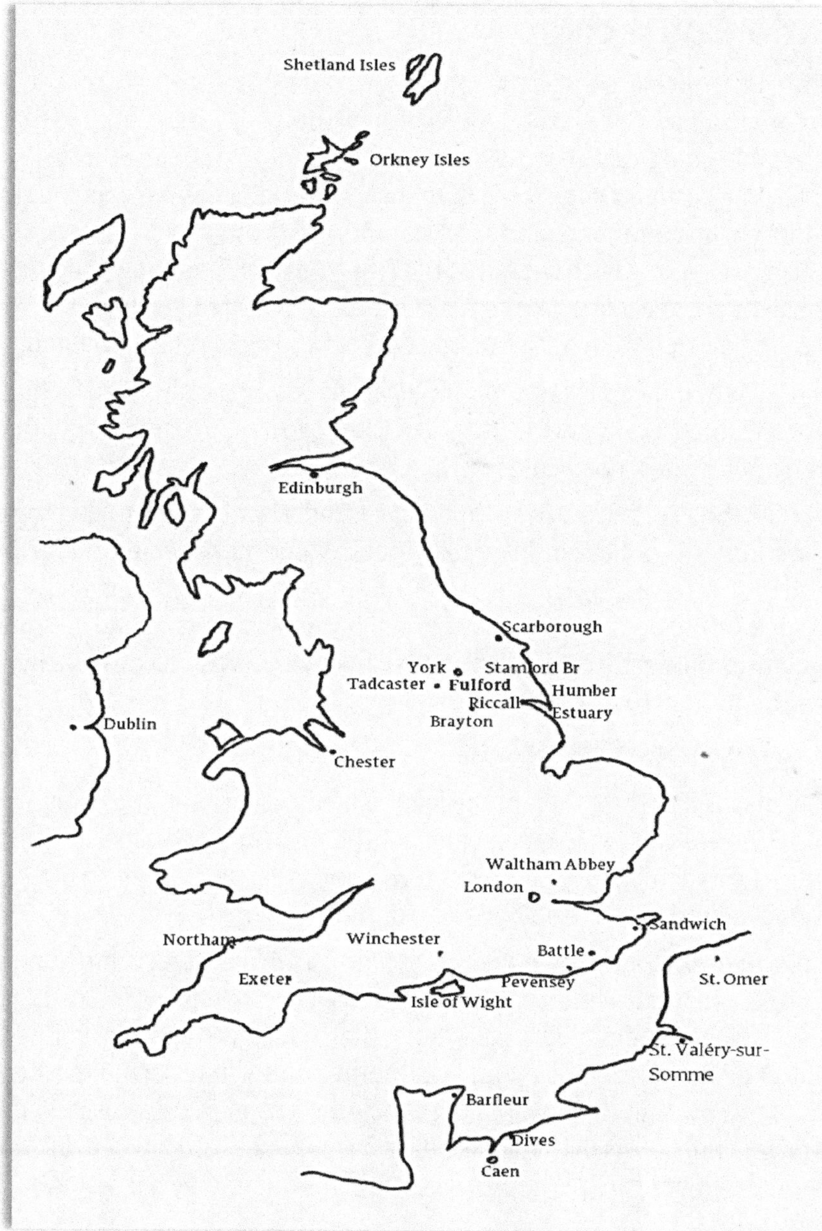

Places named in the text

Battle Postscript

Fulford, history relates, was the immediate prelude to the ambush battle at Stamford Bridge five days later. Both of the following battles of 1066 merit a proper archaeological investigation to better understand the military actions. The bonus of such work is an insight into the people who fought and those who commanded the combatants. Without such battle studies, myths persist along with the belief that the winners seemingly enjoyed some favour of the deity. The clerical chroniclers wasted few words describing battle action believing the outcome to be divinely ordained.

This northern invasion was arguable a part of Tostig's strategy to facilitate his own restoration but obviously aided the Norman invasion by dividing the English armies, north and south.

We know that York was not stormed or sacked. Harald's troops had their ships at Fulford so they could quickly access some 'home comforts'. The Riccall men faced a long trudge back to their base. Perhaps some lucky wounded would be carried back to Riccall by boat as there would be some spaces after the battle. The hall might even have served as a hospice for those too injured to move.

Clearing the battlefield

Before discussing the action of the leaders which led to the subsequent battles, the Fulford research revealed for the first time one aspect of post-battle activity which helps to explain why most battlesites left so little material behind for archaeologists to find.

The discovery of extensive evidence of post-battle metal recycling around the site of the battle action might suggest that those 'who possessed the place of slaughter' devoted what energy they had left to salvage work. While the priority for most would be finding somewhere secure to rest, they also knew that there was wealth to be won by gathering discarded weapons. Translators of the sagas often employ the word 'owned' or 'possessed' to indicate perhaps suggesting the value to be harvested after a victory.

Fulford is unique in that the activity to recover weapons is evident as is the subsequent extensive recycling of ironwork. Sadly work to investigate this discovery properly was not only prevented but once its importance was revealed the surface material was stripped and removed from the site, despite repeated objections.

From the material recovered before further investigations were banned, two narratives emerge. The first is what appears to be a well organised recycling effort. The evidence does not quite permit a confident claim that there was a production line for items such as knife blades or axe heads, but this interpretation is not unreasonable. The large number of blade-shapes, about 70 in all, were recovered close to where hearths-bottoms (PCBs) and other hearth debris such as slag and vitrified clay fragments, likely from the hearth tuyères, were found. Once again one must enter into conjecture that these blades were perhaps grave tokens even though all of Scandinavia professed Christianity. But the smiths could equally be taking advantage of quality iron available to stock the armoury with small blades.

An alternative view is that the two larger hearths identified were organised by Harald where the richest pickings were processed with some smaller scale recycling undertaken at the periphery as those hearth-bottoms were much smaller. With so much weapon-wealth in the field, it is unlikely that soldiers would have ignored this opportunity to enrich themselves. But it is speculated that scavenging was a regulated activity as there would be loot on the fallen of both sides. Organisation ensured there was no need for a greedy grab of battle debris and the recycling area required some regulating for the production of charcoal fuel, access to water, labour and transport.

Another story we might tell is that the weary and wounded warriors could recover as they recognised that there would be a fair distribution of the spoils, obviating any need for a free-for-all. They might have sought the cooling inrush of water along the beck soon after dark to have a good wash and a drink before sleeping. The cool autumn air would have woken them before first light, ready for the uninjured to start work on the battlefield.

There was wood to make charcoal as well as weapons to be gathered while tents and cloaks might have arrived from Riccall to bring some comfort to those still in the field although the area around the hall provided some shelter. The following day requisitioned carts could have carried the wounded plus some spoils of war back to their base. These carts had likely been taken from York and would have arrived with whatever food could be found. The city would perhaps want to demonstrate its value with functioning bakers and markets in order to prevent summary seizure and worse. The city leaders quickly realigned to their former earl, Tostig.

It is relevant to repeat the context and the unique conditions that prevailed after the battle of Fulford. Just five days elapsed from the day of the battle until the victors at Fulford were not simply defeated but, according to the contemporary sources, almost wiped out. At that crisis point the metalworkers had to quickly pack-up and carry away what they could in order to get back to the security of their base. This led to several assemblages, discovered during the research, being abandoned where they were quickly covered by flooding and vegetation since all of the hearth locations identified lie near the beck or on a connected paleo-channel.

If the process of recycling was completed, as one would normally expect, then all of the material would have been carried away. Under such 'normal' circumstances only some slag, hammerscale and perhaps some hearth debris might remain to be found by archaeologists. This would explain why it has proved very difficult to identify ancient battlefields based on the 'expected' finds - Battlefields were tidied up and much useful evidence for modern archaeology, removed. This is not quite to reverse the maxim about absence of proof but the post-battle, metal recycling hypothesis suggests absence of weapons is a likely condition for locating ancient battlesites.

Even at Fulford the metalworkers seemingly took away their tools as only two hammers and a few chisels were found. The exception is the number of anvils found. At this era an anvil was often shaped like a large nail which was driven into a block of wood, and these could not have been quickly withdrawn when they had to abandon the site.

An experimental archaeology project in Fulford demonstrated that hot charcoal can be extracted from a suitable pit within 24 hours. The design employed, with an access ramp, was based on one that was identified in the same area where the Northumbrians had taken temporary refuge adjacent to the hearth-finds on the recycling sites. This supports the conjecture of the post-battle metal recycling and that work could have started the day after the battle, giving them three working days before they had to abandon the site.

Several special pieces of iron were located which perhaps capture the moment of drama and sudden reversal of fortune. Five small sheets were being forge-welded together but were abandoned. Work seemingly stopped as soon as word of the fate of King Harald at nearby Stamford Bridge reached them.[115]

---

[115] The ASC notes that when King Harold arrived from the south he took steps to ensure that word of his arrival did not get out; so the metal workers at Fulford would have been left alone by the locals until the fate of the battle was clear.

Fatal Casualties

Ancient chronicles fall silent about the practical aftermath, including mentions of the way the dead and wounded were dealt with. One short note from English chronicler, Henry of Huntingdon, suggests that he might have passed through the site of the battle: 'The site of the battle is still shown on the south side of the city.'

His use of the word 'still' suggests that the battle was topical when the words were written perhaps 50 years after the battle. Later English compilers of histories chose to ignore Fulford suggesting the defeat did not survive long in the collective memory.

The comment also suggests that Henry might have passed through the site, perhaps on a journey from Lincoln sometime between 1095 and 1110. Ermine Street links Huntingdon to Lincoln and on to the south bank of the Humber. Some of the potential routes would require a short detour to pass though Fulford but when Henry VIII entered York via Fulford, the York burghers made their obeisance to him at Fulford Cross so it was obviously an established route from the south by then.

However, the scribe does not actually say that he visited the site and if he did, it is unlikely that he would have seen any physical evidence since he could not have passed through the site until at least 30 years had elapsed since the battle. Roman historians tell us that just 6 years after the Battle of the Teutoburger Forest, with a similar climatic regime, little remained of the 3 legions that had been slaughtered there.

Abandoning the bodies to wildlife and the elements was not unknown, as William of Poitiers suggests after Hastings, although Duke William arranged an 'honourable internment' for his own men while William of Jumièges talks of the English bodies being despoiled and left.

"It would have been just if wolves and vultures had devoured the flesh of these English who had rightly incurred their doom, and if the fields had received their unburied bones. But such a fate seemed cruel to the Duke and he allowed all who wished to do so to collect the bodies for burial."[116]

Both Henry and Orderic report scattered bones after Stamford Bridge. Science might yet develop techniques to identify where bodies returned to dust, but for now the victims are lost to us.

[116] William of Poitiers EHD II

Part Three: Consequences

Timetable surrounding subsequent events

After this first battle of the autumn campaign in 1066, most of the actors were still very much in play with only Earl Morcar, and to a lesser extent his brother Edwin, temporarily sidelined by their defeat. William's fleet had redeployed to St. Valéry-sur-Somme from the Normandy ports. After gathering ships and men in the estuary of the River Dives and adjacent ports during the summer, by mid-August the Papal banner to accompany this 'crusade' was received. The invasion was apparently ready, but it did not move for another month.

On the 8th of September they would all have seen the full moon, and one might speculate that this was chosen as a marker from the celestial calendar that Tostig had appointed for those taking part in his plan.

The 8th September is also suggested as the date when King Harold released the English army after the summer and autumn waiting on the Isle of Wight and the adjacent coast. This dispersal order seems a strategic response and redeployment. It was a reasonable military reaction to the departure of the Norman invasion fleet. The full moon seemingly marked the start of a great deal of activity, north and south.

One encounters suggestions, in later sources, that the Wessex army was disbanded as it was needed for the harvest. All hands were welcome whenever a harvest is gathered but the population of England was large enough to cope so any returning soldiers would be a bonus. The full moon in September, which has the folkloric title of Harvest Moon, would have allowed soldiers to travel at night and possibly do some hunting along the way. Meanwhile farm-folk would be able to harvest by the light of the moon. Early autumn dew makes the corn stalks harder to cut, so working after the sun went down on dry stems was not unknown.

The release of the English coastal guard troops is also erroneously attributed to running out of rations, forcing the army to go home. This was the prime hunting time and the harvest from the fields was being gathered. Harvest festival was just weeks away. This was the time for fattening not starving.

The ASC suggests that back in July, Harold had employed his ships at Sandwich to deploy his troops after Tostig's raid seemingly contradicting the earlier assumption that Tostig had taken all the ships. The chronicles suggest that Harold transported the mustered troops to locations along the coast to stand guard although others say the army was on the Isle of Wight. It made strategic sense to do both.

This is an example of the uncertainty with which one must cope in reconstructing past events. It is sensible to recognise that a number of options and interpretations are feasible with different chroniclers recording what was known to them, which was not necessarily the whole picture. It was earlier estimated that Tostig's raiding ended in mid-June at which point the ships taken from Sandwich 'escaped' back to their base. The chronicles report that Harold was rather slow to deploy his defence which is certainly consistent with a shortage of ships, until the 'Tostig contingent' returned.

However Harold's reported tardiness makes good military sense. He needed to wait until he was able to assess the intentions of both his brother and the Normans. Which one posed the more immediate threat? Holding his army near the ships would allow him to deploy once the threats to his kingdom were better understood and he needed to have sufficient transport available. Once again one needs to address the words employed by the chroniclers, and here 'slow' is probably descriptive rather than judgmental.

Just as when describing the battle, careful research can often allow one reasonable interpretation to be selected from among the alternatives. The battle at Fulford revealed a level of strategic, logistic and tactical sophistication that goes unreported in the chronicles. Before the end of July Harold evidently felt that deploying guard forces as well as his main army along the south coast was the appropriate response with the brother earls successful campaign to drive Tostig out of England.

The Normans redeploy

It is easy to become ensnared in the web of inconsistent speculations. For the Norman invasion the data about the ship movements comes from one reliable source.

The reports come from the '*Song of the Norman Invasion*' which is believed to have been written very soon after 1066 by bishop Guy of Amiens. Guy was out of favour with the Pope and his underemployment possibly gave him time to compose his poem that would curry favour. He is later noted as chaplain to Matilda, William's wife, at her coronation in 1068 so he might be accepted as a well-placed observer of events surrounding the launching of the southern invasion.

Using these dates and reports, we can try here to interpret the intentions of the commanders and especially William, Duke of Normandy. Guy writes that the invasion fleet was "barred by storms and constant rain' and choppy seas, even at times forcing him back to port when 'gusting east winds curl the surging waves".[117] He later reports that "at last quitting your coast you turn the fleet to another shore" and it is specific that the coast is not England but St. Valéry-sur-Somme, a wide estuarine port with space for the whole fleet. We are also told that the invasion began to leave the numerous ports in Normandy after 6th September.

Harold's navy would have been patrolling and observing, so they should have noted the stream of ships moving north which our source tells us lasted for six days. The full moon should have been of assistance to those trying to navigate the rocky coast to reach the sandy estuary of the Somme as well as any English longships perhaps hoping to intercept laden invasion vessels which they expected should be heading towards England.

Once the redeployment plan was clear however, there was no point in retaining the English coastal watch or army opposite the Norman coast.[118] They could be released after their two month deployment guarding the south coast probably with orders to muster once William's new plan was better understood.

The date of 12 September is suggested by the Norman sources for their invasion assembly to be complete and this same date has the English fleet sailing back to their base in Sandwich. Both English and Norman fleets report a storm in the channel in their chronicles. But this date suggests that the Norman fleet had almost completed their move by then and some limited Norman losses are reported, and they were probably among the last contingent to sail. The impact on the English fleet who were all out at sea, rather than hugging the coast, might have been more significant.

---

[117] The translation employed is by Kathleen Tyson published in 2014: 9781492704751

[118] The English navy possibly kept Barfleur, at the tip of the Cotentin peninsula, under observation. It was a large harbour significantly nearer England, reinforcing our understanding that the easterly redeployment was a tactical ploy, with many nautical benefits.

Returning to Guy's narrative, he specifies 15 days as the delay at St. Valéry-sur-Somme, giving a detailed weather report which includes "if the south wind blows you go back from that cause" but "if a sudden north wind opposes and hinders, you stream forth tears". The weather is generally 'cold and wet, and the sky is covered over in 'cloud and rain.' This is not unusual weather for the autumn, and the same north wind reported here would have filled the sails of the other invasion fleet successfully heading to England from Norway. Guy had family links near the fleet's new haven so would likely be well informed about timings surrounding the delays and departure of the fleet, as well as the weather.

We have a good date for the eventual departure and from this the implication is that it took six full days to move and re-consolidate the fleet after it left Normandy. The staggered departure from the various Norman ports was not the prelude to the southern invasion. Had an invasion landed in England over such an extended number of days it would have failed. This relocation was planned.

This move would have been the first trip for many of the heavily loaded ships, so would have provided a valuable experience. For some ships this might even have been their maiden voyage given the frenzy of boatbuilding documented on the Bayeux Tapestry. The wide estuary of the River Somme provided an excellent target for any novice mariners and a magnificent space to assemble the invasion fleet.[119]

Clearing the harbours in Normandy in sequence would avoid congestion at sea as well as at their final destination. Not placing the whole fleet at risk by staggering the move would also deny both the English ships and the weather the chance of wrecking the enterprise.

It is stretching credibility that some of William's fleet would not have made it to England if the plan had indeed been to launch the invasion when they departed the coast of Normandy. But there is not a single record of ships being blown across the Channel to England or any encounter with the patrolling English Navy. The Normans clearly understood the tactical need arrive together and in force as their organisation during the crossing, discussed below, illustrates. This puts beyond doubt that the relocation to

[119] It is possible that many might have chosen to walk or ride for this leg of the invasion journey. So excellent work has been published on the Norman logistics with so many mouths to feed and boats to build but they do not shed much light on the logistics of this move.

St. Valéry-sur-Somme was a planned move and not one imposed by a storm as is often suggested.

A base at St. Valéry-sur-Somme has so much to recommend itself. St Valéry was one third of the distance from the south coast of England compared with the crossing from Normandy. Indeed Orderic Vitalis notes that William returned from Dieppe, which is near St Valéry, in December 1067 'with a south wind to a harbour called Winchelsea' not far from Hastings suggesting this was his preferred crossing point.

The sandy estuary of the Somme was a benign environment in which to assemble the entire invasion fleet that had previously been divided between the many ports of Normandy. The move took them to a place where fresh supplies could have been assembled at harvest time, it was more accessible to many of those who had offered or were obliged to contribute troops, and the interlude prior to embarkation was now well away from the temptations of home life in Normandy for others.

The news that Harold had released his army could arguably have provided the cue for the Normans to risk the open sea but the dates suggest that it was William who had taken the initiative perhaps because he was working to a timetable.

If William was indeed privy to the timing of the northern invasion, he was now nicely on schedule to organise his invasion army in the assembly area and cross to coincide with the Northern invaders. On or about the 14 September Harald's invasion was making landfall in England at 'Klifland' [Cleveland]. Had things gone to plan perhaps both invasions would have made landfall on the same date.

French historians are more critical of the tales, universally accepted among histories written in the English language, that William was a victim of storms and unfavourable winds keeping him first in Normandy and then in St. Valéry. Instead they note that the re-deployment enabled the force to be gathered together for the first time, something that every commander would welcome. With many mounts for the cavalry in need of transport, a short smooth crossing was essential to the success of William's invasion. This could be accomplished with infinitely greater certainty if a shorter crossing were chosen. The sideways move would also leave the English army out of position.

The Normans were also now well placed to take advantage of the haven, the manor of Rameslie,[120] on the opposite shore for their landing. This was gifted by King Ethelred in 1015 to the Norman Abbey of Fécamp in gratitude for the refuge offered when King Sweyn, and his young son Cnut, temporarily took control of England.[121] Modern historians note the landholdings and influence of the Abbey of Fécamp as a good reason to choose Pevensey as the best landing place.

The French monastic land would probably not be patrolled or guarded against invaders since it was legally protected by Rome, a place which we might in modern parlance recognise as a demilitarised zone. Landings are vulnerable so the location required careful selection.[122] This sparsely inhabited coast was ideal from so many perspectives. It is reasonable to accept that this was always William's intended landing site.

Scarborough had been attacked on the 16 or 17 September and burnt, with the advance party occupying Riccall and securing the river on the 18th to allow King Harald to sail past Riccall in safety and onto Fulford. Possibly this was the same day that news of the northern invasion reached Harold.

William's new location was on a well-trafficked trade route compared with the more remote Normandy providing him with a faster flow of intelligence reports from England. There can be little doubt that the bad, rather than windless, weather influenced the final departure date as Guy's narrative is dominated by weather reports. The Allied invasion was postponed in June 1944 and the storm of 19 June 1944 that almost destroyed the Mulberry Harbours in Normandy after D-Day which illustrates the unpredictable power of Channel storms in all seasons.

One might however wonder why Guy protests so much about the wind which is routinely blamed for delaying the southern invasion. Pedantically, one could say that a delay can only be measured with respect to a fixed timetable. Perhaps William made so much of the enforced delay to avoid risking the taint of oath-breaking if he had indeed sworn to follow Tostig's

---

[120] There is a little confusion introduced by Domesday about whether this is an estate, a manor or village.

[121] The records are unclear as records were lost at the turbulent time but the suggestion is that the land of the Pevenisel Peninsula was gifted to the Church in Rome rather than to Normandy where it might be employed as a haven for Viking raiders. Choosing this as the site of the landing is ironic.

[122] The prompt relocation to Hastings would not violate the status of the abbey land.

timetable. William had after all made much of Harold's oath breaking in mustering support for his invasion. His enterprise could not be risked if the conditions for his heavily laden invasion fleet were unsuitable. But as a good general William would want to be seen as anxious to get on with it, even if he was secretly anxious about an agreed timetable.

Modern Pevensey is neither a port nor tidal estuary but in 1066 it was apparently a good choice for the landing of a fleet. It is estimated that the headlands have eroded between 300 to 800 metres and instead of the current shingle bank there were many shallow inlets offering easy and safe beachings for the invasion fleet. The shore of Pevensey had much to recommend it when compared with the mud flats of the south coast behind the Isle of Wight where the complex tidal regime that flows around that island posed another challenge for sailors.

William's fleet finally sailed from the Somme at dusk on Wednesday 27th September landing near Pevensey after a night crossing of the Channel to relocated along the coast within the secure enclave at Hastings, the following day. It might have been Sunday, almost a week after Harold's crushing victory at Stamford Bridge, when news reached him of William's landing.

The invasion's departure date offers just enough time for a message of Tostig's success at Fulford to reach William's ears. Any messenger, and Tostig would certainly have organised this, might have noted King Harold's army moving north as they headed south. This news would be a bonus for William. Did news of the victory at Fulford fire the starting gun for the southern invasion?[123]

This seems unlikely although because of the delayed departure, William's intelligence network could have reported the welcome news before he set sail. Had Tostig been better informed and notified of Harold's move north, the outcome of the northern invasion might have been different: The chroniclers note that Harold sealed York to prevent news of his arrival reaching the invaders so generals of the time clearly understood the need for secrecy and the military advantage of surprise. Clearly the victors of Fulford were ignorant of Harold's move, arguably because Tostig was

[123] A 2022 French biopic about William is themed around the delayed departure for England and concludes with a messenger delivering some news to which William responds by rousing the sleeping army and ordering them to sail for England.

confident that William's invasion would oblige his brother to remain in the south.

Experienced Channel sailors would have reported on the favourable coastal tide that would carry the fleet north towards England if the timing was right, and while the Channel flow was not as dramatic as along the river Ouse, this was the season of fast tides. The level of knowledge of the sea captains planning the crossing can be in no doubt. Their plan provided two separate sea-rendezvous along the way to ensure they arrived together. The fleet included sleek longships such as William's *La Mora*, gifted by Matilda, and slower freighters carrying horses and equipment. We read from Guy and others, that William, with a light burning on his mast, dropped his sail when he reached the slack tide, mid journey to allow the slower ships to catch up.

The ships gathered and then moved on but this time with all of them displaying a light to avoid collisions in the misty conditions reported. Before dawn they had reached a gravel bank where once again they paused and even deployed their anchors to hold position against what modern analysis suggests would have been a contrary tide. Anchored not far offshore to sit out a tide it allowed most of the fleet to assemble prior to landing. At dawn they moved forward to the coast that was now clearly visible. The move came at the end of the season of energetic 'spring' tides.

French historians even suggest that the timetable, with its night crossing, was subject to the same planning compromises that were faced by those planning the 1944 D-Day landings on this coast where weather, tide, rocks and sand-bars dictated the course and timing.[124] The wartime landing craft required low tide to avoid the beach obstacles whereas the Norman invasion exploited the last days of the autumnal high tide that were so decisive at Fulford. French historians also see a parallel in the deception plans employed by the Allies in 1944 with William's actions in 1066, relegating the wind to just another factor in the timing of his crossing.

The news that King Harold had departed for the north might have motivated William to make his move but it was at least another 10 days after his departure from London, or rather his base at Waltham Abbey, that William sailed. By then both the battles at Fulford and Stamford Bridge had been decided. Perhaps the winds were indeed less than favourable for his diverse fleet as there was no reason for William to delay his crossing even

---

[124] Also detailed in C & G Grainer 'The Pevensey Expedition' *The Mariner's Mirror* 1993

though during the delay, events in England all worked very much to his benefit.

There are some issues which must remain open questions unless some new evidence is uncovered. Other popular suggestions, or 'myths', surrounding the invasion can be dismissed. Was Harold bottling the Normans in the harbour with navy patrols? Seemingly not as the Normans moved north unimpeded, but English patrols might have favoured the staggered move noted. Was the English army rather publicly released to tempt William out? The redeployment of the Norman fleet was underway before Harold released his soldiers. Many speculations are possible, but the timings suggest that the Norman fleet had a plan and slipped out in stages according to that plan.

We are nowhere actually told that the English ships patrolled the sea between Normandy and England but given the tactical acumen displayed by all of the commanders discussed here, it is likely that there were regular sightings of English 'spy' ships off the coast of Normandy. Indeed the ASC says as much: King Harold 'sailed out against William with a naval force'.[125]

However, Frank Barlow records that Aelfric, Lord of Kelvedon, took part in a naval battle against William. He was arguably England's admiral. Aelfric fell sick upon his return after many ships were wrecked in the reported September storm and left his Kelevedon estate to Westminster Abbey. He then departed for the 'Low Countries' when it became clear that all those who had fought against William would be dispossessed,[126] suggesting he had been responsible for threatening or attacking the Norman invasion fleet.

There are however no records of a sea battle. Norman sources also say their own invasion fleet was sent home once their cargo of warriors, weapons and horses was delivered to their final destination, the port at Hastings, perhaps to stiffen resolve knowing that there was no escape but it also removed a tempting target for the English navy. French sources only report losses that are due to the storm during the transfer from St. Valéry -sur-Somme but they make no mention of a clash with any English ships.

It is not clear what prevented King Harold from destroying the vulnerable Norman invasion fleet once they put to sea to cross to England from Picardy. Perhaps the losses reported from the storm, or the need to refit

---

[125] ASC E (Peterborough MS) translated Guy Points

[126] Edwin, Morcar and Waltheof were spared that fate as they did not come south to confront the Norman invasion.

after a long deployment, kept them in harbour. However, it looks much more like a fundamental failure of military intelligence by Harold. They had a whole month to locate and attack the Norman invasion fleet but seemingly did nothing.

Perhaps Harold accepted the stories that a storm had severely damaged both fleets. His move to Fulford suggests they assessed that the threat for the year had passed. We do not hear of him mobilising another fyrd, as he was entitled to do under the laws of Alfred, to guard the stretch of coast that was now threatened. His brother Leofwine was the Earl of Kent and could have been alerted to the increased threat. Perhaps we cannot assign too much significance to the failure of chroniclers to record a new defensive deployment.[127] Leofwine, whose limited military experience would be fatally exposed when he met the Normans in battle, perhaps planned to contain any landing with his own mobile army but we do not read of any skirmishes or containment force being thrown around the invaders by the army of Kent.

Blockading the Normans in Hastings after their landing might be deemed a successful tactic, and perhaps it happened although the invaders cavalry seemed to have the run of the countryside to gather provisions, according to their chroniclers.

William remained in his base for a surprisingly long 16 days until challenged by Harold on 14 October. The inactivity is also puzzling as he could have marched his army to an undefended London before Harold returned after Stamford Bridge. His inactivity suggests that he was ignorant of Harold's whereabouts. However, events after his victory suggests his invasion force was not a coherent field army as their subsequent progress to London took over two months.

We know the Normans created their first prefabricated motte and bailey castle providing William with a refuge. With their advantage in cavalry, one might have expected the Normans to establish a base inland where the coming battle could be fought on terrain of their choosing. Even bringing the smaller local army to battle would recommend itself to many military minds.

---

[127] Guy of Amiens tells that while most of the natives encountered were killed except children and maidens, it notes one who was waiting under the cliff who took the news of the invasion to Harold. This suggests that a reporting and warning system had been put in place.

Perhaps William had actually made the most successful assessment of unfolding events and how they could work to his advantage. Was his plan now to await the outcome of the northern invasion once he knew he had missed the coordinated date for simultaneous north and south invasions? William was a sophisticated strategist who would have recognised the benefits of awaiting the outcome of the northern invasion before making a move.

Both commanders knew that big armies are better for battles which is likely what prompted Harold to go north to try an bolster his new brothers-in-law, leaving two of his brothers to guard the south. Harold's subsequent misjudgement was to ignore the 'biggest is best' rule and rush his understrength army to the Norman bridgehead at Hastings.

Correlation is not causality and coincidence is even further from proving there was coordination. The known timings and actions, answer as well as ask questions.

William's invasion fleet 'escaped' in stages from any English naval attempted blockade, prompting Harold to reorganise his defence which was now in the wrong place. The Norman relocation meant that William's invasion was in position to land on the same date that the Norse invasion landed in Northumbria, 17 or 18 September but the weather reportedly delayed him for 10 more days.

Harold's plan to head north worked well for William. Not only were the English resources depleted, but the attack that he must have anticipated within days of landing was delayed for two weeks. Uncertainty surrounds the cause of William's delayed departure and his failure, or reluctance, to break out of Hastings. Whether they were planned or providential, the accumulated delays served William well.

We now need to wind back time to look at the events just after the battle when the news of the northern invasion reached Harold.

King Harold (of England) arrives in York

Events surrounding King Harold's move north can be reconstructed. Messengers might have reached his family base at Waltham Abbey late on Tuesday 19th September, the eve of the Fulford battle, with news of the Norse landing and the sack of Scarborough which had happened on Sunday. If he left at dawn on Thursday, the day after the battle at Fulford, travelling on horseback he would reach Tadcaster, which was the Mercian base, at midday on Sunday.[128] This timetable allows him a full day to gather information and views, assemble his troops and give instructions for his brothers about the defence of the south before heading north.

Harold was taking a calculated risk but, then as now, he recognised the impact that weather can have on plans. He possibly appreciated that William would be kept at bay for some days and that was all the time Harold needed. He left with his southern armies in place and the new landing beach within the domain of his brother. Could he even now be reconciled with his brother, Tostig, by offering concessions? It was a task that could not be delegated, requiring his presence.[129]

Harold rode north with his cavalry who were probably his mounted housecarls and therefore full-time warriors who did not require significant time to mobilise, although the one ASC reports that he mustered troops along the way. This 'army' must have also been mounted. Fighting on horseback was an innovation that was spreading through Europe and Arab horse bloodlines, bred in Spain, were already sought after as warhorses.

There is not enough time allowed by the documented dates for an army to march north.[130] The infantry army Harold required would be provided by the Mercians most of whom, as reported earlier, had been unwilling bystanders at Fulford. Harold had doubtless hoped to arrive in time to bring his authority, military experience and forces to confront the northern invasion.

One can speculate about the impact that a significant mobile element could have brought to the battle at Fulford. Harold certainly appreciated this. His time as an unwilling guest of William in Normandy had given him time to study the evolution of mounted tactics, suggested within the narrative on the Bayeux Tapestry. Harold had in recent years been leading mounted campaigns into Wales and clearly appreciated this evolution of

---

[128] Riding 10 hours each day at 8kph (80 x 4days) =320 km. The distance 290km to York via Doncaster and Tadcaster suggesting the journey would take about 3 and a half days.

[129] One might speculate as to how Harold would have reacted with his undersized army had the Mercians not been available. In the personal chain-of-command in that era, Harold could claim the loyalty of the Mercians through his marriage to Edwin's sister, and Edwin was oath-bound not to lead his army against the Norse invaders.

[130] The author has walked it, covering 35km per day.

warfare that was introduced by mounted warriors. Fulford was perhaps the last shieldwall battle on British soil.

The surviving descriptions of the subsequent battle at Stamford Bridge reports the opening phase with Harold's cavalry charging the isolated Norse contingent with the Mercians still marching to later provide the foot soldiers.

The limited Norse force at Stamford Bridge, included their leaders Harald and Tostig, who had gone there to collect the promised hostages from the English. They had less than half the army. Norse sagas even claim they did not take their mail-coats, many of which were doubtless in need of repair after Fulford. This might be an excuse to justify their subsequent failure but Harald was probably reassured by Tostig that his brother Harold was occupied with another invasion in the south.

The Northumbrian army had been destroyed and dispersed with its leader assumed to be dead. The Mercian army was also thought to be neutralised as its leader, Edwin, was oath-bound not to lead his army against the invaders. However Harold was not bound by this oath and could command the Mercians as Edwin's kin, his brother-in-law , rather than as the King of England.

The previous day, a Sunday, the Norse army was mustered at York after a celebration the night before. The citizens submitted and agreed to join Harald to go south but not until after the winter, a timetable which raises a number of unanswerable questions. They also agreed to give a large number of hostages and Tostig appointed these as we are told he was mindful of those he did not trust.

Stamford Bridge is located at the junction of many 'Wapentakes', or administrative sub-sections of the 'Thirdings' into which the wider area was divided. This was a central location, on the River Derwent, where the hostages could be gathered. It might have been tempting for the Norse to take their boats, but the river has some tight bends which would allow only smaller ships to navigate, rather than their longships. They would not have the logistic support they enjoyed at Fulford although we are specifically told that they took bows. These are all suggestive of an overconfidence that was likely underpinned by the knowledge of the pending southern invasion.

Unlike Fulford, the ASC has much more to say about this second battle. The Norse sagas are equally informative despite being utterly defeated. Initially, both sides were playing for time. King Harald summoned his army from Riccall while Harold was waiting for the Mercians who must have marched through the night to reach Stamford Bridge around midday.

Heming provides one narrative of the battle, confirming that it was the Mercians providing the infantry. He even claims to have responded to a request from King Harold to demonstrate his prowess with the bow and shoot the King of Norway.[131] The story tells us it took two shots and even Norse sources report that it was an arrow in Harald's throat that was fatal. The 'flying razor blades' recovered at Fulford would indeed inflict such fatal wounds.

Not only was King Harald killed but Tostig, who after a second pause in the fighting for negotiations, had refused the offer from his brother to restore his earldom and was killed. The Norse army at Stamford Bridge was almost wiped out. The Norse reinforcements rushing from Riccall, led by the estimable Eystein Orre, who had led the charge across the beck at Fulford, fared no better. The Norse sources report that more died because it was such a hot day rather than 'at the hands of the Saxons' but Harold's cavalry released once the Merians arrived would have hunted down stragglers on their 24km 'Orre's storm' from Riccall.

The historian, Henry of Huntingdon, expands our record about both Yorkshire battles and introduces the story of a lone warrior holding a bridge during the Norse retreat from Stamford Bridge, adding the details of an up-thrust from a spearman, floating in a barrel, dislodged him. This is an embellishment of the one version of the ASC which mentions this incident. The Abingdon Chronicle, a component of the ASC, has the original version of this story which was inserted into that text in what is known as a gloss. It is believed that this addition was made at about the time Henry was compiling his history, and in the same locality. It is possibly not a coincidence that Waltheof, who was present at Fulford and probably at Stamford Bridge, was also the Earl of Huntingdon where these scribes were working. So Waltheof is the likely source of the story which he wanted entered into the record of the 'official' ASC.

The 'lone Viking' story is credible although the popular impression that it was the opening phase of the battle is not supported by what was written near the time. In recent times it was possible to wade across the stone ford at Stamford Bridge. A lone warrior on any bridge at that location, whose precise site has yet to be identified, would have been no impediment to an

[131] One reason for Heming's exile was defeating King Harald in an arrow shooting competition.

army crossing and certainly not to King Harold's cavalry. There are other locations on the road back to their base where the River Derwent has incised the landscape to create steep banks that provide a tactically sensible location for such a heroic defence of a bridge.[132]

King Harold had now lost two strong armies as the survivors would not be able to head south when Harold received the news of William's landing arrived a week after his triumph. The failure of the Mercians to go south has been attributed by some commentators to Harold's decision to delay the distribution of the spoils gathered from the defeated Norse, which he entrusted to the Archbishop in York.[133] Post-battle recycling evidence found at Fulford that gathered the spoils of war was evidently organised by the leadership.

The King would also have to make his way south without most of his cavalry which we can deduce because they are not mentioned in the subsequent battle. It is reasonable to suppose that they needed time to prepare themselves and their horses for another fast ride south. Harold might also have chosen to leave some trusted housecarls to oversee events in the North after the two battles where the authority of both defeated northern earls required some royal reinforcement. Maintaining law and order in a territory that had an active bloodfeud was still the responsibility of the King.

The road to Battle

A week had elapsed suggesting Harold felt no need to rush south. Riding with a handful of his guards, the three-day journey south gave Harold time to reflect and plan. Having left his brothers in charge, he could be confident that the Wessex army that he had released after a summer of waiting for William's invasion, would be reassembling after some home leave. His victory over the Norse invasion would give confidence to his southern armies and send a warning to the invaders.

From Orderic Vitalis we get the story of King Harold's decision to go to confront William: "Harold soon forgot the joy of his fatal victory in the face of grave danger, and had only a little space to feel proud and safe after his fratricide; for a messenger came bearing the news of the Norman landing. As soon as he learned that the Normans had invaded England he made

---

[132] For example both Cattons and Kexby even Elvington bridge between steep banks.

[133] Although William of Malmsbury suggest the spoils of war were entrusted to the local earls to convey to London.

haste to prepare himself for a fight to the death. For he was a brave and valiant man, strong and handsome, pleasant in speech and a good friend to his own followers.

"However, his mother Gytha, already filled with mourning at the death of her son Tostig and other good friends of his, tried to dissuade him from war; and Earl Gyrth his brother spoke these words,

" 'My dearest brother and lord, you should let discretion temper your valour. You have just returned worn out after the war against the Norwegians; are you now hastening to fight once more against the Normans? Rest I beg you. You ought to give careful thought to the oath you have taken to the Duke of Normandy. Take care that you do not commit perjury, and by this crime destroy the flower of our people with yourself and bring the shame on all our posterity. I have taken no oath and owe nothing to Count William; therefore I can boldly join combat with him for my native soil. But you, my brother, should wait peacefully wherever you like for the outcome of this war, lest the fair freedom of the English should perish through your destruction.'

"On hearing these words Harold flew into a violent rage. He rejected the counsel that seemed wise to his friends, answered his brother who was advising him for the best with reproofs, and when his mother clung to him to hold him back, insolently spurned her with his foot. Then for six days he sent far and wide to summon the populace to war, gathering a huge multitude of Englishmen around him, and hastened to battle against the enemy."[134]

Harold won the race to Hastings and occupied the ridge which blocked the exit towards London. The site is quite well understood although not yet archaeologically investigated employing the Fulford methodology. The course of the battle is well and consistently described in various Norman sources.

Harold was killed by a contingent of Norman knights that had infiltrated the English line depicted in the gory images of the Bayeux Tapestry.[135] His handfasted (first) wife, Edith, went among the dead to identify Harald 'by signs only she would know' while his pregnant wife was, we believe, with

---

[134] Orderic Vitalis, *The Ecclesiastical History book* iii, #146 tr Chibnall M

[135] Scholars have shown that the 'arrow in the eye' story was a later creation and recent analysis of the thread used shows it contains an industrial dye.

her grandmother Godiva probably in Chester. We do not know with confidence where Harold's body was buried.

Duke William of Normandy's path to the throne after the battle was not straightforward. England still had at least one undefeated army. Stranded south of the Thames for two months, Wigord an English lord, allowed some Norman troops to cross the river Thames at Wallingford and then he marched to London. Stigand, the Archbishop of Canterbury, also surrendered to William and assisted in the subsequent negotiations. After extensive discussions and concessions with the aldermen of London, terms were agreed. He accepted the surrender, or submission, of the leading English nobles at Berkhamsted and was subsequently crowned at Westminster Abbey on Christmas Day. It would take several more years for the Normans to consolidate their rule with rebellions and border skirmishes in Dover, Hereford, Nottingham, Durham, York and Peterborough and Exeter. Of the three 1066 leaders, William was the only one still standing.

Penitence

The early years of the new millennium had seen a revival in spiritual thought. One debate promoted by the Church of Rome was the justice of making war. Some churchmen felt a list of penances was always required. One such set out a detailed list covering both the battle and the subsequent conquest of England. The imposed penances can be interpreted as a spiritual rebuke for the invasion as no penances are specified for the defeated English, but ignoring the vanquished in these edicts is not unique. The penance was an ecclesiastical procedure to provide absolution for those who had killed in the course of the service, provided their cause was sanctioned by the Church. The crusades seem to have ended the debate about military killing within the Church and the need for such post facto absolution.

The ordinance, known as the Ermenfrid Penitential, is named for the Papal legate who conferred his authority on the appointed sanctions after Hastings. No penance is specified for William although we learn elsewhere that his building of the abbey at the place now known as Battle was designed as an atonement. An interesting footnote for the momentous year is provided by records showing that William was displeased when he found his abbey was being built on easier, flatter land and left his agent to ensure his instruction to build it where Harold had been killed was obeyed leaving little scope for doubt that the battlefield is accurately located.

People postscripts

In the opening section we addressed the life and significance of some actors who impacted the battle at Fulford. The consequences of the three battles some on those who survived is explored.

Widows

For Gytha, Harold's mother, it was a terrible year. Harold's army had killed Tostig at Stamford Bridge and three weeks later three sons, Harold, Gyrth, and Leofwine, were killed resisting the Norman invasion.

Only one son survived and that was Wulfnoth who had been given as a hostage to William in about 1053 and negotiating his release was possibly the motive for Earl Harold's fateful journey, depicted in the Bayeux Tapestry, when William extracted the oaths to support his claim to the English throne. Wulfnoth lived out a long life as an effective captive in Normandy until the death of William the Conqueror in 1087 when he might have been freed.

With only an indirect bearing on our story, mention should be made of another son. Swegen, the oldest Godwinson, whose actions impacted the lives of other members of the family. Clearly being groomed to inherit the role of his founding father, Earl Godwin, he dabbled in Welsh politics where he abducted the Abbess of Leominster, perhaps hoping to gain control of the estates by marrying her. King Edward refused permission and Eadgifu was returned although some chronicle entries are rather more suggestive about Swegen's actions. Late in 1047 Swegen was consequently exiled and sought refuge with Baldwin V, Count of Flanders. This enforced visit might have alerted the Godwinsons to the fact that there were two eligible women, Judith and Matilda, at the court. The former married his brother Tostig in 1051 and the latter married William about the same time, although papal objections delayed formal recognition of this latter match.

During his exile, Swegen travelled to Denmark but returned to England in 1049 to beg for forgiveness after being expelled from Denmark. His cousin Beorn, who was already based in England, might have been aware of the reasons for his Danish exile because this potential heir to the Danish throne was murdered by his wayward cousin and now Swegen was declared a man of no honour, or 'nithing'.

Again pardoned, Swegen returned just in time to join the whole Godwinson family when they were exiled in 1052 as part of King Edwards plan to prepare the kingdom for a smooth transition to William, a plan which we noted backfired. Swegen however did not return with the other Godwinsons the following year because he had perished on his way back from a penitential pilgrimage to Jerusalem.

Gytha's eldest daughter, the dowager Queen Edith, quickly submitted to William as he struggled to take control in England in the months after the invasion and critically handed over the royal treasury. Gytha's other two daughters are believed to already have become nuns.

The redoubtable Gytha seems to have been the rallying point for many noble widows. English laws gave the widows significant title to lands which impeded early attempts to reward the foreign lords who had helped in the Norman invasion. William had agreed to uphold the laws of England when he negotiated the submission of the City of London. In exchange for the throne William granted them some perpetual privileges.

Tapestry

It is arguable that the English widows, now living within the secure confines of monasteries, where most religious houses were the endowments of powerful families, provided the skills to quickly embroider a narrative tapestry. The consensus among scholars is that the design came from Canterbury with the embroidery done at several southern religious houses.

Bishop Odo, William's half-brother, is the most likely sponsor and the only recorded display was at a feast he organised to launch a crusade. There is no evidence that William ever saw himself depicted on what we call the Bayeux Tapestry. Several surviving examples suggest memorialisation through embroideries was common at the time.

Gytha & the Exeter revolt

Gytha evidently still held the considerable Godwinson portable wealth and perhaps hoped for the arrival of her grandsons, Harold's three sons Godwin, Edmund and Magnus, who had gone to Ireland to raise an army. There is evidence pointing to their attempt to organise a revolt and hold the west country where the Norman control had not yet been extended.

Late in 1067, William returned after his triumphant return to Normandy and swiftly went to Exeter, demanding the city's submission. The following year he returned and besieged the city and after 18 days it submitted again. There is evidence that William tested his political capital in the west country when he felt able to call out the traditional fyrd, or reserve army, for his occupation of the west. This is the first recorded example of native troops being deployed to fight in England, suggesting that some had accepted their new overlords.

The surrender terms were surprisingly lenient, possibly hoping to peacefully capture Gytha and her entourage with all their wealth and land titles. Marriage for these widows was William's likely plan. It is not fanciful to imagine that the Normans waited expecting Gytha to try and escape via the obvious exit along the River Exe and into the Channel towards a safe haven in Flanders.

However, Gytha evaded this trap and led these noble ladies north. Moving overland from the siege at Exeter to the Bristol Channel where she established a base on the island of Flat Holm, possibly in the hope of a rendezvous with her grandsons' expedition from Ireland. Harold's mother, Gytha, 'and the wives of many good men' as the ASC terms the widows, escaped to the rocky outcrop in the Bristol Channel, 'Steep Holm'.

The sons of Harold did not actually arrive until later in the year; Gytha's grandsons arrived with a fleet of 52 ships provided by Diarmait, the 'High King' of Ireland. The citizens of Bristol however closed their gates to them. The subsequent confrontation, known as the Battle of Bleadon, appears inconclusive although Eadnoth *the Staler* was killed. Harold's sons retreated to their ships and raided the coast before returning to Ireland with some plunder.

It is possible that this fleet met Gytha according to previous arrangements and took them into exile. Had the fleet arrived earlier, a fight for Exeter and the west country might have materialised. It is possible that William had forestalled an uprising by his show of force in the west and recruiting those who might rebel into his own employment.

At Midsummer in 1069 young Godwin and his brother Edmund returned with their army and sixty ships this time. They landed at Appledore and advanced inland to Northam where an army, now commanded by Brian of Brittany, a relative of William, quickly arrived in the area where the landscape afforded them the advantage of higher ground. The mounted mobility of a troop of Breton knights possibly provided the cover needed to move the local defenders into an advantageous tactical position and constrained the progress of Harold's sons.

Once again the tide played an important role. Not only was the tide out, but the channel was full of sandbars that could not be crossed until the high tide returned. The extreme slopes that fall down to the quay probably forced a protracted battle either beside the river or on the plateau above as they waited for high tide.

It hardly gets dark at that time of year and the tide finally returned allowing these two Haroldson brothers to escape, but as at Fulford, it was probable that a brave contingent held the attackers at bay, and the ASC terms them the 'best men', while most clambered aboard the ships and escaped to sea, one Norman source suggesting they took 1,700 casualties.[136]

That ended the Godwinson family's attempts to return with the brothers moving to Denmark, providing another footnote of these events. Marine archaeology allows a very confident identification of the longship they used. It is now known as Skuldelev 2 and can be visited in the Roskilde Ship Museum. The oak used to make the ship, originally named the Sea Serpent, can be linked by dendrochronology to Dublin and dated to this time. At the end of its life the boat was scuttled to provide defences at Roskilde. A replica has been sailed all around the British Isle and a second, *La Mora*, is under construction in Honfleur to commemorate the millennium of Duke William's birth.

The widows went to St. Omer in Flanders, where Gytha had earlier been exiled with her husband in 1051 and eventually on to her native Denmark, perhaps after her widowed daughter in law, Judith remarried and moved to Bavaria. Gytha never returned to England. Little is written about the way the issue of legal title that the widows had taken abroad with them was resolved. Did some choose to return or was the confusion over the ownership of land one motivation for the epic inquests which produced the Domesday surveys which established who owned what?

Edwin and Morcar

The brothers escaped the slaughter at Fulford but do not seem to have participated in the victory of King Harold II over Tostig and the Norwegians at Stamford Bridge. Edwin was barred by the oath he had sworn and Morcar might have felt it best to accept the presumption of his death go unchallenged while Tostig was alive. One later chronicle from John of Worcester suggest Mærleswein was appointed by Harold to replace Morcar whose whereabouts were perhaps unknown.

The timetable is really too tight to allow either earl to negotiate with their victorious brother-in-law, Harold, who had dutifully rushed north to their aid doubtless as previously agreed. The older man, recognising that size in

[136] William of Jumièges

battle counts and probably hoped to overwhelm the invasions in turn with almost the full force of the five armies he could field.

John of Worcester says they had "withdrawn themselves and their men from the [Hastings] conflict" which is harsh since the earls had suffered losses at Fulford and Stamford Bridge just weeks previously. However, the brothers seem to have mustered their armies in London not many weeks after the battle of Hastings suggesting that they were not a spent force.

Immediately after the Norman victory the brothers sent their widowed sister to Chester where granny Godiva was based. They then joined the Aldermen of London where the ASC (D) reports that the archbishop of York selected Edgar Ætheling as their next king.

The brothers initially agreed to fight for Edgar but that plan seems to have fallen apart with John of Worcester reporting: 'But while numbers were preparing to go out to fight, the earls [Edwin and Morcar] withdrew their assistance and returned home with their army.' William of Malmsbury is rather more specific implying that the brothers own ambitions had been thwarted as they 'solicited the citizens [of London] to raise one of them to the throne; failing in the attempt, they had departed for Northumberland' and implies that Edgar was not formally adopted as king. Without armies, Edgar was powerless to oppose William.

William meanwhile was playing safe and moved to Dover where the fortifications and harbour gave him a secure base, suggesting he was expecting an attack which the conflicting ambitions among the English prevented. But it would be over two months before he was able to enter London. The brothers now recognised that resistance was futile although they held out until after the coronation and submitted to the Conqueror in January 1067 at Barking which was William's temporary base while the White Tower was being constructed.

During the Easter festival later that year they were among the English nobles who were taken to Normandy to participate in William's celebrations in the duchy. William appointed Cospig, Waltheof's companion, as Earl of Northumbria but as the bloodfeud resumed, he survived only five weeks. Morcar seemingly remained in William's entourage but Orderic Vitalis chronicles the brothers rebelling in 1068, enlisting Welsh support, recalling that it was with their aid that their own father had won back his earldom. The rebellion petered out and they submitted again and were pardoned. At about the same time, the uncrowned King Edgar Ætheling took refuge with King Malcolm *Canmore*, in Scotland.

According again to Orderic Vitalis, Edwin rebelled because it was suggested William denied him genuine authority and possibly the daughter promised in marriage was seemingly withheld. If correct, it suggests a growing lack of trust between William and the surviving native English lords.

The final revolt began in 1071. Orderic describes how early in the year Morcar and Edwin were forced to flee William's court suggesting their motive was that the king's mind had been poisoned against the brothers, and they feared imprisonment. Morcar joined the revolt in the Fens, attributed in historic fiction to Hereward *the Wake*. Morcar was eventually captured and imprisoned. As was traditional, political prisoners were released on the death of a king but Morcar did not taste freedom for long as William Rufus re-arrested him and Morcar died in prison evidently too dangerous to be given his freedom.

Edwin's fate came quicker. He was betrayed, but protected by twenty faithful hearthtroops, 'all fighting desperately to the last' according to Orderic, he was killed. Other less favourable sources are ambiguous as they suggest it was one of his own who killed him.

Queen Ældgyth

Queen Ældgyth, Harold II's widow, was probably at the Godwinson base at Waltham at the time of Harold's death at Hastings. With that family decimated, her brothers Edwin and Morcar probably arranged to move her to their family base in Chester. Their grandmother, Godiva, was the surviving matriarch and tradition reports that Ældgyth gave birth, possibly to twins, although nothing has yet been securely sourced. The twins and their mother were then lost to history but they might quite reasonably have joined the children of Harold in Dublin and later gone with them to Denmark after their failed attempts to raise rebellion in England. However, Ældgyth had an elder daughter Nest, and they could have sought refuge in Wales after Godiva's death in 1069. This lady has left some interesting historical loose ends.

Dowager Queen Edith

Edith it is believed was closest to her brother Tostig so might have had mixed feeling about Harold's fate at Hastings. She was doubtless privy to the wish of her husband Edward to pass the throne to William, although she suffered confinement in Wilton Abbey, which she rebuilt for the

Benedictine Order when the Godwinson's were exiled in 1051. Without any obvious protection she submitted to William rather than joining her mother Gytha.

Immediately after 1066 she commissioned and provided much information to the scribe, probably working in St. Omer, to produce the *Vita Ædwardi Regis qui apud Westmonasterium Requiescit* or *Life of King Edward who rests at Westminster*. Ostensibly about her husband, it provides historians with an excellent source about the Godwinson family and was completed in 1067.

She died at the end of 1075 apparently spending her final years reading sacred texts. Edith's determination to be the author if not the actual scribe of the family legacy withholds much of her story such as her part in the alienation of the nobles of Northumbria by having two guests murdered. It is not improbable that she 'commuted' between Winchester and St. Omer both to dictate her encomium but also to acquire more sacred texts from the Continent.

Judith

Widowhood did not prevent the well-connected and politically astute Judith from being a key player in European politics for another 30 years after the death of Tostig. The fact that Skuli and Keitl did not return to Flanders has been interpreted by some as a suggestion that she was not their biological mother. However, their Norse names and their close companionship with King Olaf provided enough incentive for them to stay in Norway.

One of the last acts of her half-brother, Count Baldwin V, of Flanders was to negotiate her second marriage to Welf IV, Duke of Bavaria. This union produced another two sons, Welf and Henry. Duke Welf and Judith were at the eye of a decade of conflict between the Holy Roman Empire and the Papacy where they were ultimately victorious.

In her will, which was drawn up in 1094, Judith made bequests to the monastery of Weingarten where she died and was buried in March the following year. These gifts included four Anglo-Saxon gospel books where visitors can read that Judith was a widowed Queen of England, suggesting that in her version of history, Tostig had been the legitimate King of England.

Tostig

Although killed at Stamford Bridge, this short note explores why Tostig is not recognised for his pivotal role in the events of 1066. The compliers of the Norse sagas make little mention of Tostig during the battle itself perhaps illustrating the importance of taking your own skald with you into battle if you hoped for literary immortality. Tostig did not, as far as we know, have a skald to sing his praises and record his brief moment of glory.[137] The sagas provide a few detail of how Tostig sought support for his re-installation as the ruler of Northumbria. He merits one verse in *Heimskringla* but even this is mostly about his boss, King Harald.

89. OF EARL TOSTIG

"Earl Toste had come from Flanders to King Harald as soon as he arrived in England, and the earl was present at all these battles. It happened, as he had foretold the king at their first meeting, that in England many people would flock to them, as being friends and relations of Earl Tostig, and thus the king's forces were much strengthened. After the battle just described, all people in the nearest districts submitted to Harald, but some fled. Then the King advanced to take the castle [York], and laid his army at Stafnfurdubryggja [Stamford Bridge]; and as King Harald had gained so great a victory against so great chiefs and so great an army, the people were dismayed, and doubted if they could make any opposition. The men of the castle therefore determined, in a council, to send a message to King Harald, and deliver up the castle into his power. All this was soon settled; so that on Sunday the King proceeded with the whole army to the castle and appointed a Thing[138] of the people outside the castle, at which the people of the castle were to be present. At this Thing all the people accepted the condition of submitting to Harald, and gave him, as hostages, the children of the most considerable persons; for Earl Toste was well acquainted with all the people of that town. In the evening the King returned down to his ships, after this victory achieved with his own force, and was very merry."[139]

The moral of this story is that if you hope that future historians will take note of what you did, you need someone to record your version of events. Tostig signally failed either to record, or as his sister tells us, even share his thoughts, enabling others to record his plans. His widow was soon occupied elsewhere and her significant legacy was in monastic buildings

---

[137] Employing a skald in England was evidently know since Thorkill Skallason, Waltheof's skald, records the execution of his patron in 1075

[138] Thing, or Ting, was a Norse gathering, often to vote. Many Nordic countries preserve the word in the title of their modern representative assembly.

[139] This version is taken from the Online Medieval and Classical Library Release 15b translation by Samuel Laing (London, 1844) with author's alternatives noted in square brackets.

and collecting biblical texts. The monastic scribes charged with maintaining England's Chronicle saw no actions of Tostig worth recording. Tostig has suffered the fate of those whose operations are clandestine, which is probably not the legacy he intended. His sons apparently did nothing to record his place in written history.

King Alfred *the Great* writing in his translation of Boethius' *Consolations of philosophy* blames scribes who through 'sloth, carelessness or negligence leave unwritten the virtues and deeds ' of men of renown and honour. However, the limited evidence we have suggests that it was the ability to hire a scribe which determined whether a biography was written.

The sons Olaf, Skuli and Keitl

The Orkney Saga reports; "Then after the battle King Harold gave leave to Olaf Harald's son and to the Earl's [Skuli and Keitl] to quit England, and to all their men who had not fled. Olaf sailed out in the autumn from Ravenser [Hrafnesyrr – Hrafn's beach] and so to the Orkneys. And [they then learned that] on the very day at the very hour that Harald was killed, Maria his daughter died suddenly. And men say that they had but one life between them."

This tells us that after Stamford Bridge, Olaf, Skuli and Keitl, the young sons of King Harald and Earl Tostig threw themselves on King Harold's mercy. One source tells us that Olaf had been left in charge of the Riccall base. The boys, who were in their early teens, had been left at Riccall which was stripped of its defenders because every fit soldier had headed towards Stamford Bridge to rescue King Harald.

"Olaf stayed the winter in the Orkneys and lived in closest friendship with the Earls his kinsmen ; [for] Thora King Olaf's mother and Ingibjorg the Earls' mother were cousins. In the spring Olaf sailed east to Norway and was there made King along with his brother Magnus."[140]

Tostig is known to have two sons Skuli and Keitl. Some have argued that these could not have been Judith's children arguing that they would have been too young to appear at the battles of Fulford and Stamford Bridge. This is based on the assumption that they actually fought rather than simply accompanied their father.

---

[140] Taken from a facsimile of the 1873 translation by Hjaltalin & Goudie, published in 1977. The events bear a close comparison with the Taylor translation.

Skuli could have been no more than 15 while Olaf, the son of Harald *Hardrada*, was likely the same age but is recorded by the skalds as having fought at Fulford. It is likely that all the youngsters stayed with the Orkney earls guarding Riccall since they did not suffer the fate of the Norse armies which were utterly destroyed. They were old enough to carry arms and might have been arranged not just as suitable companions for Olaf but even as hostages for the paranoid Harald.

Vita Edwardii mentions Tostig arriving in Flanders after his exile in 1065, fourteen years after the marriage, 'with his wife and nursing children' so the reluctance of historians to admit them as children of the marriage can be challenged and it is recorded that Judith gave birth to healthy children into her fourth decade. The dates and ages are all consistent with both of Tostig's sons being her children.

The names are also taken as evidence that they could not have been Judith's children but this can be countered by noting that the resurgent Godwinson's had already begun to manoeuvre to take the valuable title of Northumbria in the family portfolio.

Harold's nephews, Skuli and Keitl, would make successful careers in Norway especially after Olaf became sole King of Norway following the death of his brother Magnus in 1069. He presided over a peaceful and prosperous generation, earning the by-name 'the peaceful' or 'quiet'. Perhaps these young men had already experienced enough of the uncertain consequences of warfare.

They were fortunate to survive. Few who joined Earl Orre's reinforcements rushing 24 km over difficult terrain to join Harald were left standing. The English chronicles also talk of the Mercian fleet attacking Riccall presumably from the river, and the boys evidently survived that attack on the Norse base, suggesting this was more of a nuisance raid perhaps setting fire to the Norse ships rather than a land battle.[141]

Subsequent Norse history records the rise of the Tostig-sons in Norway under Olaf's long rule. Skuli is later referred to as foster-kin to Olaf.[142] Skule helped King Olav *Kyrre* and was rewarded with several large estates in

---

[141] A day spent collecting auger samples at Riccall produced evidence of burning that has yet to be investigated.

[142] Alison Finlay's translation of *Fagrskinna* resolves a previous confusion arising from earlier translations which termed Skuli the foster-father, recognising that the term *fostri* did not uniquely define a paternal relationship.

Norway, including the large farm at Rein outside Trondheim (now Rein's monastery) and we are told he also 'took his wife'. A border dispute at Haverö led to his death.

Morkinskinna also records that King Olav "arranged a good marriage for Ketil and appointed him a district chieftain in the north", adding that "many distinguished men are descended from Ketil" founding a dynasty where their ambitious family had failed.

Norse sources note that Skuli and his brother Ketil were 'of high family in England' and were companions of the king. Morkinskinna also records that Skuli 'went west to England to ask for the return of King Harald's body 'which was granted to him'. There is strong traditional evidence to support this as Harald was reburied in Niardos, modern Trondheim. Recent excavations of Harald's traditional resting place did not however reveal any meaningful remains. Archaeology can only discover evidence that has actually survived.

Waltheof

In this narrative, Earl Edwin is confidently portrayed as the leader of the Mercians because of his senior status. But, as we noted, it is feasible that it was Waltheof who was actually giving the orders as the local commander. Since he was fighting for his native territory he would expect to take a lead.

Waltheof was the second son of Siward, Earl of Northumbria and his first wife Ælflæd, born about 1050. He was grandson of the almost mythical Earl Uhtred so a member of the house of Bamburgh which had ruled Northumbria until Cnut's fatal intervention. The death in 1054 of a much older brother, Osbearn, in the battle at Dunsinane to displace King Macbeth of Scotland made Waltheof his father's heir. He was perhaps deemed too young at about 5 years of age to succeed as earl when Siward died in 1055 opening the way eventually for the appointment of Tostig. One might conjecture that he felt some animosity towards Tostig.

Waltheof was a rare surviving Norse-Saxon who seems to have been half trusted by the Norman conqueror and this despite joining the Northern revolt in 1069. When he finally submitted, William made further efforts to win his loyalty by marrying him to his niece Judith, the daughter of Adelaide, William's half-sister making him a nephew of the king and promoting him from Earl of Huntingdon to the earldom of Northumbria in 1072.

Waltheof followed the Norse tradition of family feuding and wreaked his vengeance on the family responsible for the murder of his great grandfather Uthred in 1016 as a part of their blood feud.

Saxon England remained on the verge of rebellion and in 1075 a group of Norman knights plus the one surviving Saxon leader, Waltheof, revolted but were defeated. Waltheof gave himself up to William, who imprisoned and then beheaded him on the hill overlooking Winchester. The punishment was considered harsh as the co-conspirators had lands confiscated and were imprisoned. William the Conqueror was said to have been obsessed by guilt over his treatment of Waltheof suggesting there was a respectful relationship. We know so much about Waltheof as he was promoted as a Christian martyr ensuring that his life was well recorded in English and Norse sources by his skald.

Scotland

Having been fostered at the court of Edward *the Confessor*, Malcolm ascended the Scottish throne in 1053 with the assistance of the Northumbrian Earl Siward. It is likely that he met Margaret, the daughter of Edward *the Exile* because they were both wards of Edward and a union seemed natural although Malcolm initially made a dynastic match within Scotland. When his first wife died the way was open for Margaret although some sources suggest this forceful lady was not enthusiastic.

The names given to Margaret's many children with Malcolm are unconventional especially as their sons were expected to succeed to Scotland's throne. Edward was named after her father, Edmund for her grandfather, Ethelred for her great-grandfather then Edgar for her great-great-grandfather or possibly for her brother, Edgar *Ætheling*. Their father's longevity meant that only her youngest, Edgar, would occupy the Scottish throne.

Many trivial changes, such as the introduction of the dining fork, are attributed to Margaret but her impacts on Scotland was significant and long-lasting, among them being the adoption of the same language spoken south of the border. But it was a daughter of this marriage that most impacted the English royal house as William's youngest son, Henry, married their eldest daughter introducing the bloodline of Alfred *the Great* to the Norman conquerors. Through their daughter Matilda, who history has denied the title of first female sovereign of England, the Plantagenet line would later assert their right to rule Scotland, through Edward I, *the Hammer of the Scots*.

Annex A: Army organisation, tactics and weapons

This section should, arguably, precede any description of the battle. It is appended here so that the focus in the battle would be on the people and their actions. Placing it after the battle permits some analysis of how well they performed.

This annex is designed to provide another context for the battle at Fulford, including army organisation, weaponry and tactics. One purpose is to dispel some popular misconceptions which can often be traced to the creative industries, where elaborate headgear and uniforms are photogenic while mythic 'berserkers' provide good action sequences. The reality of the events at Fulford, based on careful re-creation, were arguably just as exciting as the products of fictional creativity.

Fulford is currently one of the very few ancient battles to have been investigated systematically which has also provided weapon fragments. These physical finds have permitted the confident description of the tactics and weapons that was explained in the narrative of the battle with the caveat that the extent to which Fulford is unique cannot be assessed until other sites have been similarly investigated.

Army sizes

It is surprising that nothing is written in contemporary sources to tell us how big the armies were. We have several statements about the number of ships that brought the invading Norse but even that data varies so much as to make it of limited use because longships come in many shapes and lengths. Therefore estimates have to be made set in the context of this battle.

It is a military maxim that victory goes to whoever can bring superior numbers to bear. Tactics and plans are designed to focus the force and provide local numerical superiority over an enemy in order to break their formation. Attempting this when long lines of shields clash is difficult but King Harald was the expert at focusing his force on a weak point, as he did at Fulford. While size matters, it is no guarantee of victory.

The fact that the ancients seldom recorded the numbers involved in battles possibly suggests that it was not something that was thought to be important, unlike ship numbers. Occasional references to bigger or stronger might be taken as guides to relative army size but the only qualifier provided at Fulford is a single reference to the weaker troops being assigned to Tostig.

In the context of descriptors one could consider quantity and quality and again there is just a single comment made during the reported debate in Oslo when Tostig's proposition to invade was being discussed – One warrior warns that a single Saxon warrior is worth 10 Norsemen while another notes that the English, probably thinking of Tostig, cannot be trusted.

Numbers do matter when it comes to the push and shove of shieldwalls but in such close quarter fighting, there is nothing to suggest that either side held the advantage. This battle was one of manoeuvre where both sides were at times successful in bringing superior numbers to bear on weak points in the opposing defences. Harald was just a better practitioner which is why he won. A line could be stretched to appear large or contract to give it depth. So the width of a battlefield cannot be used as an analogue for an army's size.

The calculations of army sizes is necessarily imprecise but the consensus estimate suggests we know that the Northumbrian army, led by their new, young Earl Morcar and the Mercian army under his brother Earl Edwin both fielded between four and six thousand trained and armed soldiers.

King Harald brought several hundred ships allowing an estimate of the average size and the number of 'benches' or oarsmen. The upper estimate of this invasion force is 10 thousand warriors including the contingents supplied by Earl Tostig plus the army from the Orkney earls. With space for no more than 60 ships along the gently sloping banks on the outside of the bend at Fulford, Harald could have had no more than 2,500 quality troops with him when he landed. This was insufficient to engage in battle but strong enough to deter a surprise, dawn attack, which was also constrained by the imminent arrival of the tidal bore, about two hours after first light and the English tactical deployments to address other threats. Superficially, Harald, might have appeared a tempting target.

Orkney was a stopping off point on the journey and their earls, two brothers Paul and Erland, owed allegiance to the kings of Norway. Their force was tasked with going ahead to secure the bases and they are reported to have fought one battle in Holderness before going on to occupy and secure the planned landing at Riccall. The Orkney sagas do not report the action at either Fulford or Stamford Bridge, reinforcing other suggestions that their role was to guard the base.

There are a number of good reasons why Harald might have decided to take the Orkney army even if he only planned to use them to defend his base. The Orkney mariners probably were more familiar with the local coast and rivers. Plus their early arrival would not reveal to true intent of the Norse invasion. But the wily Harald had also left his wife and two daughters in the Orkneys, taking by way of security, at least one noble Orkney woman.

This is how one saga reports this: "Now King Haraldr sailed first to Orkney, and left behind there his wife Elsvetta and his daughter Maria. He took away with him from there Jarl Pall, son of Jarl Thorfinnr and of Ingibjorg, daughter of Jarl Finnr Arnason." Obliging the Orkney earls to accompany this invasion ensured that they could not take advantage and perhaps try to seize some land in Norway or ally themselves with Denmark to assert their independence. As a schemer himself, Harald might be described as paranoid. The saga continues, "From there King Haraldr took his army south to England... "[143]

So not everyone who arrived was available to fight at Fulford. Texts record seamen and it is likely that artisans and other support personnel would arrive as non-combatants with the fleet. This compounds the problem of estimating army sizes. A range of estimates is advisable, and another method looks at the space available at either landing or on the battlefield.

The space for the Norse landing and the size of the shieldwalls that can fit into the understood landscape suggests that both sides had about six thousand soldiers on the east bank and taking an active part in the battle.

Armies were not the uniform centralised national organisations we know today. Loyalty was still to their local leader who was known to them. For a Northumbrian soldier, the king was a remote concept. Their leader had probably inherited an obligation to bear arms and these obligations rippled down the social hierarchy. A local leader would owe their loyalty to another more powerful overlord and so on up perhaps to the king. The king's festive gatherings that took place at Christmas and Easter where probably matched locally because these gatherings served to establish and reinforce military control that evolved as titleholders died or were replaced. This system of military obligations was then reinforced through gifts, appointments and with grants of land.

While the chain of command was passed through the governing power, a soldier took his orders from someone he knew. The death of a king or leader

---

[143] *Fagrskinna* Tr Alison Finlay 2004 edition 9004131728 Brill Chapter 63

could therefore lead to the disintegrations or defeat of an army as people would not take orders or risk their life for someone to whom they owed no obligation. In 1013 when King Sweyn *Forkbeard* of Denmark died suddenly, the army did not stay to support his son Cnut who had to leave England and raise his own army to successfully re-invade England.

Although the army sizes are unknowable, Fulford can arguably claim to be the biggest of these three, autumn battle of 1066.

- Four fresh armies took part at Fulford: Northumbrian, Mercian, Norwegian, Orkney plus Tostig's contingent. At Stamford Bridge there were two armies, minus some casualties from Fulford, plus King Harold's cavalry. At Hastings the Norman army faced three English armies from Kent, East Anglian and Wessex armies and it is suggested that the size of Kent and East Anglian contingents did not match those raised in the three great earldoms.
- Time – Fulford lasted effectively 24 hours starting from the time Harald landed at Fulford with battle action lasting about 6 hours for all of three battles.
- The area covered by the battlefields is harder to compare. Fulford is similar to Hastings in size while the Stamford Bridge was an ambush and a running battle over an extensive area all the way back to the Riccall base.

Fyrd

The Anglo-Saxon *fyrd* was an 'expeditionary' force whose organisation developed to meet changing external threats as well as domestic power dynamics. King Alfred answered the threats posed by Norse invasions by expanding the system of fortified *burhs* and he reformed the *fyrd* to become an ever-ready guard, backed by a standby army. This system was later expanded from Wessex into Mercia formally dividing soldiers into 'ready' and 'reserve' contingents providing an army that could be quickly deployed.[144]

As an exemplary administrator, Alfred specified details such as the numbers required to defend walls in the burhs and the time of service obligations on the basis of one man from every hide of their land.[145] This

---

[144] Anglo-Saxon Chronicles in 894 tell us: 'The king divided his army into two, so that always half of its men were at home, half on service, apart from the men who guarded the boroughs.'

[145] The taxation unit of land was the *hyde*. It was not of a fixed size but represented the land that would support one extended family.

guard duty appears to be in addition to the landowner's obligations to serve in the king's *fyrd.* Similarities with a Home Guard can be imagined where training and weapons were provided.

Military service was codified, under the laws of king Ine and updated under the Alfred to provide what was called a *select-fyrd.* Many studies have failed to identify a set of rules or organisation for the fyrd suggesting it was subject to change but it is likely that service was time-limited by logistics as much as by contractual obligation. But the fyrd was always much more than an assemblage of peasant soldiers. Personnel were identified and obliged to be ready. When mustered it was an effective force.

Rather than raising emergency levies to respond to a crisis, from Alfred's time the rules made it possible to maintain an army in the field, whenever necessary. However, it is likely that 150 years later kings did not have an army permanently in the field and there is no clear evidence how by the time of Ethelred the king could deploy an army at all. The ruler had become dependent upon their nobles for troops in time of crisis.

Most free men it seems had some obligation to carry arms and train. If a threat loomed, the local thane might perhaps expand the number of retained, full-time 'heath-companions' and possibly these would undertake the training and lead these local bands acting rather like NCOs[146] in a modern army.

Hearthtroops

Lords were literally 'loaf givers' if one traces the etymology of the title. They were responsible for the wellbeing of their people. But there are also references in Norse literature to 'ring givers' although gifts by this time were more often of temporary title to land rather than silver. Previously the arm-rings given as reward for service had value as silver that could be 'hacked' to pay a debt or purchase goods but also displayed prestige and royal favour.

In Anglo-Saxon England, in common with other Celtic cultures, there was an understanding that with any gift came duties. There was a reciprocity: The lord owed a duty to protect his people while the people owed the lord a range of services. This would change under the subsequent feudal system

---

[146] A Non-Commissioned Officer (NCO) include sergeants and corporals and are those who lead the soldiers in the field.

where the people became subjects who owed everything to their overlord and where rulers increasingly distanced themselves from their people.

Leaders at all levels of society had a group of retainers to do their bidding. They were rather more than companions or drinking buddies. Lords still lived in halls to which many ordinary people would have access to seek redress or answer charges, while the lucky ones would have a seat at feasts. In theory all free people could approach their lord and the hearthtroops would provide a bodyguard or bouncer when necessary. There is no manual listing the duties of hearthtroops, or *huscarls*, except that in battle they were expected the protect their lord with their life and at Fulford, Morcar's men were exemplary in the way they performed this duty. At the battle of Maldon these troops remained faithful even when their lord was slain.

However, one might imagine that these retainers had other roles, from carrying messages to collecting taxes as well as training and perhaps selecting those who were to form the army if it was called to action. In normal times this might have been an attractive career option and when danger was present their role would be to lead troops in any fight and ultimately guard their patron with their life. Written evidence is absent but one can speculate that this retinue played a vital role in the gathering and deployment of local troops in the field. Once troops were in position and battle commenced the hearthtroops remained close to their lord perhaps leaving the task of local leadership to thanes.

Arms

The Germanic tribes, from whom the Norse nations as well as the Angles and Saxons derive, allowed free men to carry arms, literally putting power in the hands of the folk. It was not exactly democracy but gave a degree of empowerment which is recognised on maps into the 19th century which divided northern counties into 'wapentaks', with 'hundreds' as the southern counterpart, where freemen could gather and 'vote'.[147]

The right or duty to bear arms

We read of rules where a king would take the weapons as a death duty, or death tax, gifting them to the next generation provided they were loyal, male and also old enough to join his army thus keeping weapons in circulation and in the right hands.

[147] The location of these gatherings, known as tings, can be found in surviving place and field names.

The martial culture that evolved has, for better or worse, been fundamental to the evolution of Europe. Fighting was not however the normal way of life. People survived by farming and trade. External threats or internal challenges meant that weapons were maintained both as a precaution and as an expression of authority. The latter is still embodied in the mace which has evolved into a decoration that is processed, and remains in place, while the British House of Commons is in session. A mace was a blunt, but potentially lethal, weapon that was permitted in places where edged weapons were banned, an early example of health and safety regulations.

We read of early law specifying the arms and equipment that must be maintained. Other laws specify that these revert to the ruler upon the death of their holder who would normally assign them to the successor but gave the king some control of who was armed. England had enjoyed almost a generation of stability so the state of preparation can be questioned. However, the uprising and surge south in late 1065 meant that the army who would do battle at Fulford, had 10 months to refine, repair and train suggesting that they should have been well prepared.

Spear

Tacitus writes of the Germanic tribes "Only a very few use swords or lances. The spears that they carry *frameae* is the native word - have short and narrow heads, but are so sharp and easy to handle, that the same weapon serves at need for close or distant fighting. The horseman asks no more than his shield and spear, but the infantry have also javelins to shower, several per man, and they can hurl them to a great distance; for they are either naked or only lightly clad in their cloaks. There is nothing ostentatious in their turn out. Only the shields are picked out with carefully selected colours. Few have body armour; only here and there will you see a helmet of metal or hide. Their horses are not distinguished either for beauty or for speed, nor are they trained in Roman fashion to execute various turns. They ride them straight ahead or with a single swing to the right, keeping the wheeling line so perfect that no one drops behind the rest. On general survey, their strength is seen to lie rather in their infantry, and that is why they combine the two arms in battle. The men who they select from the whole force and station in the van are fleet of foot and fit admirably into cavalry action. The number of these chosen men is exactly fixed. A hundred are drawn from each district, and 'the hundred' is the name they bear at home."

The spear was the honoured weapon of the era. It served for hunting as well as warfare. It was economical in its use of material and allowed an enemy to be engaged at a distance. Evidence of shafts survive in graves which suggests they varied from 1.5 to almost 3 metres in length.

The length of the shaft was a compromise. A longer shaft would permit those in the second or third rank of the shield-wall to engage opportunity targets that presented themselves when shields clashed. A shorter shaft would be easier to control and manoeuvre in a close-quarter battle. Perhaps different shafts were prepared to suit the needs of war, or hunting.

Ash was the preferred wood for the shaft. It produced excellent, knot-free shafts for tools and implements of all sorts. Species such as ash, beech and willow were harvested by coppicing on a rotation for fuel, fencing and building as well as shafts for tools and weapons in the medieval economy. These tree shoots would be cut back to the stump. The following years, a new set of shafts would sprout and grow until the requisite size for harvest some seasons later.

Fulford produced only a single spearhead, and this was of a type designed for throwing and was indeed recovered among the scatter of arrowheads. Illustrations suggest that some warriors carried these throwing spears in a quiver ready to act as projectiles, in the same fashion reported by Tacitus. There were many designs for spearheads, ranging from finely tapered to broad flat blades. No large spearheads were recovered from the Fulford site.

The addition of 'wings' which were short protrusions at the base of a spear-blade might have developed from hunting. The momentum of a charging boar or stag would not stop the animal landing on top of the spear-carrier as it was impaled or 'run through' with a spear. In battle array, such wings could have been employed to good effect to hook opposing shields, spear shafts or limbs as battle was joined. If the trailing edge of the weapon was given a sharp edge it would have inflicted nasty wounds as it was drawn back. In addition to their use in defence or close quarter fighting, a charging line of long spears could impact and disrupt an opposing shieldwall while remaining out of range of sword stroke or the slash of an axe.

Again, we lack records of how they were used but such speculation respects the intelligence and ingenuity of the ancient warriors who doubtless trained in a repertoire of moves with their spear. However, we have the benefit from a generation of reenactors who are dedicated to authenticity. Although they employ intrinsically safe copies of ancient finds it does allow the way lethal weapons were probably employed to be observed.

The drawback of a long-shafted spear in battle is that most required two hands to control and thrust. Therefore spearmen would have to sling their shield onto their back. Spear carriers would be vulnerable at the front, and their employment was best deployed from behind a line of shields.

The base of the spear might have another small piece of iron known as a ferule which could serve two purposes: If the original head was chopped off it provided another penetrating point. But more commonly it would allow the spear to be stuck into the ground to provide a formidable fringe of points to deter both charging horses and warriors. At Stamford Bridge King Harald's army was short of shields and his men were ordered to create such a spear-wall by ramming the shafts into the earth.

The spear was almost certainly the most common weapon at this time to judge from the number found in grave burials and they illustrate different designs although the purpose was always the same. A spearman would be a well-trained warrior whose action would be critical in both defence and attack.

Swords

Swords were status weapons with early references to blades being bequeathed, giving them a long life, provided they were not subject to the fatigue of battle too often. Swords were expensive because they were difficult to make, requiring a large bloom of iron to beat into shape.

The blade had undergone steady technological development through the centuries. From the cast bronze sword to the short stiff stabbing swords of the Romans which were replaced by longer slashing weapons with thin cutting blades, both made from wrought iron. Iron was produced by first removing most of the oxygen from the rust-red ore in a furnace and then by repeated heating and hitting to drive out the slag trapped inside the iron-bloom produced in the hearths.

Long slender slashing blades were first made possible by the process of pattern welding. At a metallurgical level, the mixing and folding of pieces of iron allowed a grain structure to be imparted which increased fatigue resistance by limiting the propagation of micro-cracks in the blade as it was bent and bashed in battle. Forge welding gave the blade the right balance of weight, strength and flexibility to make it an effective weapon.

Technological improvements during the tenth century in Europe meant that swords could be beaten out using a single bloom of quality wrought-iron and this is the technology found at Fulford. The stranded filaments of iron are visible at the core of these blades. These flat, thin blades followed the established design with a channel or fuller running from the hilt to the tip which made the sword both lighter and more flexible.

These were slashing rather than stabbing weapons. The cross-section of the limited samples of sword blades recovered from the heart of the battle action in the ford demonstrated some remarkable craftsmanship. The thickness of the blades is a little over 2mm and the channel of the fuller compresses the iron running the length of the blade to about 1mm. Anyone lucky enough to have handled a realistic copy of these blades will recognise that these would be capable of slicing off a limb or removing a head at a single stroke, as often reported in the literature.

Around the time of the Fulford battle steel blades formed from iron that had probably come from India, although it is known as Damascus steel, allowed narrower blades which were still strong and flexible. They were manufactured without a fuller, so these blades are known as lenticular or lens shaped. All of the blade fragments recovered at Fulford have fullers.

Modern reproductions of swords are typically twice the thickness suggested by the Fulford finds. There is increasing evidence that many grave finds of swords were symbolic rather than practical weapons because placing a good blade in the burial would invite robbers. These grave-goods might have inflated the perceived dimensions which are compounded by the way iron rusts and rots. It is not easy to identify the surface.

While swords and spears might have defined a warrior's primary role, they also carried secondary weapons.

Axes

Two types of axes are recognised. The first was the fierce and long handled swinging axe that was said to be favoured by King Harald. The 'bearded axe', so-called because the base of the blade seems to protrude rather like a beard. This is not the natural shape for chopping wood where a straighter blade-edge would be more suitable. The shape and the length of the front edge of a war axe made it well suited for slicing whatever came in its swinging radius.

This weapon could not be used in the press of a shieldwall but was perfect for cutting through shield-planks, helmets and even armour. The warrior needed enough space to swing his weapon. So the long-handled axe was a weapon to lead a charge or for felling warriors who had broken into a shieldwall.

As with the long-shafted spear, the warrior could not benefit from a protective shield as both hands were employed to steer a battle axe. This illustrates the need for practiced teamwork as well as coordination in the battle ranks. There can be little doubt that battle drills were regularly practised perhaps with wooden weapons.

A second sort of axe we recognise from finds had a smaller and shorter handle. This could be operated while holding a shield and could be used in close quarter fighting by those who did not own a sword. It is also possible such an axe could be thrown but this would deprive the user of a valuable weapon and provide the enemy with ammunition.

It is possible that such an axe would double up as a practical tool for chopping wood. However many sets of craftsmen tool have been found which suggest some specialised styles of wood-working axe that are generally termed 'adze'. Such weapons are often illustrated attached to a holster on the warrior's belt.

Seaxe

Another close-protection weapon was the seax, a form of short stabbing or chopping blade. Like the axe, this was likely a secondary weapon carried by most warriors. A few illustrations show it hanging in a scabbard, but reenactors commonly attach it to the back or front of their belt so that it could be drawn when pressed in the shield wall.

It was at this stage of close-quarter fighting that the sturdy blade would be employed. The blade was stout enough to withstand impacts and parry the slash of a sword. It could be used to hack the shaft of an intrusive spear but would be most lethal when stabbing.

These weapons are not well represented in grave burial finds suggesting they enjoyed a lower status as a weapon. Even if it was commonplace and unloved, it would be a lifesaver in battle.

Arrows and bows

At both Hastings and Stamford Bridge battles the use of arrows is well recorded. Ironically there is no mention of arrows in the accounts of the Fulford battle although it is at this site that many arrowheads have been recovered, unlike at the two subsequent battles where no arrows have yet been discovered. The way these arrows were employed was discussed in the context of the battle with more details later in the archaeology annex.

Arrows and bows were universally carried for both hunting and sport while their use in battle would disrupt or injure their opponents and in Beowulf 'the iron-tipped arrow shower' is mentioned in the context of battle. The limited evidence in literature and illustrations give little prominence to the use of bows in a battle array but Fulford suggests it was a weapon of tactical importance. The bowmen deployed at Hastings were a specialist group of mercenaries rather than ordinary foot soldiers. At Stamford Bridge we have a record of the bow being used like a sniper weapon to fatally wound King Harald.[148]

The manoeuvres preceding the battle at Fulford are relevant to understanding the location of the assemblage of arrowheads discovered. The Mercian army was effectively unable to participate in the battle when it became evident that the Norse did not intend to cross the river. The arrow finds suggest that participation in the battle for this stranded component of the Mercian army was limited to firing arrows at the Norse army when the ebbing tide permitted them to charge to encircle the Northumbrians. The arrows identified are all of the tanged type rather than the socketed arrows which would make the English archers famous in later centuries.

The tang was an extension behind the blade which was pushed, rather like a nail, into the shaft where it was bound in place. The fragile, un-ridged leaf-shaped arrowheads discovered might not have been the projectile of choice. Later arrows would have a hollow socket into which the shaft of the arrow could be fitted so that all of the kinetic energy in the shaft was transferred through the arrow point to provide penetration One example is the bodkin type that is better suited to penetrate a mail shirt. It is feasible that the flat arrowheads were employed because they were available as these arrows were also well suited for hunting birds.

What makes these Fulford arrows unusual is their very thin cross section which led them to being dubbed 'flying razor blades'. Tanged arrowheads are not well documented in museum collections. The fragile state of the thin metal recovered might explain why so few have been identified but Fulford has shown that they can survive. Those that have been studied have produced a 'standard' morphology, known in the UK as type 1a, which has a trapezoidal cross-section. All of the arrowheads that left enough metal to permit them to be measured and drawn had, by contrast, a flat blade.[149]

---

[148] The story that King Harold was killed by an arrow in the eye is largely discredited and whose origin has been traced back to what might now call some marketing literature produced by a group of archers employed by William at Hastings.

[149] It proved possible to estimate the way these arrows were forged from a thin bar of iron.

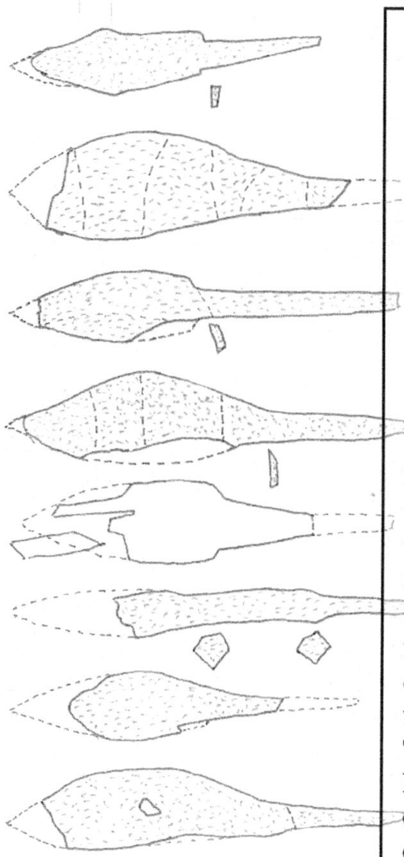

At least 40 tanged arrows were identified but the fragmentary nature of these finds after 20 years in conservation (sic) meant only 8 could be accurately drawn. There is so little surviving iron that xray assessment was of little use.
The metal of the arrowhead is always less than 2mm thick, so the rust encrusted was left in place for sketching which required multiple measurements and plotting to represent the surviving shapes.
The illustrations note any breaks and the original shape is sometimes only visible in the surrounding crust Subsequently, the outlines were plotted suggesting how they might have been made as the cross-section is remarkable consistent along its whole length and the points were a consistent 45 degrees.
There were two concentrations of arrow heads. No arrows were identified outside the battle zones in the extensive area surveyed during the project.

These missiles would cut through any cloth and inflict serious wounds on exposed flesh. The find assemblages suggest that these were aimed at the unprotected backs of the advancing Norse invaders. While few hits would be immediately fatal, the impact of a shower would be disruptive and incapacitating, causing casualties requiring attention to bind wounds.

Arrowhead finds from burials in Lydam, Hederby, Birka and Ladby might suggest that a mix of types was normally carried by archers and it would be reasonable to speculate that the Mercians, who had been deployed months before, also carried a range of arrow types. They possibly employed the most appropriate arrowheads in the circumstances.

The arrowhead assemblages from graves were kept in pouches, rather than shafted.[150] The shafts would have to be procured, seasoned and prepared with their fletchings. So it is again reasonable to speculate that archers would tip their projectiles with a suitable arrowhead shortly before they were employed.

The blade-like arrowheads found might have been employed because their lightweight gave them some extra range dictated by the tactical contexts. The arrowhead choice might have been dictated by the nature of the target, shooting from the back or the side of the enemy. The unique tactical setting of the Fulford battle, where the river provided a protective moat with a soft, and relatively static targets a bowshot away, the warriors evidently judged the leaf arrowhead as the optimal choice.

Although there was a single bodkin, the other arrowheads recovered in this area would have inflicted injury by cutting through clothing and flesh. The bodkin could have struck through a shield or passed between the links of chainmail. The arrowheads recovered could have buckled or broken if they hit anything solid but would slash any flesh encountered. All of the surviving projectiles display fractured or bent points.[151] Some limited experiments with replica arrowheads, made by the arrowsmith Hector Cole, suggest that they were capable of embedding themselves into the wood of a shield. Do the tip fractures observed represent damage done when the arrows were hastily knocked off shields?

---

[150] Wegraeus E, Die Pfeilspitzen von Birka, in Birka vol II ed Arwidsson, 1986

[151] In addition to the 7 items drawn, perhaps 40 were noted where the fractured nature rendering drawing impractical.

Protective equipment

Shield

A shield was the warrior's friend. In the heat of battle, the shield provided some sense of invulnerability. The use of the shield also had a fundamental effect on tactics. The shield was not just there for defence but was useful as a weapon in its own right. The shield could be used to parry or push weapons aside rather like the buckler of the later era.

Shields were carried by every soldier and indeed there is evidence that spare shields were available on the battlefield and a second shield slung over the back can be seen in illustrations. Shields gave their user the illusion of security but the boards of light lime wood were only thick enough to stop an arrow.[152] Had they been made thick enough to stop a spear thrust they would be too heavy to use.

A shield could however deflect a spear thrust and even a sword slash provided the user got the impact-angle right. One interesting find from Fulford are a set of anvils that would have been perfect for knocking dents out of the iron boss which would protect the warrior's fist where he gripped the shield. The anvils suggest that it is possible that some running repairs were carried out during the battle.

The shield was not only for personal defence but provides collective protection for those beside and behind. When the sword or spear was raised to strike, one side of the attacker's body would be exposed. The same advice to strike to the right must have been drilled into every army since they made an art of warfare. If shields were closed up, interlocking allowed the impact point of a charge to be spread, making the name 'shieldwall' appropriate.

Evidence suggests that the kite-shaped shield associated with the Normans was familiar among the English and Vikings of the 11th century. The advantage of the shape was the protection it afforded not only to those on horseback but also to the vulnerable legs of foot soldiers. There is always an element of fashion in arms and armaments, and it is possible that the kite shield was more popular in the south so few would have been employed at Fulford among these northern warriors.

---

[152] The consensus estimate based on the rivets used to fix the shield boss in lace that the boards were 6mm thick producing a shield weighing 6-8kg.

However, the loss of one's shield would require a very quick rethink in tactics. Stripped of this protection, attack was probably the only form of defence. A glorious and defiant burst of aggressive energy might just create a gap into which your comrades could pour and behind which you could then retreat. The likely fate however would be a spear thrust or axe blow and a few lines in the tales told round the hearths during coming winters of reckless bravery. Immortalised in a saga, such acts might comfort others who might in the future be obliged to emulate such sacrifice.

The size of the shield can be inferred by examining the pattern of nails and fittings in graves. The best guess is that the planks were glued together then covered in leather to hold the structure in place with an edging of animal sinews nailed round the perimeter to provide the rim with reinforcement against the hack of a sword. The assumption is that shields were flat even though the illustrations often suggest a domed shape. It is not clear that this is artistic licence as the construction of a domed shield would have presented a challenge to the woodworking technology of the time.

In the centre of every shield was a boss of iron. These varied in shape, depending on the technology available. Some were sheets made into cones while by the time of Fulford they appear to be domes beaten from one piece of iron. The boss would protect the hand of the warrior and perhaps employed like a boxing glove when confronting the enemy.

Armour

Starting at the top, an iron helmet was likely a luxury for the rich or those qualified by rank or occupation to stand in the front row of a shieldwall. Because helmets were durable, their use probably increased over the generations but near-contemporary illustrations suggest many were just an iron framework. Hardened, thick leather might have filled the gaps between the iron frame as it was only in later centuries that metallurgical technology allowed a single sheet of iron to be formed into a helmet.

Design and construction probably depended on the wealth of the warrior. Surprisingly few helmets have survived so once again it is drawings from the time that suggest front line warriors had iron helmets, many from this era with nose or eye guards. The foot soldiers in the deeper ranks of the shieldwall might have only limited head protection, relying on those in front to keep swords and axe blows out of range, and they would raise their shield to protect against airborne threats from short spears or arrows.

The short range, intimate weapons offered limited threat to the rear ranks of the shieldwall whose job was to lend their weight to shove when shieldwalls met and to be ready to stab or chop any opposing warriors that broke through. However the modest foot soldier in the rear never knew when they would be promoted by events to face the enemy, so it is likely that helmets were a coveted accessory. Perhaps they would hope to acquire one from a casualty if the opportunity presented itself.

Any blow to a head encased in iron would have been traumatic. The stunning effects could have been reduced by some padding, but there is little evidence that much space was left for any shock absorbing material. The surviving helmets suggest nose guards, eye protection, cheek flaps and attachments for some chainmail to protect the neck were 'normal'. But these prestigious survivals might not be representative of the headgear worn by most warriors.

The other key item of protection was the chain-mail shirt or byrne as they were called. These were expensive items that only those at the front of a shieldwall could possess. This suit, made from rings of wrought iron, would mitigate the effect of a slashing blow. Each ring was closed with a small rivet after it was connected to adjacent rings. These were impressive demonstrations of the craft skill of ironworkers. The resources invested in a suit of armour can be appreciated by noting that in the margins of the Bayeux Tapestry the fallen are depicted already being stripped of their chainmail.

This iron shirt could stop the slash of the sword or the thrust of a spear from causing a fatal injury. The effectiveness was enhanced by the garments worn below to disperse the energy from blows. The padded 'jack' or jacket below the armour that would absorb and spread the energy to mitigate the damage to flesh and bone.

Experiments have shown that chain-mail would not be effective at stopping the thrust from acute spear points but might well limit its penetration and a bodkin (thin) arrowhead would probably penetrate while the bladed-arrowheads found at Fulford would be ineffective against chain-mail.

Armour would limit injuries during close quarter battle. If the opponent could not swing their axe, make an effective stroke with their sword and was limited to prodding and poking with their spear, the riveted links could prevent serious injury.

A jacket, padded with wool, would also be hard for a sword to slash or stab and such padded armour was probably normal for ordinary soldiers to judge by surviving images. Some illustrations show a thick jacket covered in triangular, stuffed pockets.

With all protective equipment there is a design compromise. Movement and mobility were keys to survival. Battle is exhausting and overheating a serious risk making decisions about protection a balancing act. Several commentators have noted that the all-up weight of arms, equipment and protective equipment has remained remarkably similar through the ages. Thirty kilograms is about as much as a fit man can carry and remain active during a battle. It is interesting to observe that soldiers on the modern battlefield are again being equipped with armour.

While their armour conferred some protective benefits to the wearer, their very best protection was afforded by remaining as part of a coherent unit. So it is worth briefly examining how this worked as the multiple phases and the different fights that took place at Fulford are best understood in the context of the tactics of the time.

Tactics

Because a soldier's immediate survival and longer-term prosperity depended on the outcome of battle, warriors unsurprisingly devoted much thought and preparation to maximise their prospects of survival and victory.

Films portray battle between long lines of uniformly equipped warriors who are well drilled to play their part in a wall of interlocked shields. There were several different walls of warriors formed on the battlefield at Fulford each designed to meet specific local threats. The narrative of the Fulford battle does not describe a protracted slugging match between two sets of warriors. Instead different shield walls formed to block the clever series of manoeuvres by each side.

Because the subtlety of the tactics at Fulford, here we briefly address how shieldwalls worked and look at the options available noting how each tactical device worked and how it could be countered. Within the battle just described these are the range of tactical option practiced at the time. Fulford is arguably not exceptional in the variety of tactics employed because the two battles that quickly followed Fulford, at Stamford Bridge five days later and Hastings three weeks later, illustrate the tricks and tactics that were also deployed by the different commanders.

During a battle, danger can come from many directions. Those wielding their swords at the front had their focus on the man opposite them. However, behind the front man might be a warrior armed with a spear whose long shaft of ash would allow him to jab any one of half a dozen warriors fighting in the first few lines of the opposition. They could attack not only those to their front but those either side if an oblique gap in the shields was spotted.

Survival depended on being quick-witted and observant plus good teamwork. The well-protected front rank would focus to the front while the spearman behind the protection of the shield wall, whose vision might not be blinkered inside a helmet, could thrust their spear to open the opportunity for the leading swordsmen and perhaps these actions were coordinated.

Battle spears with 'wings' could hook a shield edge and expose its carrier. Both shield walls would be engaged in this lethal search for exposed body-part that they could attack. A spear thrust might immobilise a shield and unbalance both its carrier and the attacker whose shaft was temporarily stuck fast. Such micro battles punctuated the action in a shield wall. One response was to step back out of range, a manoeuvre that would certainly have been rehearsed as it had to be conducted as a unit.

In such tight formation injuries were surprisingly limited but two issues meant they would require local reorganisation from time to time while still in contact. The inevitable attrition on bodies as well as weapons and shields plus the sheer exhaustion necessitated some shuffling. This was when numbers mattered. A wall that was 10 warriors deep would apply more 'pressure' than one with half that number. It would also be easier to insert a replacement allowing a few comrades to disengage or to help a warrior with a serious wound to the rear.

Size also mattered especially as a battle continued when lines would tend to contract as weapons and warriors became incapacitated. This is where good control was essential. A mobile force could lend their weight to any section under stress allowing the line to be stabilised and straightened since kinks in the line exposed warriors to assault from the side. So maintaining a straight wall of wood and steel at the front was important.

Reports of battles lasting for hours, as they did at Fulford, implies that a warrior's engagement was continuous. However, ten minutes of ducking, thrusting and resisting the push of the opposition was exhausting. So frenzied activity would be interspersed with times when both sides would draw breath and reorganise. Any thinning of the line might easily offer a temporary gap which an experienced, observant leader might exploit whereas if the line had depth, no easy gaps should present themselves. Once again, size and organisation mattered.

Holding the line was perhaps the first imperative. Pushing forward however offering several tactical advantages. It could advance past those who had been injured it allowed them easily to retire to attend to their wounds or weapons. Conversely, the retreating line risked losing their wounded to a fatal thrust from the advancing foe.

But if just one section of the line advanced into the enemy, its own line would stretch and thin reversing their local numeric advantage. There was one tactic which exploited the value of concentrating an assault force. This is known by a number of names but 'the boar's snout' graphically describes this tactic.

A group of experienced warriors would pack tightly together and rush the opposition in a spear-shaped formation whose sheer momentum would likely drive a wedge into the opposing shield wall. Once 'inside' the wall those within the boar's would attack the hinter-ranks whose spear-carriers were likely unarmoured perhaps with both hands committed to controlling their spear shaft. Either a quick retreat to allow those better equipped to engage the break-in or a rapid transition to their close quarter weapons was called for to prevent the wedge expanding to expose more of those whose armaments were designed to support the shieldwall.

Experimentation by re-enactors has demonstrated how effective this formation could be. The warriors at the point of the wedge would lean back into the rest of the wedge to make sure it was a compact formation. This wedge would give the attackers a slight numeric and weapon superiority at the point of impact.

To counter this, a brave warrior swinging a two-handed bearded axe might arrest the progress. A carelessly successful boar's snout might detach itself from its own shieldwall exposing their unprotected backs to attack allowing the insurgents to be cut down. Such details go unreported in the royal chronicles but within the shieldwall these manoeuvres would test the opposition with the aim of destroying its coherence. Perhaps tentative at first, these ploys would be practiced by a strong army when strength and stamina was being tested.

Once a line was broken, a warrior lost protection from their sides and back. Coherence was synonymous with survival. Every warrior knew that an isolated warrior was close to death. Battle required teamwork and that needed someone to give orders. No military manual survives so one must employ conjecture and tactics tested by modern reenactors.

The role of commanders and the signals they employed are limited in the written record to mentions of blasts on a horn and banners that marked rallying points so that a leader could show the direction of advance, or retreat to other soldiers. Although it is unreported, it is safe to assume that there was a chain of command that ultimately relied upon a leadership class of warriors, akin to NCOs, who would muster the 20 or so soldiers around them, to accomplish the tactics they had practised. Their vital role would be to order replacement shields to be passed forward, or for a someone to take over the weapons and role of an injured comrade and to move the warriors to support their leader.

In summary, a shieldwall was a series of micro-battles that followed some simple rules, foremost of which was keep cohesion. The issue of flanks and isolation are dealt with in the battle narrative itself.

Casualties

The consequence of armies wielding such wounding weapons was casualties. The scribes and storytellers seem careless about making such records just as they were with noting the size of the forces. This suggests a fatalistic acceptance of death and how irrelevant such reports were considered. Modern psychotherapists might interpret this neglect as escapism or suppression of painful memory.

At Fulford all the key players survived this long and hard battle. But the records all agree that the casualties on both sides were high. Given the reckless charges undertaken by both sides across the exposed deep ditch of Germany beck, high casualties were inevitable. The English would have lost all of the rearguard once they were surrounded as reported in ghoulish detail in the sagas.

There was much healing to be done after a battle and we have one example of a military medical service. 'After the battle the King [Magnus] ordered the wounds of his men to be bound; but there were not so many doctors in the army as were necessary, so the King himself went round, and felt the hands of those he thought best suited for the business; and when he had thus stroked their palms, he named twelve men, who, he thought, had the softest hands, and told them to bind the wounds of the people; and although none of them had ever tried it before, they all became afterwards the best of doctors. There were two Iceland men among them; the one was

Thorkil, a son of Geire, from Lyngar; the other was Atle, father of Bard Svarte of Selardal, from whom many good doctors are descended.'

Those who were wounded early in the battle would be able to withdraw in the lulls that followed each assault. A collection of 13 skeletons was excavated at St. Andrewgate, on the road from Fulford to York which can be dated close to the time of this battle. Some show multiple wounds, including a high proportion delivered while the victim was prone, and probably mortally wounded or already dead. It is conjecture that these might have been a few who had left the battle as walking wounded but had been overtaken and killed after the Norse breakthrough, late in the battle. They might also have been survivors of a group left to guard the city.

It now seems strange that so little was done, and almost nothing recorded, about those who fell in battle. It was however only the trauma of the killing of soldiers at an industrial scale during World War I that promoted extensive memorialisation and attempts to record the individual resting place of those who died.

While battles were bloody and very personal, casualties in 'normal battles' are believed to have been surprisingly low, perhaps 5-10%. Had they been higher, it would have been impossible to maintain the many campaigns by insurgents reported in the literature. Provided armies held their formation, it was hard for either side to kill their opponents. As long as soldiers stood shield beside shield, they could defend each other. The danger came when lines were broken, or armies started to flee. If a warrior turned his back to run away he could no longer see the danger. Speed and distance were then his only defence.

Command and control

The written sources are silent about the way armies were organised and controlled. Therefore we must surmise how things worked based on the social organisation and the limited narratives of the way battles were conducted. In England, earls were appointed by and beholden to the king. Their appointment had become largely hereditary although there was scope for appointments of the minor earldoms to favour certain families or local dynasties.

Three major earldoms are recognised, Wessex, Mercia and Northumbria. Within these there were nested about another 10 earls who generally owed allegiance through their overlord to the King and Edward had employed such appointments to exert some political control through the minor earldoms. The structure below the earls is less well documented.

Land holdings note thanes as the local lords, based on the tax records. There might also have been an informal hierarchy among the thanes based on the size of their holding or population but for our purposes it is reasonable to assume that for warriors it was their local thane that they would follow and whose instructions they would obey. They were probably under no obligation to obey an outsider whose rank they did not know.

We noted earls had a group of hearthtroops whose primary role was to protect their chief with their life. While one can picture them forming a cordon around their lord, and it is clear that during the coming battle these brave warriors fulfilled this contract, it is possible that they served the role as messengers both in times of peace and war. Gathering all the thanes to pass instructions would be to leave the army leaderless so housecarls might have been employed to pass instructions during the action but stationed near their lord, they were ready to react if a threat developed.

Whatever the system, it worked well in the 18 hours after the arrival of King Harald's army at Fulford with a series of sensible and effective deployments, even if they ultimately failed. This suggests that there was good intelligence gathering and senior military leaders to assess the implications before issuing effective instructions.

These manoeuvres were complex and required coordination and the plotting that happened suggests they were achieved in a timely and effective fashion. The employment of archery by the Mercians who were enforced bystanders during the battle and the subtleties of the Northumbrian retreat tell us that there were sufficient tactically aware warriors in the army who had the authority and ability to get the army to respond in a coordinated way. It was a team effort.

One might contrast the two armies. At Fulford, Harald *Hardrada* ordered several well-timed interventions but he held the initiative and had a battle plan while the natives were reacting to his moves. This is the conventional, if simplistic, role of the general.

It is relevant to note how effectively the English armies responded to cover each move, correctly anticipating every vulnerability in their position. This could only be accomplished if there was a competent group in charge with the capacity to implement their plan through what we would now call a 'chain of command'.

The popular image of two shield walls, slogging it out does not capture the sophistication of the way this battle unfolded and was fought. It is frustrating that we do not have the drills or procedures that formed a part of the ordinary warriors training documented. The battle suggests that both sides were well drilled despite the fact that most of the native soldiers this was their first battle.

We noted that these warriors were not farmers whom circumstances had forced to bear arms. Preparing for war and arming oneself to protect hearth and home from bandits, raiders or a full-scale invasion was a duty that came with rank and local position. The action at Fulford tell us that they took this responsibility seriously as they did not fight like part-time or unprepared warriors.

We have no record of any speeches delivered but the leaders would have made sure that their troops understood what was at stake. The serious talking would likely have been done in the weeks before the battle. Communication, other than simple instructions during the battle, was impractical. Once in action a warrior needed to respond to the actions of those around and to follow banners that marked the position of their various leaders.

Annex B: Archaeology - Swords, arrows, recycling

This essay addresses some interpretive aspects of the investigations. Because of the unique nature of so much of what was uncovered a final paper has so far been replaced with progress reports. Battlefields of this era were believed devoid of finds. Fulford has shown that perception was wrong, but change is a challenge.

A formal method was employed to locate the site of a 1066 battlefield in England because there was a low expectation of conventional physical finds, for the very good reasons that no other sites of this era had produced any battle-finds. The focus of the project was initially not on artefacts. Instead early investigations included landscape, climate, tide, the built and the natural environment.

The surface and actions reported in near-contemporary sources allowed some written passages to be archaeologically tested. It is unusual to test early literature in this way, but it provided the opportunity to precisely locate landscape features and then check their accuracy. Remarkably, no errors were detected, and several ambiguities were satisfactorily resolved through these tests.[153] It was even possible to suggest the location on the battlefield of the different surviving reports.

There exists an archaeological preference for items to be excavated from a known context. A rigorous application of such a rule could arguably exclude the arrowheads, sword fragments and recycling debris from consideration as battle artefacts. But we have to work with what is found and each assemblage, such as the arrowheads, come from a relevant context with the surface scatter providing a two-dimensional map of events. It is relevant to report that an extensive surface area was investigated as a part of the methodology and the various assemblages reported were only found in places that fitted the interpreted action of this battle. In the context of a battle, quantity is relevant, and concentrations give such assemblages meaning. The finds often helped to refine the interpretation presented here.

The National Lottery funded first phases which was designed to locate the site. Subsequent work was devoted to confirming this location. Both phases took a decade each of which half was field work and half was deskwork or report writing.

---

[153] However, the early sources were often wrong is reporting names and relationships of the 'enemy'.

It is easy for projects to be driven by pre-conceptions rather than being evidence led. The structured approach employed at Fulford included the need for regular iteration to assess emerging evidence against what was already recorded. It also required the testing of all previously published hypotheses. Such a formal approach is arguably necessary to address the needs of civic society where decision-makers prefer confident, binary answers.

At Fulford, a one-meter square, test pit was dug in 2013 at a place thought to be near the heart of the battle and where extensive auger samples revealed buried, crunchy layers of iron, just above a stone base. Could the source of this iron be from weapons that had rusted away? This was a one-person operation with barely space to crouch to use a trowel. It yielded some exciting finds but seemingly no rusty weapons, at least initially.
The complex biochemistry that encases any iron lost in running water gradually revealed some exceptional objects when the recovered material was assessed.

Battlefields are big. The possible landscape, until one has localised the site of the action, is enormous. At Fulford the area to be investigated was defined by the work of those who had published possible locations for the battle.[154] It makes little sense to excavate until there is high confidence that there is a viable target. Only 15 years into the project did systematic excavation begin and this was only justified because a single site had been confidently identified by literature and landscape studies. These excavations served to dramatically confirm the location with sword and

[154] A chapter in *Finding Fulford* is devoted to assessing all of the suggested location for the battle none of which were feasible.

dating evidence, plus a wide, stone-surfaced road across the ford itself which gave its name to the battle .

Some pieces from the deep layer of 'iron' were removed for testing. Examining the iron showed it had all the appearance of natural iron pan. In an anaerobic environment, such as the alluvial mud being deposited by tidal flooding, bacteria takes the oxygen attached to the iron oxide leaving the iron to drift through the column to settle and form a layer with visibly enhanced iron. These bacteria played a critical role in the evolution of life on earth, and our red/brown soil owes its colour to this ubiquitous mix of iron oxides.

This large stone from the trial trench revealed a pattern of striations on its flat base caused by the glacial scraping actions that transported it. The domed upper surface (right) was covered in iron from which some sword tips detached while others could be traced. Fulford's 'Rossetta Stone'.

However, two stones deeply encrusted with iron were being studied which concealed some surprises. One morning, as the stones dried, they fell apart and shed four pieces which looked very much like the tips of swords. X-rays of these items and a trip to the British Museum confirmed that they were likely 'the tips of edged weapons'. This is certainly not the way that a good archaeologist should locate 'finds' but keen eyes, curiosity and an open mind are necessary qualifications for any investigations. The largest stone which unlocked the physical archaeology of the battle now provides the doorstop to my office.

Over the following summers, the area was excavated, confirming this was at the heart of the battle where an embanked, 10 meter wide road led into the ford.[155] It had the hallmarks of a Roman construction and the few datable finds suggest that it remained in use into the 16th century. It was exciting to identify sets of cartwheel ruts on the upstream side of the road.

The stone, ford-road had two more surprises. Anybody who excavates must assume the responsibility to document everything, regardless of its relevance to their particular search. Just below the Roman road surface a flat stone, standing on a trilith, was found which aligned with the ancient centre of the stream. A very short distance upstream a set of stepping stones was later discovered. An Iron Age settlement two kilometres south suggests that this crossing point has been in use for several thousand years.

The importance of the stone-built ford discovery cannot be overstated. Much early effort had been expended during the project looking for a road since the name of the battle tells us that it happened at a ford which had to be linked to a road. Armies move slowly across open country so they employ roads to bring them to battles.

The ford was also the location of all of the weapon fragments found. While the evidence from Fulford is that battle debris was gathered, only within the water and mud of the ford did a few fragments escape post-battle recycling.

The systematic way that the battlesite was cleared offers both a consolation and challenge to those who have searched in vain for early battlefields and found nothing. It tells us that most of the material was removed. But this clearing is a challenge to modern researchers since any pieces that escaped collection are likely to be small and lost somewhere inaccessible. Fulford shows that significant finds can be located on ancient battlefields.[156]

Many Fulford finds posed a particular challenge as there are obstacles to be crossed when a new class of artefact is identified. Metal detecting revealed a scatter of arrowheads typical of the era along the southern bank of the short, east/west section of the Ouse beside Fulford Hall and it is sensible to interpret these as being fired from the opposing, north bank. The assemblages by themselves did not initially contribute to the quest. It was only when the landing and deployment of the Norse army on the evening

---

[155] Repeated requests to excavate the opposite bank were ignored and is now buried below the access road to a new housing estate.

[156] The dedication, expertise and determination of the metal detectorist who undertook this task cannot be overstated.

before the battle at this location that these missiles could be related to the battle.

The Fulford arrowheads are much thinner in profile but are at present the largest collection of field finds of, presumably, 'used' missiles. The fragility of these artefacts whose external shape is distorted by a millennium of rusting, makes them hard to identify not least because there is so little metal to cast a shadow on any x-ray plate.[157]

The crossed swords on the road sign that greets those visiting Fulford are good representations of the weapons employed during the battle. The fuller, a channel running the length of the blade, was noted on all the sword tips found. This fuller both lightened the blade and gave it the flexibility required on these 'beaten blades'. The Fulford finds suggest the blades were very thin, 2 to 3 mm thick.

The sword tips pose different and unresolved challenges related more to the study of martial culture. They seem to have been purposefully, and in two cases with a lot of effort, broken. The location of these finds was where this battle interpretations says some brave warriors stood their ground to allow their earl to escape along the ditch with much of the army.

No matching tipless swords were identified in any accessible collections which again makes it difficult to address some of the questions raised by these fragments although the fibrous internal structure tells us much

[157] It would be unfair to dwell on the early expert assessment of the arrowheads as knives or forks, based on the very feint x-ray image cast by these ultra-thin tanged arrowheads. It did however lead me to suggest to an audience at the British Museum that we had found where the invaders held their celebratory tea party, as they looked not unlike the little butter knives that one used to find in cutlery drawers.

about the way these swords were beaten from a fresh iron-bloom, so typical for that time and how they were broken.

There was another class of find that proved challenging to identify. Nine substantial anvils were located during the excavations at the ford. These anvils would have been driven into a substantial block of wood to be employed by metalsmiths. Their find-location and shape posed interpretive problems.

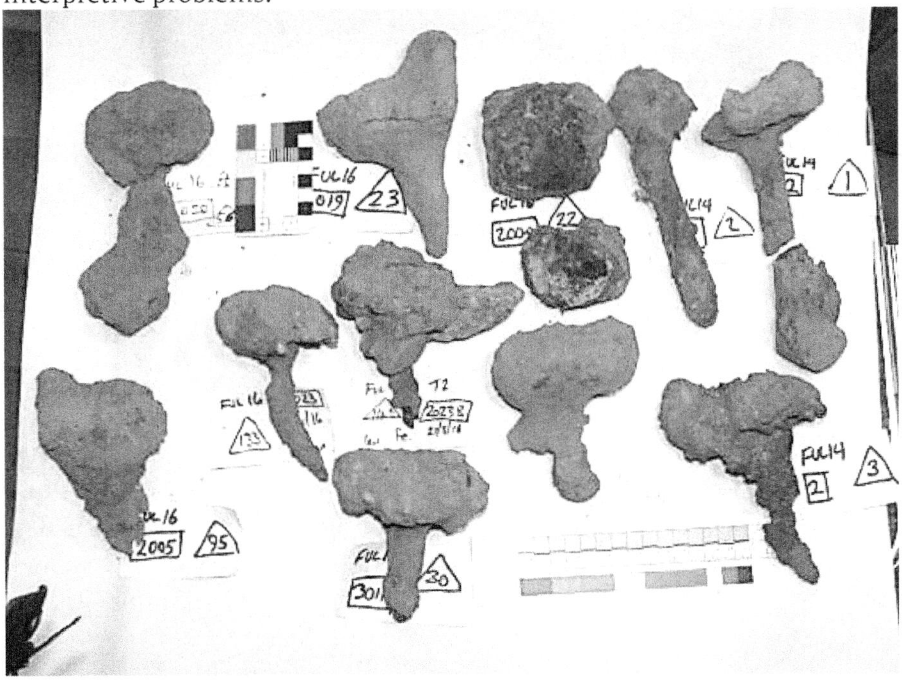

Eleven possible planishing anvils have been recovered from the stone surface close to the stone crossing at the ford. None have yet been conserved as X-ray shows the internal structure is fragmented. Their pointed ends were embedded in wood which was necessary before they could be used for beating iron. Most grounded at bends with the head of the anvil acting as an anchor for the block of wood.

In their haste the Norse metalworkers it is probable that these items were abandoned as it would take too long to extract them when news of the defeat arrived from Stamford Bridge, forcing their retreat to Riccall.

The subsequent flood tides could have flushed the wooden blocks towards the river. These large lumps had seemingly grounded at bends in the beck with the heavy iron anchoring them in place. Analysis has revealed mineralised wood around the tips of the pointed shafts, certainly confirming these anvils had been driven into the wood. This translocation by the beck can explain the various find concentrations.

There are no similar surviving examples of the Fulford anvils in the many catalogues of early metalwork consulted. Their use as planishing anvils to beat out dents in iron plate was suggested at a gathering of Scandinavian Museum conservators.

The project was extremely fortunate to have been able to have two early finds examined in a CT scanner which revealed just how much of the iron of the shaft has fragmented. The image produced represents the best form of conservation currently available with the possibility of 3D printing a copy based on the CT scan, a form of virtual conservation. They are among the items that will be stored until they are better understood.

The anvils were all at the same level (context) as the sword fragments, suggesting that they reached their find-location soon after the battle. These anvils suggest that they were in use in and around the battle, possibly even allowing for some running repairs on dented helmets or shield bosses.

When the site was hastily abandoned by the metalworkers when the Norse army was defeated at Stamford Bridge, the task of extracting their anvils from the wood might have been impractical. The debris left behind in the recycling area suggests they were in a hurry as they abandoned mostly unfinished, least valuable items when they had to flee back to their base.[158]

Discovery archaeology

Discovering the location of ephemeral human activity, such as a battlefield, can use found objects as pointers on which to build an interpretation. The received opinion at the time when the project was launched was that no battle objects would be found. Fulford has shown that this view is wrong. However, the expectation of no physical evidence promoted the development of a method for 'Discovery Archaeology' to identify and interpret the stories left to us. It used an holistic approach to evidence, which included finds from near the surface.

[158] The possibility that subsequent scavengers were selective in what they removed before the whole area was buried by the tidal floods.

There are two problems. First, surface finds tell centuries of human stories which are jumbled and out of their likely loss-context. This is why archaeologists prefer limited contexts such as buildings or graves. Second, one piece of rusty iron does not tell much of a tale, unlike perhaps a coin or piece of pottery which can be dated. When concentrations of 'rusty lumps', or scrap iron as my patient metal collectors termed them, are found it becomes possible to attempt an interpretation of collections in the context of the site. At Fulford, in the areas subsequently identified as the locus of the battle action, concentrations of iron objects were recorded that were hundreds or even thousands of times the background level helping to alert an observer to the exceptional nature of the area. Sadly find-concentration is not a metric that is currently recorded as it was a valuable pointer during this project.

Iron is particularly challenging for field archaeologists because it rusts. Large pieces maintain their identity much better than small items such as arrowheads. Work will continue for many more years to interpret all of the material and the processes that have transformed them during nearly a millennium buried in different environments.

Despite the challenges presented, iron had to be the research focus. The battle was fought by men, clad in iron and using iron weapons. The first story it told was about the recycling of battle debris gathered together after the action. This was followed by the narrative of the arrow scatters and the weapon fragments from the excavations at the ford. Each added substance to the written record.

Why bother?

The outcome of a conflict is often determined by marginal, and sometimes, random factors which can only be appreciated when the landscape is identified and scientifically examined. Studies of ancient battles that are confined to what was written do not permit the consummate skills or subtle, tactical intelligence of the opponents to be recognised. These discoveries can subsequently be employed to enhance the detailed narrative for battles to address the eternal question of 'why did it happen like that?'

If the words are not themselves studied within their physical context, we risk perpetuating the view expressed by many of the ancient scribes that the outcome was the will of a supernatural power rather than the consequence of the context, plus the cunning and courage of the combatants.

A study of the action that purports to resolve a conflict is best set in the socio-political context that promoted it. However, even if the focus is confined to the battle itself there is often much to be learned about the politics, people and relationships that led to the conflict. One lesson that those who promote conflict to resolve disputes might learn from 1066 is that it is a very uncertain method as the 'wrong side' often emerges victorious.

It might also seem unlikely that a modern soldier could take lessons from studying the tactics employed at Fulford but the project's first mentor who kicked open a few doors for the project, the late Prof. Richard Holmes, was well known for taking modern military leaders to old battlefields to draw out some timeless lessons of warfare and soldiering.[159] Perhaps the key lesson he would draw from Fulford is not to expect the enemy to react in the way you anticipate as the opposing leaders are also cunning and want to survive the battle.

[159] Many have been immortalised in the BBC series of 'War Walks' although in real life he conducted many of them on horseback.

Annex C: Geology

The familiar surface around York was formed as little as 10,000 years ago when the last great ice sheet was withdrawing. When this glacier retreated it moulded the local landscape, shaping the Fulford surface. Fulford's fascinating geology reflects its location near the southern limit of the last ice event.

The geological timescale is not normally recognised as relevant to the study of a medieval battle. However, the battle at Fulford took place on a surface that was sculptured by the complex interaction of ice and meltwater. The retreating icesheet around the world raised the sea level by many metres and is still imposing changes on the Fulford surface. Planners permitted 600 homes to be built here and chose to ignore the area's geology where a rise of 1.6mm on the Ings each year will be progressively impactful.[160]

Slopes, marshes and natural obstacles play an important part in most battles. At Fulford, the landscape dictated the location, as well as the course of the battle. So an understanding of the underlying geology was worth investigating. The results proved invaluable to both locating and interpreting the battle. A bonus from understanding the wider geological landscape came when assessing all other locations that had been proposed for the battle and excluded most of them.[161]

While the ice sheet was covering York to a depth of many hundreds of metres, a channel carrying meltwater ran underneath and carried with it material that formed the high ground upon which the main road between York and Fulford was built. This feature is known as an esker. The terminal of this esker, as it emerged from the retreating ice sheet, formed something similar to a river delta but in this case, it is known as an esker field with 'islands' formed from graded sands and gravels.

It is perhaps unjust to reference geology as a footnote since it was the match between the literature and the landscape from a millennium ago that focused the research. Mike Wood must take the credit for leading this fascinating research.

---

[160] A pumping station at the heart of the battle action is planned for 2027 to prevent the access road to the houses from flooding.
[161] However the methodology being followed made it necessary to test all of the other sites suggested by historians for the battle.

The big picture

York stands at the centre of the largest river valley in northern England drained by the Ouse and several significant tributaries. The last ice sheet paused twice in this area during its retreat and produced the York and Escrick moraines with Fulford equidistant between the two.

During the past two million years, the icesheets have grown and swept over much of the Northern Hemisphere, frequently covering and sculpting the British Isles in the process. Between 13,400 BP and 12,900BP when the Younger Dryas, brought the ice back to parts of northern Europe seemingly in a matter of years, brought a freeze that would last for about 1400 years.[162] Radiocarbon dates suggest that the ice had moved north of York by about 13000 BCE.

This last great sheet flowed through the Stainmore Gap where it was split into two flows by the Cleveland Hills and North York Moors which stood clear of the ice. The retreating ice allowed humans to migrate to northern latitudes often driven by the rising sea levels as their coastal homes and hunting grounds flooded.

The North Yorks Moors diverted the ice flow down the East Coast, blocking the rivers and leading to the formation of the Lakes Humber and Pickering in which clays were deposited up to 20m deep contributing to the flat landscape east of York. Water from Lake Pickering carved Kirkham Gorge as its meltwater cut a path to the River Derwent. The ice blocked the Humber so Yorkshires coastal rivers flow inland and away from the sea.

Geology imparts humility to those who employ it to interpret recent history. The clay is formed when granite, and other volcanic materials, weather over eons which transforms the rock chemistry. This is the clay upon which all the land around Fulford is built. Examining this clay under a microscope revealed the bones of creatures suggesting that some of this clay could have been formed 160 million years ago, being moved to this location by forces of unimaginable power and a geological patience.

---

[162] 'Meltwater from retreating glaciers upset the AMOC whose surface manifestation is the Gulf Stream, brings the warm water from the tropics to Europe. Dilution of the salty water reducing the density which provided the motive power driving the system' - William Patterson University of Saskatchewan 2009

Germany Beck

Germany Beck is the main drain for the extensive low-lying land to the east of the esker high ground with numerous channels. Its tortuous course is dictated by the outwash of the esker material of stone, sand and clay in the esker field with some limited channelling in recent centuries. The course of the beck where it flows through the battle area has changed very little.

Ings

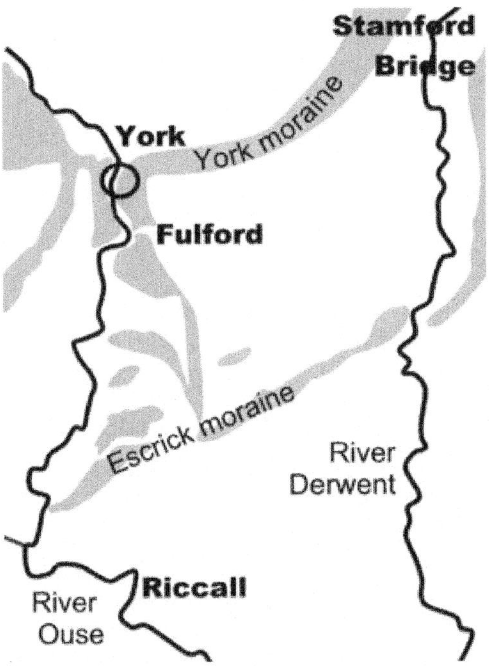

Two moraines, created by retreating ice, have formed a complex pattern around Fulford. Linking the two local moraines is an esker or sub-glacial river that carried material leaving the surface manifestation where roads and villages have been established. Below the ice-sheet, meltwater carried and later deposited material along the line of the modern A19. Esrick was the maximum extent of the Devensian glaciation.

The Ings feature extensively in the narrative of the battle. These are floodplains that sit either side of the River Ouse north and south of York. What makes them exceptional is that the water does not spill over the land but is constrained by an earlier geological deposit. These therefore become liner ponds at each flood event.

Over the millennia the Ings have been regularly flooded with water coming from two separate directions. A tidal bore along the Humber used to bring river mud, rich in organic material known as alluvium, to spill onto the landscape. Since the construction of an 18th century lock downstream from Fulford, floods now only come from upstream when the catchment overwhelms the capacity of the river. This downstream flooding is not a recent phenomenon as dangerous levels of lead and zinc are found in the mud layer which can be traced back to the ancient mines in the Dales.

One interesting observation about these regular floods is that the heaviest, larger material settles first creating what is called a levée beside rivers. This provided the firm footpath at the top of the bank that feature prominently in the tactical account of the Fulford battle. The process provides positive feedback since walkers consolidate it to create a barrier trapping finer sediment as it flowed further from the levée constrained by the eskers to the east which confines the flood water.

Left is an image of core samples being extracted from the ings which allowed the rate at which flood-alluvial material had been deposited to be calculated.

Below is an image of the Ings, looking towards Fulford.

Germany Beck was formed to drain the area to the east as far as Lawrence St, which has all the appearance of being another esker. The course of the beck has been subject to some manual adjustments but these changes amount to little more than some straightening since the material on either bank is very hard, glacial clay. The bends in the beck follow the glacial clay, sand and gravel deposits.

PEAT

Peat played its part in the battle. This material has an attraction for archaeologists since the carbon it sequestrates allows its formation to be dated, providing an analogue for the way the surrounding countryside has evolved. The environment within peat is also interesting for the way it preserves organic material but sadly by the time of the battle the layer was covered to a depth of over a metre by four centuries of flooding.

Samples were taken from the top and the base of the peat. At the base, an alder twig was dated to 2060+ –35BP (73BCE) and a sedge nutlet from the top sample gave a date of 1385+-35BP (636CE) 150. This timescale spans the late Iron Age to the Anglian or mid Saxon era. This was not a long-lived peat accumulation but is consistent with the dynamic flooding history of this waterway.

Roundabout 600CE the Ings was no longer able to hold all of the flood water as millennia of deposits had raised its level. Now flood-water began to spill along Germany Beck to reach and in due course to smother the peat and stop it growing. It is quite possible that it was this regular inflow of mud which gave Fulford its name since this would have been indeed the 'muddy ford'.

The one peat area investigated did not disappoint as it conserved the tips of wooden stakes that predated the stone ford at the heart of the battle and a matted wood crossing 80m upstream of stone crossing which was dated to the century after the departure of the Romans from York.

The interpretation is that a line of wood stakes led to a place where the peat could be crossed during the second century. By the sixth century, the peat crossing had to be covered in matted wood so this route could be used when the stone-ford was flooded.

Annex D: What's in a name?

Every year emails or txts arrive enquiring where they can find Fulford Gate so they can visit the battlefield. This poses a serious problem because Fulford Gate has never existed as a place except in the imagination and the writings of some modern historians. It is of course the battlesite of Fulford that people want to visit.

Versions of the Anglo-Saxon Chronicle (ASC) provide York (C, D, E), Stamford Bridge (C, E) and Hastings (D) as sites of the three 1066 battles. The authority normally accorded the ASC does not explain why York was omitted from the popular memory as the first for this trilogy of battles. Norse sources call Fulford the 'battle at the Humber'. So it is evident that the naming of battles is not just a matter of geography.

We must seek another explanation to explain why York is not recognised as the name of the first battle of 1066 and also why confusion has arisen about the name, Fulford, just as in the 18th century Stamford Bridge was regularly renamed 'Battlebridge,' but this error has seemingly realigned with reality.

Hastings is recognised as the operating base for the Normans and historians agree that the battle took place some 10 km away on Senlac ridge, which is now known as Battle, and is the site of William's commemorative or penitential abbey. French historians were referring to the 'battle of Hastings' in the century after the battle and that has become its accepted name.

Given such a loose association between geography and events, there is much fascinating cultural archaeology to be done to explain how battles adopt their names. It must be the work of others to explain why popular history has generally overlooked the first of the battles of 1066 which took place at Fulford.[163]

However, Fulford provides another interesting twist since historians have actually invented the name, Fulford Gate, for this battle placing it somewhere that has never existed in any traceable record. The name of the

---

[163] Stickland write "the ways in which certain battles were selected...for memorialisation ....indicate the central significance of battles as key cultural markers.' suggesting Fulford did not pass this test in *Writing Battles* Ed Naismith et al Bloomsbury 2020 9781350253162

battle is transcribed from two early sources as Fuelford although the National Archive indexes Fulford as Foleforde/Fuleford/Fuleforde.

Gate Fulford is not recorded until the 16th Century and no record of Fulfordgate has yet been noted. Fulford Gate seems to be a modern affectation first noted in E A Freeman's *History of the Norman Conquest of England* circa 1870. It is ironic that Freeman, who branded the Norse sagas as 'near fiction', seems to be guilty of inventing and mis-naming the battle which others have uncritically followed.

When the church of St. Oswald's was consecrated in 1866 the surrounding village 'adopted' the title Gate Fulford for the surrounding houses as the previous church was located in Gate Fulford which was probably the outer point of entry to Roman York.[164] The new St Oswald's church replaced the 10th century church located much nearer York and where archaeology has shown there was an outer palisade dated to Roman times, making the location of the first church a credible claimant to the name as this was the Roman era 'Gate at Fulford'. But this church and therefore the original Gate Fulford was nearly 2km from the battlefield. Interestingly, this happened just at a time when Anglo-Saxon scholarship, such as the work of Freeman, was illuminating this era by employing the emerging Norse saga compilations.

But in 1895 the East Riding Council decreed that the place around their new church, that was calling itself Gate Fulford, should rightly be called Water Fulford since it was within that parish. Perhaps unwittingly the new settlement had strayed into the territory of the East Yorkshire 'Thirding'. Contemporary Kelly's trade directories reflect the adoption of the 'official' name. The battle could therefore sensibly be called Water Fulford, but it is 'legally' incorrect to apply the name Gate Fulford, let alone the other permutations, to the battle which two ancient sources tell us took place at Fulford.

However the prosperous citizens who had relocated 'Gate Fulford' were unhappy with their official address of Water Fulford. Various linguistic compromises were attempted locally, such as Ambo (Both) Fulford, which appear in various documents to avoid association with the failed settlement of Water Fulford where part of the hall of King Harold II's brother, Earl Tostig, survives inside Water Fulford Hall. In 1935 the East

---

[164] This deconsecrated church still stands and is the place where the Mercians contingent who went to block the flank beside the River Ouse would have accessed the levee to move into position.

Riding Review published an order abolishing all prefixes so, as in the 11th century, the whole area was once again known as Fulford. [165]

For a critical four decades, 1860-1900, the place of the battle was illegitimately called Gate Fulford and this was followed by a similar period when it was 'officially' Water Fulford. Perhaps this explains why the 'wrong' name came to be associated with the battle since it coincides with the early versions of Anglo-Saxon history.

None of this explains why modern writers have chosen to use the Fulford Gate when no ancient source, gazetteer or satnav can find such a fictional place.

In the interests of clarity and historical accuracy it would help rescue the forgotten battle of 1066 at Fulford if historians could agree to use the name of the place where archaeology has shown the battle took place. It would certainly help rescue Fulford from obscurity if we could all agree to use the name for a place that actually exists, especially as it matches the only name used in early sources.

---

[165] The parish of Fulford at the time was so extensive that the annual 'beating of the parish bounds' took two days..

Annex E: Whose version of history? You can decide

The Land-waster flag[166]

During the foregoing narrative there have been occasions when credibility is challenged by improbability. Perhaps a position, midway between rejection and acceptance is necessary. Interpreted history should rarely be accepted as 'true'. The early written sources employed to discover the Fulford battlesite demonstrated what one observer recorded also needed a physical context.[167]

For example we may examine the possibility that the banner carried by the victor at Fulford is the same as the Scotland's famous *Fairy Flag*. There are two versions about the origin of the banner that brought armies victory: For those who believe in fairies, the Fairy Flag was, as the name suggests, a gift from the fairy folk. Alternatively it is the silk banner acquired by Harald when travelling in the Holy Land, possibly in the hope that it would have the miraculous life that was ascribed to it by its owner, at least until he was slain.

This origin story can be documented. King Harald *Hardrada's* banner was carried at Stamford Bridge by Croven, son of Harald *the Black of Iceland*. He was one of the few to escape from the battle and before 1079, had established himself as King on the Isle of Man. Later the Western Isles [of Scotland] came under control and the chiefs of Clan MacLeod claim this antecedent. This piece of cloth survives and this credible line of possession now places it in Dunvagan Castle and was carried by the Leod clan into several hard battles.

Nineteenth century academic inspection of the surviving fabric of the *Fairy Flag* confirms it is made of silk fabric, now rather willowish in colour, probably of eastern origin with no scientific dating. Such testing might eliminate or illuminate aspects of this story. Whatever the facts they have no practical significant but certainly add an emotional link.

---

[166] The name of the banner can also be translated as *Land-Ravager* just as *Hardrada* can be interpreted literally as 'hard-ruler' but is better expressed as 'tyrant'.

[167] Some legal jurisdictions allowed a verdict of 'not proven' which nicely expresses the ambiguity where matters are known but cannot be proved that underlies so much of what is reported by historians.

In composing this Fulford battle story, most emphasis has been placed on detailing evidence impactful to our understanding of the location and course of the action. But that is not the whole human story. In the retelling of history, which is after all *everyman's* story, different interpretations based on the available evidence can often be credible.

However, the real story of 1066, revealed at Fulford, requires no dramatisation; it is an exceptional story.

Annex F: Timelines

December 1065	28	Abbey Minster of St Peter, the West minster, consecrated with Queen Edith and Earl Harold 'dux et subregulus' present
Key	*	*Estimated date*
January		**1066**
3		Edward slips into coma
5	Thursday	The dying king has a fit and makes final dispositions relating his prophecy of doom
6	Epiphany	Funeral and Coronation had to be rushed before the end of the Christmas festival assembly
20*		William's ambassador tells King Harold II that his 'usurpation' would be challenged
30*		King Harold II rejects William's demands effectively accepting that they were going to fight
February		
5*		Gilbert sent as legate to ask for papal blessing on an enterprise to punish King Harold
15*		The leading Lords of Normandy agree support but ask William to call a counsel of all knights to get their assent for an overseas attack
20*		Second Norman ambassador demands Harold marry William's daughter as they had agreed
*		Tostig heads to visit his cousin King Swein of Denmark seeking support
25*		King Harold II & Bishop Wulfstan head to York
March		Tostig moves on to persuade King Harald in Norway to invade England
1*		Northumbrian Witan is swayed by Wulfstan to support Harold and England
Mid*		Tostig with King Harald in Norway
Mid*		Ceremony and festivities in York for wedding of King Harold II
		King Harold II tours Northumbria to cement loyalty
Late*		War token sent to summon Norwegian levy

Late*		Tostig returns to Flanders
April		Easter was on 13 April
"Spring"		Tostig sets out on raids on south coast
16		King Harold back at Westminster
24		The 'hairy star' appears
May		Tostig attacks Isle of Wight
*		Possible secret meeting with William
*		Tostig in Flanders or Sandwich to await confirmation of plans and make arrangements
June		Tostig attacks and holds Sandwich
Late*		Tostig leaves Sandwich when Harold mobilises
		Tostig starts raiding on the east coast
		Dedication of Holy Trinity in Caen
		William wins support for his invasion
Late*		Progressive mobilisation of fyrd begins
July		Ecclesiastical council in Caen
Mid*		Tostig's raids 'driven off ' by Mercian and Northumbrian armies
Late*		Tostig reaches Scotland
Mid*		King Harold II's army installed on Isle of Wight
August		
12		William's fleet is completed and gathers in the estuary of the River Dives
Late		King Harald of Norway's fleet sets sail from The Solunds, near Bergen
September		Harvest season
6		Ships in Normandy start to leave for St. Valéry-sur-Somme
8		Full moon. Around this time the Norse invasion fleet visits Orkney and Shetland Isles
8*		King Harold II releases some of his army and redeploys others after news that Norman fleet has relocated
10*		King Harald of Norway reached the Firth of Forth to meet Tostig
12		King Harold II's fleet leaves the Isle of Wight.
13		William's fleet all relocated to St. Valéry-sur-Somme

14*	Thursday	The Norse fleet makes landfall, probably near Tynemouth
16*	Saturday	Scarborough is attacked and burnt
17*	Sunday	Holderness, a base of one of the northern rebel earls, is destroyed
18*	Monday	Tostig's army re-board ships in Humber and move with tidal bore swiftly inland: Riccall occupied by Orkney contingent who have moved ahead.
19*	Tuesday	News of the northern invasion reaches King Harold II
19		Tostig's fleet arrives at Riccall from midday until tide turns – 8 hours on this date
19		King Harald of Norway re-boards his ships at Brayton and rides the tidal bore on the River Ouse past Riccall to land at Fulford in the evening
19		Overnight Mercian army mobilised from Tadcaster to move to Middlethorpe
20	Wed	King Harald of Norway defeats the combined army of the northern earls at Fulford
21*	Thursday	Southern mounted army sets out 10 hours x 8kph=80 x 4days=320 km -distance 290 So it takes 3.6 travel days
22	Fri	Post-battle activities
23	Sat	Norse celebrate
24	Sun	King Harald parades army and accepts the submission of York
24	Sunday evening	King Harold II arrives in York in the evening and takes steps to ensure that the presence of his army is not revealed . Mercian army mobilised from Tadcaster to move to York and onwards
25	Monday	King Harold defeats and kills the Harald and Tostig at Stamford Bridge.
25		'Spring' tides peak
26	Tue	Tostig buried and King Harold holds a council
27	Wed	William's fleet sails from the Somme at dusk
28	Thursday	William lands near Pevensey after a night crossing of the Channel

29	Friday	William moves along the coast to Hastings
30	Sat	Invasion fleet heads home after unloading
October	Sun	News of Wiliam's landing reaches Harold late assuming 4 days hard riding (120km per day)
2*	Mon	Some foot soldiers set out for the south needing 7 days to cover the distance
3	Tue	Harold and some housecarls set out on horseback
4	Wed	
5	Thur	10hrs for 8 hours of daylight=80km per day = 3.6 days riding
6*	Fri	King Harold II reaches Waltham Abbey in the evening
7	Sat	
8	Sun	Any soldiers walking from York could reach London, footsore
9*	Mon	Army bound for battle mustered possibly at Southwark and march toward Hastings
10	Tue	140km at 35 km per day = 4 days
11*	Wed	King Harold II leaves London
12	Thur	
13	Fri	The English muster to block the valley road some 10k from William's camp
14	Sat	Battle with Norman invaders results in the death of King Harold II and much of the south Saxon nobility
29		Canterbury submits
November		William based in Canterbury
		Dowager Edith surrenders her treasury
December	mid*	Submission of clergy and the London merchants to William at Berkhamsted
	25	Coronation in Westminster of King William I

Dates discussed in this book

King Edward's long reign began (He was 62 when he died in 1066)	1042 but coronation was April 1043 when Edward was aged 40.
King Edward rode to Winchester with all the leading earls, accused his mother, Emma, of treason and deprived her of lands and titles.	1042 Having asserted his authority, Edward later restored her lands. Dowager Queen Emma died in March 1052.
Edith Godwindottir's marriage to King Edward.	Jan 1045
Swegen Godwinson's first exile	March 1047 -1049
Exile the Godwinsons as King Edward again asserts his authority.	September 1051: Suggested date for a visit by Duke William.
Swegen Godwinsons' second exile, this time for life.	1051 Exiled. Died or was killed returning from Jerusalem
Return of the Godwinsons with popular support.	1052
Death of Godwin, Earl of Wessex.	April 1053 when feasting with King Edward.
Death of Siward, of Northumbria.	March 1055
Ælfgar, Earl of East Anglia exiled opening way for Tostig to become Earl of Northumbria.	1055
Earl Ælfgar restored after attacking England.	Late in 1055
Macbeth defeated at Lumphanan	1057
Death of Leofric, Earl of Mercia to be succeeded by his son Earl Ælfgar.	September 1057
Death of Ælfgar, Leofric's son, Earl of Mercia.	*1062*, Succeeded by his son Edwin.
Tostig's pilgrimage and 'business trip' to Rome.	1061
Harald Godwinson's fateful trip to Normandy seemingly to negotiate the return of hostages given at the time of the family's exile.	1064 where he secured the release of his nephew Hakon's but not his brother Wulf held as hostages by Duke William
Northern rebellion against Tostig.	3 October 1065
Tostig's exile accepted by King Edward.	28 October 1065

Estimated battle timetable

18:00	Harald Lands at Fulford the day before the battle
19:00	Darkness falls
20:00	Mercian army leaves Tadcaster
02:00	Mercians in position on Middlethorpe Ings
05:30	Dawn tide surge due
06:00	First light: Troops start to move from Riccall
09:00	Some Mercians redeploy to block east bank
10:00	First sight of troops arriving from Riccall
11:00	Northumbrians set out to Fulford
12:00	Tostig deploys along the ditch
13:00	Morcar attacks after wading across the ford
14:00	Peak of Morcar's advance
15:00	Fierce battle
16:00	Harald's men charge
16:30	Battle with Mercians beside the river
16:45	Control of ford threatened
17:00	Retreat begins
17:30	Rearguard holds the ford
17:47	Sunset -completely dark by 19:00
18:00	Surge tide returns flooding the battlefield
18:30	Edwin submits to Harald
19:00	Surviving Northumbrians disperse to the east

Would these sailing timings work?

Invasion timings		Nautical miles				
From	To	Dist km	Days	Dist per day	Sailing time day	Speed required Knots
The Solunds	Orkneys	500	5	100	24	4.2
Orkneys	Dunbar	210	2	105	24	4.4
Dunbar	Tynemouth	85	1	85	24	3.5
Tynemouth	Scarborough	74	1	74	14	5.3
Scarborough	Humber	70	1	70	14	5.0
Humber	Flaxfleet	35	0.2	35	5.45	6.4
Flaxfleet	Riccall	30	0.2	30	7	4.3

- These crossing speeds are feasible under sail. Sources report an 'apartic'/northern wind which is good for square-rigged sails.
- The complex tidal flow favours boats heading south during daylight but limits sailing time due to pattern of on-shore, off-shore winds. But the coastal time could be achieved using oars if the wind failed them.
- River speeds are achievable. Flow speed of tide during a bore is 8-12 knots.
- Actual speed possibly quite high especially near the head of the river bore. They might have arrived a bit earlier than projected.
- If a 5-minute gap is allowed between longships to avoid congestion at the landing place, 480 boats could reach Riccall during the 4 hours while the river flows upstream. Later arrivals would have to row once the water is static but before the ebb.

List of illustrations

Index

Printed in Dunstable, United Kingdom

68561788R00147